The Social Reality of Violence and Violent Crime

Henry H. Brownstein

*University of Baltimore and National Development
and Research Institutes, Inc.*

Allyn and Bacon

Boston • London • Toronto • Sydney • Tokyo • Singapore

Editor in Chief, Social Sciences: *Karen Hanson*
Editorial Assistant: *Karen Corday*
Marketing Manager: *Brooke Stoner*
Editorial-Production Administrator: *Annette Joseph*
Editorial-Production Coordinator: *Susan Freese*
Editorial-Production Service and Electronic Composition: *Modern Graphics, Inc.*
Composition Buyer: *Linda Cox*
Manufacturing Buyer: *Megan Cochran*
Cover Designer: *Jenny Hart*

Copyright © 2000 by Allyn & Bacon
A Pearson Education Company
160 Gould Street
Needham Heights, MA 02494

Internet: www.abacon.com

Library of Congress Cataloging-in-Publication Data

Brownstein, Henry H.
   The social reality of violence and violent crime / Henry H. Brownstein
      p.   cm.
   Includes bibliographical references and index.
   ISBN 0-205-28807-3
      1. Violence—United States—Public opinion.   2. Violent crimes—United States—Public opinion.   3. Family violence—United States. 4. Youth and violence—United States.   5. Public opinion—United States.   I. Title.
   HN90.V5B78   1999
   303.6'0973—dc21
                                                      99–26300
                                                          CIP

Printed in the United States of America

10   9   8   7   6   5   4   3   2   1   04   03   02   01   00   99

Permission Credits: Materials from NDRI research projects are used with permission of the National Development and Research Institutes, Inc. (formerly named Narcotic and Drug Research, Inc.).
Pages 78–80   From *Complete Directory to Prime Time Network and Cable TV Shows* by Tim Brooks and Earle Marsh. Copyright © 1995 by Tim Brooks and Earle Marsh. Reprinted by permission of Ballantine Books, a Division of Random House Inc.

To Cindy, Becky, and Liz

Contents

Preface

The University of Baltimore is located just beyond the city's downtown section, about a mile north of the most popular tourist attractions and amidst the most popular cultural institutions. Adjacent to the university is the Lyric Opera House, down the street is the Meyerhoff Concert Hall, and within walking distance is the Maryland Institute of Art and the Walters Gallery. Add to this a growing number of interesting restaurants and shops, and to an urban mind, it is a wonderful location. To people who live in the suburbs, however, it's the city. So, for the university, what should be a recruitment advantage becomes a recruitment problem. As Director of the Graduate Program in Criminal Justice and a member of the Marketing Committee of the College of Liberal Arts, I am often asked about the safety of the campus by students who are thinking about admission. I offer them statistics that reveal a few thefts from unlocked offices and automobiles but show no record of violent crime on campus or involving university students. No matter. Prospective students read the newspapers and watch the evening news, and they know the city is not a safe place.

This book is about violence in U.S. society. But, as the story above suggests, violence means different things to different people, and people think about violence in different ways. So this book is really about how we *think* about violence and how we have come to think about violence during the twentieth century in the United States. It is a book about the stories we tell about violence and how we use those stories to help understand what violence is, where it is located, and how much of it there is. It is about the ways people in society use stories to make claims about violence and the nature and extent of violence as a social problem. It is about why people act as individuals and as representatives of larger social institutions, such as the media and government, to tell these stories and to use them to make particular claims about violence.

The stories I tell and the arguments I make can and should also be viewed as claims about violence and about the social processes through which violence is defined and measured in society. This book, then, ultimately reflects on how I look at violence in particular and social life in general. Consequently, a reflexive statement is in order. For you to be able to adequately assess the value and merit of my claims, you should know something about the work and experience on which they are based.

After four years of teaching fourth grade in the Bushwick section of Brooklyn, New York, I returned to graduate school in 1972. From what I had learned as an undergraduate sociology major at Brooklyn College, and from what I had seen working with kids living in the inner city of New York, I was angry. I wanted to change the world, not an uncommon career objective for sociology students in the late 1960s and early 1970s. By the time I earned my Ph.D. in sociology at Temple University in 1977, I had learned a few things about research. Foremost, I saw research as a tool I could use to attack the problems of the world. I would uncover the truths of social life and expose the predicaments and injustices of our society. Knowing the truth, people would work on fixing the problems. (I still get upset when I think about the widening social and cultural gap between the most impoverished and the most enriched among us, but I know now that nothing I say or do will make much difference.)

After just over four years of teaching and trying, with limited success, to do research at a small college in upstate New York, I took a position in 1982 doing research with the New York State Division of Criminal Justice Services (DCJS). What appealed to me about the job was that it was in an office Governor Hugh Carey had established to provide information and advice about crime and justice directly to him. When Mario Cuomo became governor of New York in 1983, the arrangement got even better. Governor Cuomo created the position of director of criminal justice as the head of all criminal justice agencies in the executive branch of the state government. The DCJS commissioner served simultaneously as director, strengthening our ties to the governor's office. Our office included one bureau that collected and maintained the state's official crime and justice statistics, another that used those statistics to do research, and a third that used the findings of that research to develop programs and policy recommendations for the director.

My first role at DCJS was to supervise teams doing evaluations of alternative-to-incarceration programs in New York. Over three years, we evaluated two programs: one an alternative to prison and the other an alternative to jail. When we tried to share our findings with government officials, we learned that they were most interested in what we had to say when it was consistent with what they wanted to hear. So much for research contributing to a better world.

Around 1985, not yet totally disillusioned, I met Paul Goldstein, who was working at Narcotic and Drug Research Institutes (NDRI) in New York City. Paul had written about the connection between drugs and violence and had developed a framework for understanding that relationship. We had common interests and talked about doing research together. Through NDRI, Paul was in a good position to seek federal funds for research. Through DCJS, I was in a position to gain access to whatever data we would need to do the research.

Since 1985, I have been doing research with federally funded grants awarded to NDRI for the study of the relationship between drugs and violence. Paul left for the University of Illinois at Chicago, and I began a collaboration with Barry Spunt. Barry left for John Jay College, and Susan Crimmins and I began a collaboration that continues to the present, despite the fact that I left DCJS for the University of Baltimore and despite the fact that NDRI changed its name to National Development and Research Institutes.

Our first studies examined homicide data collected from police departments throughout New York State. Later studies involved interviews with people who were under the custody of the state for having participated in violence. All the studies focused on how drugs are involved in violence, but each asked general questions about violence, as well. Throughout this book, I refer to findings from this research, and occasionally I tell a story about things we did or people we interviewed. Research findings are cited and interview accounts are noted by the acronyms of the studies from which they are taken. The following is a listing of the studies with acknowledgment of the funding agencies and the names of the principal collaborators:

- Drug Related Crime Analysis—Homicide 1 (DRCAH1) was funded by the National Institute of Justice, Grant Number 85-IJ-CX-0052, 1985–86. Paul Goldstein and I directed the collection of data from police departments around New York State for every homicide reported to the state under the Uniform Crime Reports program for the year 1984.

- Drug Related Crime Analysis—Homicide 2 (DRCAH2) was funded by the National Institute of Justice, Grant Number 87-IJ-CX-0046, 1987–89. As a follow-up to DRCAH1, Paul and I, with Pat Ryan as our project director, collected data from New York City Police Department detectives during the active investigation of 414 homicides from 17 precincts over 8 months in 1988.

- Drug Relationships in Murder (DREIM) was funded by the National Institute on Drug Abuse, Grant Number 2 RO1 DA4017-03, 1988–91. DREIM was also a follow-up to DRCAH1. Paul and I, with Barry Spunt as our project director and Michael Fendrich as our senior data analyst, directed the interviewing of 268 people (mostly men) incarcerated in New York State for one or more of the homicides committed in the state in 1984 and included in our earlier study.

- Female Drug Relationships in Murder (FEMDREIM) was funded by the National Institute on Drug Abuse, Grant Number 1 RO1 DA07374-01, 1991–94. Barry Spunt and I, with Susan Crimmins as our senior project director and Sandy Langley as our senior data analyst, directed the interviewing of 215 women incarcerated or under active parole supervision in New York State for homicide.

- Learning About Violence and Drugs Among Adolescents (LAVIDA) was funded by the National Institute on Drug Abuse, Grant Number

R1DA08679A, 1994–98. Susan Crimmins, Barry Spunt, and I, with Judith Ryder as our senior project director directed the interviewing of 414 youngsters under custody in New York State for murder, robbery, assault, or sexual assault.

• Female Drug Relationships in Murder 2 (FEMDREIM2) was funded by the National Institute on Drug Abuse, Grant Number 2 RO1 DA07374-04, 1995–98. Barry Spunt and I joined with Debbie Baskin and Ira Sommers, then of John Jay College, to conduct a study involving interviews with 319 women either in prison, in jail, under arrest, or in a community rehabilitation program about their participation in robbery and assault.

Other studies have been funded, but they are still underway, and neither findings nor stories from those studies are used in this book.

In addition to my immediate interest in doing research in a policymaking setting, I was also attracted to the job at DCJS because I wanted to learn about official records of crime and justice and how they could contribute to informed decision making in policy and practice. Throughout the years I was "on loan" to NDRI for the drugs and violence studies, I continued to participate in agency business. Because of my research, I was routinely involved in providing information to policy makers about drugs and violence. I also worked with the executive deputy commissioner of the agency, Barry Sample, on a number of special assignments, including reviewing budget proposals, reviewing reports by other agency staff, and filling in for bureau chiefs who took extended leave. Eventually, almost three years before I left DCJS for Baltimore, I became chief of the Bureau of Statistical Services.

While continuing to participate in the research with NDRI, as bureau chief, I was responsible for a staff of about 25 people whose job it was to collect data from various criminal justice agencies around the state, create and maintain official databases derived from those data, routinely prepare statistical reports for distribution to policy makers and practitioners, and respond to requests from the hundred or so people who called our office every month for information that could be culled from our data or statistics about crime and justice. We also worked with the research and policy bureaus on special reports requested by the governor's office or the state legislature. In terms of our ability to contribute to policy making and practice, I came to view the process as a variation of the television game show *Jeopardy*. We were not asked to use the data and statistics we had to provide answers to research questions that would then be used to inform policy and practice. Instead, policy makers and practitioners came to us with answers to questions or solutions to problems, and it was our job to use our data and statistics to find the questions that would result in their answers or solutions.

As you read this book, keep in mind that the things I say have been influenced by my work and experience. When I write that something is clear, ask yourself whether it is really clear to you. When I suggest that a conclusion should be reached, ask yourself whether you think I reached that conclusion on the basis of the evidence I presented (assuming you agree that the evidence says what I say it says) or on the basis of what I said about myself in this Preface. Actually, you should do this with everything you read. If you start to do that after reading this book, I will have accomplished what I set out to when I first sat down to write this book.

Acknowledgments

Walking through the book exhibit at a meeting of the American Society of Criminology, I was talking to Marty Schwartz about an idea I had for a book about violence. Marty is not one to waste time, and before I knew it, he was introducing me to people he thought might be interested in the book. So, as usual, I thank Marty for helping me to transform an idea into a project.

Once I completed a prospectus for the book, I sent it to a few publishers, and almost immediately, several expressed interest. That was good, but it was also confusing, and several people were willing to listen to my happy dilemma and to talk to me about their own experiences. For that I thank Niki Benokraitis, Gregg Barak, Walter DeKeseredy, and again, Marty Schwartz. I am especially grateful to Roz Lichter for helping me put the situation in perspective.

In the end, I reached an agreement to write the book with Allyn and Bacon. In large part, I think it was because of Karen Hanson, Editor in Chief of Social Sciences. When we first talked, she expressed enthusiasm for the project and seemed to share my understanding of what the book might become and where it might fit. As an editor, she quietly encouraged me and guided me through the process of creating a book from an idea. All the good things people told me about her are true. In particular, I also thank Michael Granger of Modern Graphics, Inc., who showed me how a good copyeditor can improve the quality of a manuscript.

Included in the book are references to research projects in which I have participated over the past 15 years or so. Most of that work was done through National Development and Research Institutes in New York City with funding from the National Institute on Drug Abuse and the National Institute of Justice. I thank all the people I worked with on those projects, particularly Barry Spunt, Susan Crimmins, Pat Ryan, Paul Goldstein, Michael Fendrich, Sandy Langley, and Judi Ryder. In addition, several people at various times read various parts of the manuscript and offered comments and suggestions. For that I am grateful to Niki Benokraitis, my colleague at the University of Baltimore, and to the following individuals who reviewed this book for Allyn and Bacon: Barbara H. Chasin, Montclair State University; B. Keith Crew, University of Northern Iowa; and Angelo Tritini, Passaic County Community College. I took all comments seriously and made changes where necessary and appropriate. Of course, the decisions, and hence the responsibility, for the final product is mine. Further, opinions and points of view are mine alone and do not necessarily reflect those of any reviewer, anyone I have worked with, or any agency that has supported my work.

Finally, I want to thank my family. My wife Cindy and my daughters Becky and Liz put up with my long hours and grumpy moods while I worked, and sometimes struggled, to figure out how to put into words what I wanted to say. Without their love and support, this work would not have been possible.

1

The Social Meaning of Violence and Violent Crime

On a damp and cloudy day late in 1989, I took the train from Albany, New York, and followed the Hudson River south to Ossining, where a correctional facility of the same name is located. The massive walls of the prison better known as Sing Sing are set on a craggy slope overlooking the tranquil waters of the Hudson. I walked down the slope to a small but forbidding entrance for visitors. Inside the doorway, I showed an officer behind a desk the card that identified me as part of a research team that had been approved entry to interview inmates for a study of drugs and homicide.[1]

After answering the officer's questions to his satisfaction, I passed through a metal detector without setting off any alarm. My hand was then stamped, and a second officer sitting in a cage at a console surrounded by video monitors automatically opened the first gate of bars that I would pass through that day. The bars slid to the side for me to pass, so I stepped in, before the bars quickly slid back to their original position, which left me in a small space with metal bars behind and in front of me, a concrete wall to my left, and to my right a window behind which sat the officer at the console. I showed my stamped hand to the officer and the next gate of metal bars opened to a long corridor, which my assigned guide and I followed into the prison.

After passing an assortment of additional security stations, I finally was brought to an area of offices that normally were used to counsel inmates with alcohol and other substance abuse problems. I met with my liaison officer, a treatment counselor, who found me an office in which to conduct interviews and began calling for the inmates who would be my respondents.

First to arrive was a middle-aged white man who was serving a life sentence for killing his wife. He was college educated and retired from the military. I told him about the project, explained the meaning of informed

1

consent, and with his approval began to ask him my questions. Among other things, I asked him to tell me about the murder. He proceeded to tell me the following story.

In the earliest hours of a summer morning in 1984, the respondent's wife was found brutally murdered in her own home. She had been beaten with a fireplace poker, strangled, and stabbed several times. Just before 2 A.M., a neighbor heard screams coming from the house and called the police. The police arrived within minutes, but not until after the same neighbor claims to have heard the footsteps of someone running from the house.

The respondent and his wife were going through a divorce, so he no longer lived in the house. He did, however, stop by every day to care for his numerous plants. The night before the early morning murder of his wife, he was in the house for a few hours. While there, he did see his wife's son from a previous marriage and did call one of his two ex-wives. No one saw him leave that night, but he said he did. Before 10 P.M., he drove the short distance back to where he was living with his new girlfriend. By his account, when his wife was murdered, he was home in bed with his girlfriend. Nonetheless, before the sun rose the next morning he was picked up by the police and taken to the local police station where he was questioned for almost 20 hours. Besides unexplained scratches on his arms, no firm evidence linked him to the crime and he was released, though he was told not to visit the murder scene and not to attend the funeral.

The respondent considered himself a social drinker at the time and admits that he probably had a few beers with lunch the afternoon before the murder. He might also have smoked a few joints of marijuana during the days before that. And he did snort two lines of cocaine that evening when he was at the house, in addition to the two lines he had done that morning. His wife, he recalled, did not like cocaine, but in his opinion probably had been smoking marijuana. Still, he does not think that either one of them was high at the time of the murder.

This was not an easy case for the police to solve. There was no record of any items missing from the home, so burglary was ruled out. The wife's new boyfriend might have been a suspect, but he had a solid alibi and no evidence pointed to him. For more than a year, no arrest was made.

Then, about 15 months after the murder, the neighbor who originally called the police called again. Fearful that a vicious killer might still be on the loose, she demanded action. She threatened to take the story of the failed police investigation in a middle-class suburb to the media. Piecing together a circumstantial case and highlighting a cocaine–violence connection, the police arrested the respondent and charged him with murder.

The police broke the story of the arrest, and the media reported it. The theme was that the respondent had a $3,000-a-month cocaine habit and was high the night of the killing. Of course, the respondent called that story ridiculous. He had been a cocaine user but used only the small amount he could afford with his salary and his military pension. Besides, at the time of the murder, he was in a drug treatment program that his employer recommended he try.

Questions remain. If he was in drug treatment at the time, why did he snort four lines of cocaine the day before the killing? If he was home in bed with his girlfriend when his wife was killed, why did no one believe her? No matter. The story that accompanied his arrest easily explains how a white, middle-class and middle-aged, college-educated man with a good job and an honorable military career could do something so wicked. Every violent act must have its devil, and in 1985 in the United States, cocaine was one of the most fearsome.

To understand and explain complex social phenomena, social scientists, public officials, and the mass media simplify and condense the lives and experiences of countless individuals. Through numbers and words, they typify reality to make comprehensible what is inherently complicated and obscure. In doing so, they tell stories that render intelligible the phenomenon in question while at the same time trivializing the thoughts, feelings, beliefs, and actions of those who participate in its social realization.[2] Effectively, the various literary forms of the storyteller are used to shape public opinion and to make public policy. In the case of the social phenomenon of violence, the theme of these stories inevitably is one of good versus evil.

This is a book about violence and violent crime. More precisely, it is about the social meaning of violence in American society in the twentieth century. Building on the theoretical notion that reality is socially constructed, this book illustrates from the American experience those *stories* that have been used in the social construction of drug-related violence, stranger violence, family violence, female violence, youthful violence, violence by the poor and minorities, and violence of the workplace. To tell these stories, the book weaves together official statistics, media reports, and research findings, including personal accounts from interviews conducted for my own research with people who have experienced violence as victims, offenders, and witnesses.

This chapter describes and explains the process by which violence is socially constructed. It demonstrates how and why we have come to define and measure violence primarily in terms of violent crime.

The Social Construction of Reality

In the introduction to the essays in their book *Constructing Crime*, Gary Potter and Victor Kappeler ask, "What does the public really know about crime and how do they know it?"[3] The authors ask this question because they wonder how people, most of whom have never been and never will be the direct victim of crime, can be so convinced of the risk to their personal safety that they adjust the patterns of their lives in response to that risk. The answer, Potter and Kappeler suggest, is that people learn about crime from what they are told, not only through personal interaction with others but also through the mass media. In other words, people do not really know much about crime, but from what they learn from others, they think they do. Individually and collectively, they construct the problem of crime and declare it to be real. The idea that reality is a social construction is not new.

There was a time, not too many decades ago, when thousands of students of sociology were introduced to the study of society through a brief but persuasive book by Peter Berger. In his *Invitation to Sociology*, Berger explains and describes the seemingly paradoxical nature of society. Yes, it is possible to view society as "the walls of our imprisonment in history,"[4] but, as Berger makes clear, "Our bondage to society is not so much established by conquest as by collusion."[5] Simply, that means that society may appear to us as an objective reality, but, in fact, we subjectively contribute to making it what it is. As Peter and Brigitte Berger write in their introductory sociology textbook, "Something is objectively real when everyone (or nearly everyone) agrees that it is actually there, and that it is there in a certain way."[6] Society appears to us to have that quality. However, it has that quality because we subjectively—through our actions, through the decisions we make, through the way we interpret things, for example—give it that quality. We construct social reality.

As those invited by Peter Berger to enter the field of sociology grew to their professional maturity, his thesis was not lost on them. Consequently, as we reach the close of the twentieth century, it is not surprising that social constructionism has come to dominate social problems theory and has made significant inroads into scholarly thinking about crime. This perspective is particularly useful for understanding violence.

From the social constructionist perspective, social reality is a product of social interaction in the form of individual decisions, interpretations, and actions. In that individuals act and interact, make decisions, and interpret their experience in the context of their unique social positions and interests, social reality and hence all social phenomena are necessarily constructed in an ideological and political context.[7] That is, the social world in which we live is designed by us in the context of our own values and interests, or, more precisely, by those among us who have the power to design that world in the context of their own values and interests.

How is it that images and ideas constructed subjectively in our individual and collective consciousnesses appear to us objectively as things existing outside of us? From a variety of positions and in support of a variety of interests, interacting individuals collaborate and compete in the social arena to define and construct social reality.[8] In the language of social problems theory, they make *claims* about social reality.[9] The purpose of this claims making is to construct from subjective experience a representation of some particular social phenomenon that will confront other members of society as objectively real.[10] Claims makers generate from their subjective experience all sorts of social phenomena that become objectified in that they are "available both to their producers and to other men as elements of a common world."[11]

To rephrase the question raised by Potter and Kappeler, what do people know about violence, how do they know it, and why do they respond the way they do? The answer is that violence has been socially constructed in the United States in response to various claims made about what violence is, where it is found, who is affected by it, and so on. Those claims have been made by a wide variety of claims makers—not only people we know personally or the mass media—within various sociological and political contexts to give meaning to particular acts, action, or activity as violent. It is on the basis of those claims that we define the nature of violence and measure its scope in our society.

The Meaning of Violence

Consider the following news accounts, all of which appeared in the *Washington Post* on Thursday, June 4, 1998.

- On page D7, an article by Wendy Melillo, "Teen Admits Role in Gang-Related Killing," tells how yesterday a 17-year-old boy from Fredericksburg, Virginia, "acknowledged his role as the driver in the Feb. 27 attack at Marshall High School that resulted in the shooting death of David C. Albrecht, of Falls Church."
- On page D1, "In Frostburg, Wreckage and Relief," by Paul W. Valentine, tells how a man "surveyed what was left of his house—a modest bungalow with shattered windows, gaping holes in the walls, and doors ripped from their hinges—mute testimony to Tuesday night's freak tornado."
- On page A1 is a picture of a "High-Speed Catastrophe," a story about a train wreck in Germany described in an article on page A25 called "High-Speed Train Crash Kills Scores in Germany."
- Also on page A1 is a story by Christine Spolar called "Albanians in Border Towns Gird for War" about the intensification of fighting in a Serbian province that is "forcing thousands of ethnic Albanian refugees to flee to Albania."
- The lead story on page A2, "U.S. Takes Alleged Terrorist Into Custody Years After Pan Am Blast," is about the indictment of a man believed to have prepared the bomb 15 years ago that caused an American airline to explode 26,000 feet in the air.

- An article by John F. Harris on page A8, "Clinton Presses for Tobacco Bill," quotes President Bill Clinton as saying, "Smoking-related illnesses kill more people every year than AIDS, alcohol, car accidents, murder, suicides, drugs and fires combined."

Which of these news reports tells a story about violence?

Violence is one of those things that you may not be able to describe in words, but you know it when you see it. This is true in part because violence is not just one thing but rather many things, making it easier to give examples of violence than to say exactly what it is. In a book about the difficulty of understanding violence, Graeme Newman identifies a number of forms of violence, "from political violence, through the violence of occupations, criminal violence, violence in the home, to the violence of those who are sick, and many other different forms of violence."[12] The examples from the newspaper presented above illustrate various events that could be defined as forms of violence. There is a gang killing, a natural disaster that destroyed property and lives, a collision that caused death and destruction, an act of war, an act of terrorism, and a product being sold that is acknowledged to be responsible for widespread death and illness.

Examples help illustrate what we mean by violence but do not specify the conditions that are necessary and sufficient for members of a society to agree that particular acts, action, or activity are violent. For that purpose, a definition of violence is needed, and several are available. Some are broad and encompassing, such as Graeme Newman's definition of violence as the use of force to gain dominance over another or others.[13] Others are more limited in scope, such as the definition of the National Research Council's Panel on the Understanding and Prevention of Violence, which confined its attention to violent behavior and interpersonal violence and therefore defined violence as "behavior by persons against persons that intentionally threatens, attempts, or actually inflicts physical harm."[14] In trying to define violence for their book of essays on its patterns and causes, Neil Alan Weiner and his associates acknowledge the difficulty of connecting a conceptual definition of violence to examples of social activity that could be called violent. They begin their definition with a two-page listing of hypothetical vignettes describing different patterns of behavior finally concluding with a definition of violence as "the threat, attempt, or use of physical force by one or more persons that results in physical or nonphysical harm to one or more other persons."[15]

From these definitions, it is possible to conclude that violence refers to something that involves social activity; the threat, attempt, or use of physical force; and the intent of gaining dominance over another or others. As noted earlier, there are many forms of social activity that may or may not be defined as violent in terms of these criteria. However, these examples suggest that many natural or accidental events that cannot be described as social or intentional may be viewed as violent. Newman raises a number of questions about the meaning of violence that evince a broader definition.[16] Must violence be inclusive of physical force and, to the extent that it must, what constitutes physical force? Are the violent consequences of acts of nature distinct from human acts of violence? To what extent must violent acts by humans be related to violent emotions such as anger, hate, or rage? In the end, the decisions, interpretations, and actions that define what to us is violence depend on our place in history and our place in society. In the case of social activity, in particular, what we view as violent is determined in the ideological and political contexts of values and interests, not by the nature of the act alone.[17] That is, the forms of social activity that we consider violent are those that in our judgment symbolize and represent physical force and domination.

While recognizing that violence may be more broadly defined, our attention in this book is on violence in the social realm. That is, we focus specifically on how social activity is defined as violence. We use examples of activity in a variety of social realms to explore how what we individually and collectively consider violence depends on who we are and where we are placed in public life and on claims about the nature of violence to which we are exposed. It also depends on how we measure the extent of violence in our society, though how we measure violence itself depends on what we are trying to accomplish with that measurement.

The Measurement of Violence and Violent Crime

The measurement of violence is important for two reasons. First, assuming that members of a society have mutually agreed on and accepted a common definition of violence, any subsequent social or public response to violence requires knowledge of its scope, magnitude, and location in society. Second, in that measures of violence are themselves grounded in the actions, decisions, and interpretations of those individuals who measure it, the very act of measurement is itself an aspect of reality construction. That is, how we measure violence has an impact on where in society we say it is located, how extensive we believe it to be, and therefore what we propose to do about it.

The determination that it is possible to assess the scope, magnitude, and location of violence in society implies that particular forms or elements of social activity not only constitute violence but are observable and measurable as well. In the United States in the late twentieth century, violence as a social phenomenon is observed, measured, and therefore studied and addressed primarily in two realms of social activity: criminal justice and public health.[18] Some argue that the primary focus should be on mortality and morbidity statistics.[19] Nonetheless, violence in the United States is formally and officially recognized and addressed first as a crime problem and then, to a lesser extent, as a health problem.

When the federal government established in the late 1960s the National Commission on the Causes and Prevention of Violence, the renowned members of the commission immediately turned to the available data and statistics on violent crime.[20] Similarly, the President's Commission on Law Enforcement and Administration of Justice, formed by Executive Order in 1965, defined and examined violence in terms of violent crime.[21] Since that era, violent crime has become the principal measure of violence in the United States. As Albert Reiss and Jeffrey Roth write in their report for the Panel on Understanding and Preventing Violence of the National Research Council, "Violent behaviors that society identifies as crimes are counted more completely and classified more accurately than those that are not."[22]

For most of this century, the Uniform Crime Reports (UCR), prepared annually by the Federal Bureau of Investigation (FBI) since the 1930s, has been the official measure of violent crime in the nation.[23] Statistics are collected and compiled by the FBI from every state in the nation, with each state collecting and compiling its statistics from local law enforcement jurisdictions. The most familiar and widely used component of the UCR is its count of crimes known to the police, particularly its index of seven major crimes.[24] The crime index is separated into violent and property indices, with the index of violent crime including nationwide counts of murder or nonnegligent manslaughter, forcible rape, robbery, and aggravated assault. Whenever a news account suggests that violence or violent crime is up or down in a particular location, it is usually referring to a change in the violent crime index of the UCR in that location. Also included in the UCR are counts of arrests reported by police departments around the country. Counts of crimes known to the police, including those for violent crimes, are broken down for the UCR by location; arrests made by the police are also broken down by location and by age, gender, and race of offenders.

Over the years, questions have been raised about the reliability and validity of UCR statistics.[25] These concerns have been exacerbated in recent years by the introduction of another measure of violent crime, the National Crime Victimization Survey (NCVS). Established in 1973 by the Bureau of Justice Statistics (BJS), the NCVS (sometimes identified as the NCS) is a victimization survey of a sample of individuals older than age 11 and their households. The purpose of the NCVS is "to learn more about crimes and the victims of crime, . . . to measure crimes not reported to the police as well as those that are reported."[26]

Inevitably, the number of violent victimizations reported by the NCVS is going to be greater than the number of violent crimes known to the police reported by the UCR, suggesting that the UCR may not be an adequate measure of violent crime. However, a more thoughtful interpretation of the inconsistency between these statistical reports concludes that while neither the UCR nor the NCVS is by itself an adequate measure of violence, each in some way is an estimate of the scope and nature of violent crime.[27] That conclusion leads to the recognition that there must be other measures of violence, as well, and in recent years, more attention has been given in the United States to public health statistics as measures of violence.[28] Specifically, students of violence have paid more attention to mortality and morbidity statistics, particularly in the area of what are called intentional injuries.

In that no one measure of violence adequately represents the true scope and nature of the phenomenon, it seems reasonable to make use of a variety of measures to arrive at a best estimate. The problem is that the vast differences in quantity observed among the variety of measures are not statistically reconcilable. For example, the UCR reported that there were 1,864,168 violent crimes known to the police in all of the United States in 1994.[29] For that same year, the NCVS reported that there were 9,796,920 incidents of violent victimization in the United States, of which 2,922,850 were actually completed.[30] For 1993, the UCR reported that 32 percent of all murders, robberies, and aggravated assaults involved firearms,[31] while the Public Health Service reported for that same year 15.6 firearm injuries per 100,000 population.[32] To understand the relationship between the variety of measures of violence, then, it is necessary to understand how they are socially constructed and why they are constructed as they are.

Arguing that measurement is not an end in itself but rather an element in the service of scientific inquiry, Abraham Kaplan writes, "The failure to recognize this instrumentality of measurement makes for a kind of *mystique of quantity*, which corresponds to numbers as though they were the repositories of occult powers"[33] (emphasis in original). That is, the measure itself does not possess an intrinsic scientific value but rather serves as a tool by which the scientist may standardize and categorize the social phenomena that are the objects of study.[34]

Violence takes many forms, and no one measure can or should be expected to adequately represent it. In social life, what we consider to be violence is the product of individual and group decisions, interpretations, and actions. Through similar processes we determine how we can and should count those occurrences of violence and how we can then arrive at the best estimate of violence in society. Immediately, a problem becomes apparent. Writing a review of a book about how students are admitted to elite colleges, David Nyberg writes, "We can't measure all the important things, so we make what we can measure more important than it is."[35] That has been the case with the measurement of violence. The statistic representative of violence that has been most accessible and easiest to calculate has been the UCR violent crime index. So the greatest emphasis in the social construction of a measure of violence in the United States has been given to the UCR index.

Measuring violence in terms of the measurement of violent crime does not, however, prove to be as simple or straightforward as it would appear. In addition to the introduction of the NCVS, the debate over the validity of UCR statistics was stimulated by an article by John Kitsuse and Aaron Cicourel in which they suggest that the UCR official crime statistics were in fact social constructions.[36] They write that these statistics "specifically [reflect] organizational contingencies which condition the application of specific statutes to actual conduct through the interpretations, decisions, and actions of law enforcement personnel."[37] The UCR violent crime index is the product of the interpretations, decisions, and actions of public officials, researchers, law enforcement officers, bureaucrats, and even data entry clerks.[38] Different decisions are made in different jurisdictions, different actions are taken in different offices, different people interpret things differently, and so on. A simple decision by a bureaucrat in state government such as when to close a file and stop accepting data from individual police departments that are delinquent in submitting monthly UCR reports, for example, could have an significant impact on the number of violent crimes reported for that state.

Nonetheless, in the United States in the late twentieth century, violent crime largely has become a proxy for all violence. The public and its social representatives have constructed the social meaning of violence in terms of violent crime. There are notable examples in which other forms of violence had to be criminalized before becoming recognized as violence, as was done with domestic violence over the last 30 years.[39] The answer to the question of how we measure the nature and extent of violence in our lives, then, is that we measure it in terms that are most easily observable and quantifiable: We measure it in terms of violent crime.

Why We Tell the Stories We Tell about Violence

The question that remains is why we tell the stories we tell about violence in our society. Ultimately, public opinion, public policy, and public practice with regard to violence are the products of claims making. Claims are made through stories that are told by government officials, the media, and other social actors with a stake in the meaning given to violence in order to support a representation of violence that is favorable to their own values and interests. For example, to address the problem of violence, we must first define and measure it. It should be clear at this point that violence is essentially a subjective phenomenon and that these are not simple tasks. Still, for those among us with the responsibility to manage the problem, the nature of violence and the difficulty of these tasks cannot be an impediment to action. What would appear to be a dilemma, however, can inadvertently protect public officials from public judgment. Public officials are best served when a problem is defined in simple terms and measures of its magnitude are easily quantifiable.[40] The subjective nature of violence and the resulting difficulty in its definition and measurement give officials responsible for the management of violence in society the ability to define and measure it in ways that best serve their own goals and objectives.

In the early 1900s, Max Weber suggested that the basis for social action can be rational or nonrational. The reason for making claims or telling stories that represent violence one way or another similarly can be rational or nonrational. For Weber, action is rational when the actor "tries to achieve certain ends by choosing appropriate means on the basis of the facts of the situation as experience has accustomed us to interpret them."[41] Following Weber's distinction, the reason for making a claim through a particular story is rational when the purpose of the story is to achieve an objective that is reasonable in the context of the experience of the storyteller. The reason for making a claim through the telling of a story is nonrational when the purpose cannot necessarily be understood in the context of who the storyteller is, such as in the case of a story told in support of tradition or emotion. Stories that have been told in the United States in support of claims about violence have been told for both rational and nonrational reasons.

Stories that reflect and support the values and interests of the storyteller arguably are rational in that they are told in support of claims consistent with the experience of the storyteller. Such storytelling is inherently compatible with the way policy is made and programs are developed in the United States. Making policy, designing programs, and establishing practices in the public arena are actually processes of prioritization and resource allocation.[42] To get higher priority and more resources for their favored goals and projects, individuals and agencies involved in these processes must assert their claims on behalf of their values and interests. This process is illustrated in terms of violence policy through an example I witnessed when I worked for the state government in New York.

One fall day during the early 1990s, Governor Mario Cuomo of New York called together several of the commissioners of his various agencies to work together on The Governor's Agenda to Reduce and Prevent Violence. Commissioners came from the Departments and Divisions of Health, Mental Health, Social Services, Housing and Community Renewal, Education, Human Rights, Alcoholism and Substance Abuse, Urban Development, and Youth among others. They also came from Criminal Justice, State Police, Parole, Probation, and Corrections. As staff to the project, I was present while the most powerful officials of the executive branch of the state government were asked to provide ideas, recommendations, and proposed initiatives toward the governor's agenda. It was the State Director of Criminal Justice, also Commissioner of the Division of Criminal Justice Services, who had called them together, and it was he who was chairing the meeting.

Over the next few weeks, the various agencies each submitted ideas, recommendations, and initiatives, and these were consolidated into a single preliminary report to the governor. This preliminary report, prepared by staff of the Division of Criminal Justice Services, was the basis of the second meeting, at which several commissioners were represented by their deputies. The report was supposed to be an integration of the material submitted in the form of a reasonable and intelligent strategy for dealing with the problem of violence. They looked at the listing of more than 100 proposals. As a discussion ensued, the criminal justice agency heads argued for a strong emphasis on enforcement. Most other agency officials argued for an integrated approach, giving as much attention to prevention as to enforcement. But it was the staff from Criminal Justice who were putting the report together. When everyone else left, their commissioner turned to them and said, "If the governor wanted prevention, he would have given this project to the 'quiche eaters.' But he gave it to me. So he wants enforcement." Other agencies continued to provide data and statistics for the report, but in the end, *The Governor's Agenda to Reduce and Prevent Violence* was essentially a report about violent crime with an emphasis on law enforcement.

Stories told in support of claims about violence are nonrational to the extent that they are grounded in something other than experience of the claims maker or storyteller. For example, a story may be told in response to an emotional need, such as fear. Typically, however, they are told in support of some moral claim about right and wrong or good and evil.

In an analysis of morality and politics in terms of social deviance, Nachman Ben-Yehuda defines morality as "the process through which an object or process is evaluated as good or evil."[43] In that same context, he suggests that sociologically the main function of morality is "to orient and direct social actions toward specified goals" through a "complicated structure of symbols . . . attached to various societal issues."[44] Thus claims can be made through stories told to symbolically link violence to any number of social actions or phenomena in the name of moral dogma. In any society, there are people who act as moral crusaders or moral entrepreneurs who, as defined by Howard Becker, find some evil in the world that so "profoundly disturbs" them that they feel "nothing can be right in the world until rules are made to correct it."[45] When these moral entrepreneurs see what they believe to be evil overtaking good in society, they create a moral panic[46] aimed at stigmatizing the social action or phenomena that so offends them. Defining some form of social action as violent or linking violence to a social phenomenon is a simple way of symbolically associating that action or phenomenon with evil.

The following chapters of this book all tell stories of the social construction of a particular form or manifestation of violence in U.S. society in the twentieth century. Not all are specifically about violent crime, but because of the centrality of violent crime to the way we view violence, to some extent, every one is told through its connection to crime and the criminal justice system. Stories are included that clearly have a rational basis for having been told, such as the story in Chapter 2 about how Harry Anslinger, the first head of the Federal Bureau of Narcotics, used a campaign against marijuana to build his agency and his own reputation. Stories also are included that clearly demonstrate a nonrational basis for having been told, such as the story in Chapter 7 about the coming age of youthful super-predators, pitting good people against bad. However, in the end it should be clear that all the stories told about violence are told for both rational and nonrational reasons. The concluding chapter considers how public policy and public opinion on violence and violent crime, as mediated by official records and news accounts, are typically formed in the wake of urgency and in the absence of knowledge and are oriented to the values and interests of those who make the claims and tell the stories of violence in the United States.

Endnotes

1. Throughout this book, I will refer to findings and interview responses from a series of studies I have participated in since 1985. I was coprincipal investigator for two studies conducted through National Development and Research Institutes (NDRI) and funded by grants from the National Institute of Justice (NIJ) involving data from almost 1,800 homicide case records and more than 400 active homicide investigations. I was coinvestigator for five additional studies involving interviews with more than 1,000 individuals incarcerated or detained in New York State for a violent offense, most conducted through NDRI (one was conducted through John Jay College of the City University of New York) and all funded by grants from the National Institute on Drug Abuse (NIDA). The interviews provided detailed information not only about the violent event in which the individual participated but also about their prior experiences with violence, drugs, crime, personal maltreatment, and so on. The studies were all in some way about the relationship between violence and drugs. More detail about these studies is provided in the preface to this book. When stories from them are used, they are cited using an acronym (defined in the preface) and an identification number. The story that follows is from DREIM #246.

2. Compare Beckett, K. (1997). *Making Crime Pay—Law and Order in Contemporary American Politics*. New York: Oxford University Press. Kappeler, V. E., Blumberg, M. and Potter, G. W. (1996). *The Mythology of Crime and Criminal Justice*. Prospect Heights, IL: Waveland. Pepinsky, H. and Jesilow, P. (1985). *Myths That Cause Crime*. Cabin John, MD: Seven Locks.

3. Potter, G. W. and Kappeler, V. E. (1998). *Constructing Crime—Perspectives on Making News and Social Problems*. Prospect Heights, IL: Waveland, p. 2.

4. Berger, P. L. (1963). *Invitation to Sociology: A Humanistic Perspective*. Garden City, NY: Anchor Books, p. 92. See also Durkheim, E. (1938). *The Rules of Sociological Method*. Tr. by S. A. Solovay and J. H. Mueller and ed. by G. E. G. Catlin. New York: Free Press, p. 13.

5. Berger 1963: See also Weber, M. (1947). *The Theory of Social and Economic Organization*. Tr. by A. M. Henderson and T. Parsons and ed. with an introduction by T. Parsons. New York: The Free Press, p. 88.

6. Berger, P. L. and Berger, B. (1975). *Sociology—A Biographical Approach*. Second, Expanded Edition. New York. Basic Books, p. 77. See also Berger, P. L. and Luckmann, T.

(1966). *The Social Construction of Reality—A Treatise in the Sociology of Knowledge*. Garden City, NY: Doubleday, p. 17.

7. Compare Quinney, R. (1970). *The Social Reality of Crime*. Boston: Little, Brown.

8. See Best, J. (1989). *Images of Issues: Typifying Contemporary Social Problems*. New York: Aldine and Gruyter. Best, J. (1990). *Threatened Children—Rhetoric and Concern about Child Victims*. Chicago: University of Chicago. Brownstein, H. H. (1995). "The Social Construction of Crime Problems: Insiders and the Use of Official Statistics." *Journal of Crime and Justice* 18:17–30. Brownstein, H. H. (1996). *The Rise and Fall of a Violent Crime Wave: Crack Cocaine and the Social Construction of a Crime Problem*. Guilderland, NY: Harrow and Heston. Miller, G. and Holstein, J. A. (1993). "Constructing Social Problems: Context and Legacy." In G. Miller and J. A. Holstein (eds.), *Constructionist Controversies—Issues in Social Problems Theory*. New York: Aldine de Gruyter. Rafter, N. H. (1990). "The Social Construction of Crime and Crime Control." *Journal of Research in Crime and Delinquency* 27:376–89. Spector, M. and Kitsuse, J. I. (1987). *Constructing Social Problems*. New York: Aldine de Gruyter. Woolgar, S. and Pawluch, D. (1985). "Ontological Gerrymandering: The Anatomy of Social Problems Explanations." *Social Problems* 33:159–62.

9. See Best 1989, 1990. Best, J. and Horiuchi, G. T. (1985). "The Razor Blade in the Apple: The Social Construction of Urban Legends." *Social Problems* 32:488–99. Brownstein 1995; Jenkins, P. (1994). "The 'Ice Age'—The Social Construction of a Drug Panic." *Justice Quarterly* 11:7–31. Rafter, N. H. (1992). "Claims-Making and Socio-Cultural Context in the First U.S. Eugenics Campaign." *Social Problems* 39:17–34.

10. Compare Blumer, H. (1971). "Social Problems as Collective Behavior." *Social Problems* 18:302–3.

11. Berger and Luckmann 1966:33.

12. Newman G. (1979). *Understanding Violence*. New York: J. B. Lippincott, p. 5.

13. Newman 1979:1.

14. Reiss, A. J. and Roth, J. A. (1993). *Understanding and Preventing Violence*. Washington, DC: National Academy Press.

15. Weiner, N. A., Zahn, M. A. and Sagi, R. J. (1990). *Violence: Patterns, Causes, Public Policy*. San Diego: Harcourt Brace Jovanovich, p. xiii.

16. Newman 1979:1–3.

17. See Arendt, H. (1969). *On Violence*. New York: Harcourt, Brace & World, p. 4. Stigliano, T. (1983). "Jean-Paul Sartre on Understanding Violence." *Crime and Social Justice* 19:53. Sorel, G. (1950). *Reflections on Violence*. Tr. by T. E. Hulme and J. Roth. Glencoe, IL: Free Press, p. 70.

18. See Curtis, L. A. (1974). *Criminal Violence*. Lexington, MA: Lexington. American Psychological Association (1993). *Youth and Violence: Psychology's Response*. Vol. 1: Summary Report of the American Psychological Association Commission on Violence and Youth. Washington, DC: APA Commission on Violence and Youth. (1974); President's Commission on Law Enforcement and Administration of Justice. (1968). *The Challenge of Crime in a Free Society*. New York: Avon. Reiss and Roth. (1993). Rosenberg, M. L. and Fenley, M. A. (1991). *Violence in America—A Public Health Approach*. New York: Oxford University Press. Roth, J. A. (1994a). *Understanding and Preventing Violence*. National Institute of Justice Research in Brief. Washington, DC: Office of Justice Programs. Roth, J. A. and Moore, M. H. (1995). *Reducing Violent Crimes and Intentional Injuries*. National Institute of Justice Research in Action. Washington, DC: Office of Justice Programs.

19. Rosenberg, M. A. and Mercy, J. A. (1991). "Introduction." In Rosenberg, M. L. and Fenley, M. A. (eds.), *Violence in America—A Public Health Approach*. New York: Oxford University Press, pp. 3–13.

20. Curtis 1974.

21. President's Commission on Law Enforcement and Administration of Justice, 1968.

22. Reiss and Roth 1993:2.

23. Bureau of Justice Statistics. (1988). *Report to the Nation on Crime and Justice*. NCJ–105506. Washington, D.C.: U.S. Department of Justice. Maltz, M. D. (1977). "Crime Statistics: A Historical Perspective." *Crime and Delinquency* 23:32–40.

24. The UCR crime index includes the crimes of murder or nonnegligent manslaughter, forcible rape, robbery, aggravated assault, burglary, larceny–theft, and motor vehicle theft. Attempts in the 1970s to add arson as an eighth component of the index were not entirely successful, and today, for the federal government, arson is only part of the modified index, and some states do not include arson at all. See Federal Bureau of Investigation. (1996). *Crime in the United States, 1995.* Washington, DC: U.S. Department of Justice.

25. See Blumstein, A., Cohen, J. and Rosenfeld, R. (1991). "Trend and Deviation in Crime Rates: A Comparison of UCR and NCS Data for Burglary and Robbery." *Criminology* 29:237–63. Blumstein, A., Cohen, J. and Rosenfeld, R. (1992). "The UCR-NCS Relationship Revisited: A Reply to Menard." *Criminology* 30:115–24. Brownstein 1996. Eck, J. E. and Riccio, L. J. (1979). "Relationship between Reported Crime Rates and Victimization Survey Results: An Empirical and Analytic Study." *Journal of Criminal Justice* 7:293–308. Gove, W. R., Hughes, M. and Geerken, M. (1985). "Are Uniform Crime Reports a Valid Indicator of the Index Crimes? An Affirmative Answer with Minor Qualifications." *Criminology* 23:451–501. Hindelang, M. J., Hirschi, T. and Weis, J. G. (1979). "Correlates of Delinquency: The Illusion of Discrepancy Between Self-Report and Official Measures." *American Sociological Review* 44:995–1014. Jensen, G. F. and Karpos M. (1993). "Managing Rape: Exploratory Research on the Behavior of Rape Statistics." *Criminology* 31:363–85. Maltz, M. (1975). "Crime Statistics: A Mathematical Perspective." *Journal of Criminal Justice* 3:177–94. McDowall, D. and Loftin, C. (1992). "Comparing the UCR and NCS over Time." *Criminology* 30:125–32. Menard, S. (1991). "Encouraging News for Criminologists (in the Year 2050)? A Comment on O'Brien." *Journal of Criminal Justice* 19:563–67. Menard, S. (1992). "Residual Gains, Reliability, and the UCR-NCS Relationship: A Comment on Blumstein, Cohen, and Rosenfeld." *Criminology* 30:105–13. Menard, S. and Covey, H. C. (1988). "UCR and NCS: Comparison over Space and Time." *Journal of Criminal Justice* 16:371–84. O'Brien, R.M. (1990). "Comparing Detrended UCR and NCS Crime Rates over Time: 1973–1986." *Journal of Criminal Justice* 16:229–38. O'Brien, R. M. (1991). "Detrended UCR and NCS Crime Rates: Their Utility and Meaning." *Journal of Criminal Justice* 19:569–74. O'Brien, R. M. (1996). "Police Productivity and Crime Rates: 1973–1992." *Criminology* 34:183–207. Skogan, W. (1974). "The Validity of Official Crime Statistics: An Empirical Investigation." *Social Science Quarterly* 55:25–38. Thornberry, T. P. and Farnworth, M. (1982). "Social Correlates of Crime Involvement: Further Evidence of the Relationship Between Social Status and Criminal Behavior." *American Sociological Review* 47:505–18.

26. Bureau of Justice Statistics 1988:11.

27. Compare Hindelang, Hirschi, and Weis 1979; McDowall and Loftin 1992; Thornberry and Farnworth 1982.

28. See Rand, M. R. (1997). *Violence-Related Injuries Treated in Hospital Emergency Departments.* Special Report. August. Washington, DC: Bureau of Justice Statistics. Roth and Moore 1995.

29. Maguire, K. and Pastore, A. L. (1996). *Sourcebook of Criminal Justice Statistics 1995.* Washington, DC: U.S. Government Printing Office, p. 336.

30. Maguire and Pastore 1996:232.

31. Federal Bureau of Investigation (1994). *Crime in the United States, 1993.* Washington, DC: U.S. Department of Justice, p. 11.

32. National Center for Health Statistics (1996). *Health, United States 1995.* Hyattsville, MD: Public Health Service, p. 155.

33. Kaplan, A. (1964). *The Conduct of Inquiry—Methodology for Behavioral Science.* San Francisco: Chandler, p. 172.

34. Kaplan 1964: 172–4.

35. Nyberg, D. (1985). "Lucking into Harvard." A review of *Choosing Elites* by R. Klitgaard. *New York Times Book Review* May 5:7.

36. Kitsuse, J. I. and Cicourel, A. V. (1963). "A Note on the Uses of Official Statistics." *Social Problems* 11:131–39.

37. Kitsuse and Cicourel 1963:137.

38. Brownstein 1996:21–24.

39. Fagan, J. (1996). *The Criminalization of Domestic Violence: Promises and Limits*. National Institute of Justice Research Report. Washington, DC: U.S. Department of Justice.

40. Compare Beckett 1997; Brownstein 1996; Kappeler et al. 1996.

41. Weber 1947:91.

42. Brownstein 1995:22.

43. Ben-Yehuda, N. (1990). *The Politics and Morality of Deviance—Moral Panics, Drug Abuse, Deviant Science, and Reversed Stigmatization*. Albany, NY: State University of New York, p. 50.

44. Ben-Yehuda 1990:50.

45. Becker, H. S. (1963). *Outsiders—Studies in the Sociology of Deviance*. New York: Free Press, pp. 147–8.

46. Ben-Yehuda 1990:98.

2

The Legend of the Drug-Crazed Killer

The Library of Congress is located just east of the Capitol Building along Independence Avenue in Washington, D.C. According to the tour guides stationed at any of the public entrances to its several buildings, its halls contain 110 million items, including 17 million cataloged books. One sunny morning early in 1998, I drove to Union Station, parked my car, and walked along First Street to the Jefferson Building of the library. I asked a succession of reference librarians for direction, until finally they sent me to explore the ancient card catalogs hidden in catacombs behind the alcoves of the main reading room. When that search ended without success, I made my way through the labyrinth of tunnels under the three buildings of libraries to the law library in the Madison Building, where I finally found what I was looking for.

About 25 years ago, when even a man who would later become president of the United States felt comfortable enough to at least try smoking (though not necessarily inhaling) marijuana, I read a book by John Kaplan, a professor of law at Stanford University. In *Marijuana—The New Prohibition*, Kaplan describes how Harry Anslinger, the commissioner of the Treasury Department's Federal Bureau of Narcotics from 1930 into the early 1960s, vigorously pursued the argument before Congress and the nation that marijuana use inevitably results in violence.[1] What struck me was how Anslinger built an agency and a career on what he discovered and then promoted from what a few newspaper articles had been suggesting, never feeling the need to support his argument with evidence.[2]

After years of procrastinating, I finally had a good reason to locate the records of the original hearings and to read for myself what Anslinger actually had said to Congress when our nation's legislators were considering the passage of the Marijuana Tax Act. What I found would have been amusing, except that it was too similar to what I observed as a New York State government employee when the case linking crack cocaine use to violence was being made. Both of these stories—how marijuana use was connected to violence in the 1930s and how crack cocaine use was similarly linked to violence in the 1980s—are told in this chapter. In both cases, the connection to violence was more firmly grounded in politics than science. Public policy eventually was made not on the basis of empirical evidence about the relationship between drugs and violence, but rather in response to the legend of the drug-crazed killer. That legend lives in the stories we tell about violence in America.

An article titled "Couple held in death of volunteer" appeared in the *Arizona Republic* on February 27, 1998. A woman was "allegedly bound, sexually assaulted, and murdered" by a man and woman to whom she was delivering groceries after they called her church to ask for help for their hungry family. The murdered woman from the Phoenix area was described as decent and dedicated to her children, someone who loved people and loved helping them. Little was written about the people who had brutalized her, except that they had done so in front of their own children and that the man was on probation after earlier having plead guilty to a misdemeanor charge of marijuana possession. In a follow-up article in the same newspaper the next day, "Outreach to needy to continue," Clay Thompson told how the people of the church would not let the evil that befell one of their own deter them from helping others in the future. While neither *Republic* article attempted to name the root of that evil, an Associated Press news report, written by Kate Hunger and released on February 28, suggested that the villain was drugs. According to that account, the man ran from the scene of the assault to his sister's house where he told her that, at the time of the attack, he was high on crack.

This chapter reviews the various claims about violence by people who use drugs and shows how those claims have caught the attention of the American public during this century. Those claims are contrasted to the evidence of research and official statistics and to the record of history.

Defining Drug Users as Violent Offenders

Both its imposing physical structure and its image in popular culture make Sing Sing prison in New York a particularly fearsome place. Even more fearsome is its Special Housing Unit, where inmates who are too troublesome to remain in the general population of prisoners are kept. There, I went to meet a man who would tell me a story about one night when he was high and someone was killed.[3]

After passing through the many security gates and checkpoints at the entrance to Sing Sing, I was taken down a long hallway to an office where I was introduced to a captain of the guard, who would decide whether I could continue on to the Special Housing Unit. He agreed, as long as my escort stayed with me, and suggested to the correctional officer accompanying us that if he thought the inmate would get violent during the interview he should be put in shackles. At the end of the hall, a gate was opened, and we were permitted to descend a flight of stairs leading to a wall of bars. The wall opened into an antechamber surrounded by entrances to several other rooms and hallways, many locked behind gates that could only be opened by the officer seated at the desk in the center of the room. After a brief discussion with the officer, my escort was permitted to enter the cell block to find the inmate I wanted to speak to and to ask him through the bars of his cell if he would be willing to talk to me. I do not imagine he was interested in contributing to the body of scientific knowledge, but an extra 45 minutes out of a cell where he normally spent 23 hours every day probably sounded like a good idea.

We were introduced and placed in a small room off the central area. The door was closed behind us. My initial trepidation gave way to appreciation for the privacy when I found before me a person who seemed to be a perfectly gentle man. His story, however, told of a time when perhaps he was not quite such good company.

Early in 1984, he had been arrested for killing a man outside of a bar in New York City. He was 26 years old and living with his wife. One winter day he felt restless, bored, and needed to get out of the house. Earlier in the day, he had ingested a small amount of heroin and, in retrospect, realized that it was probably the need for more that had made him feel so uneasy. That evening a friend, maybe really just an acquaintance, came to the door with the offer of a ride in his car; the inmate jumped at the opportunity.

They drove around and ended up at a club where you could buy anything you wanted. They started with Bacardi. Throughout the evening they shared, besides the half-pint of rum, six quarts of beer, five quarts of Old English, and six bags of reefer. When they finally left the club, they were both, in his words, "real high."

In the early morning hours, they left the club and stood outside near their car. They watched as another man walked toward the car and began to urinate on it. The friend who owned the car became angry, and a fight ensued. Soon, all three men were fighting. A gun fell from the jacket pocket of the man who had urinated on the car. The owner of the car ran around to the driver's side. The man I was speaking to had tried to run, but the stranger was holding his coat. He pulled loose, leaving his coat with his keys in the pocket on the ground. The man chased after them and was killed by a gunshot that came from the passenger side of the car. In his account of the story, this would not have happened had they not been so high.

While it is not possible to know exactly how many, it is a safe bet that on any given day in the United States lots of people get high. A safer bet is that the overwhelming number of those people who get high do not kill someone else because they are high. Certainly, some do get violent,[4] but even that is probably a very small proportion of all the people who get high.[5] In one noteworthy study of heroin users in New York City and Baltimore, David Nurco and his associates found that only a small percentage of all the addicts in their sample regularly engaged in violence, and those few accounted for most of the violence committed by all of the people in the sample.[6]

In the first pages of his book on the war on drugs in the United States, James Inciardi tells the story of how we in the United States came to equate drugs with crime and thereby to define drug users as criminals, particularly violent criminals. From the period of the Revolution through the last years of the nineteenth century, a populace fearful and suspicious of the prevailing medical practices of bleeding and purging welcomed home remedies available in general stores to cure their ailments, illnesses, and especially pains.[7] With no legal requirement that they do so, the manufacturers of these medicines did not report their ingredients, and their products commonly included derivatives of opium or cocaine.[8] Inciardi describes how in 1897 the Sears Roebuck catalog sold hypodermic kits for morphine users, how, in 1885 a new soft drink named Coca-Cola included extracts of coca to provide the product with a stimulant effect, and how, just before the turn of the century, Bayer and Company began to market a new product trade named Heroin for coughs and other chest ailments, and even as a treatment for morphine addiction.[9] David Musto, perhaps the most prominent historian to study drug use in the United States, called this period "an era of wide availability and unrestrained advertising."[10]

Early in the twentieth century, when users of these home medical remedies were still considered legitimate and respectable citizens, concerns about the addiction potential of using drugs such as cocaine and opium surfaced. The medical community of the time was quick to define addiction as a health problem and hence drug users as people in need of medical attention.[11] The law enforcement community, on the other hand, saw the problem in terms of crime, with an underworld of people profiting from the addiction of others to drugs.[12]

According to Inciardi, despite a lack of knowledge of how many people were actually having problems with these drugs, "by the early 1920s readers of the popular media were confronted, almost on a daily basis, with how drug use, and particularly heroin use, had become a national epidemic."[13] Calling something an epidemic is one way to get policy makers to respond to it. In 1906, the Pure Food and Drug Act was passed, imposing "standards for quality, packaging, and labeling " and making it possible for people to avoid those products that included ingredients defined by the mass media as harmful or addictive.[14] In 1914, the Harrison Act was passed, and in 1937, the Marijuana Tax Act, together giving the federal government the authority to regulate and control the production, importation, sale, purchase, and free distribution of first narcotics (erroneously defined to include a wide variety of drugs) and then marijuana.[15] By the early twentieth century, drug use had evolved from a normal form of conduct to a condition requiring medical attention to a class of criminal behavior.[16]

Debate certainly continued during the second half of the twentieth century. Some have continued to argue that intoxication has a legitimate place in society. Arguing for the pleasures of intoxication, Aldous Huxley once wrote, "That humanity at large will ever be able to dispense with Artificial Paradises seems very unlikely. Most men and women lead lives at worst so painful, at the best so monotonous, poor and limited that the urge to escape, the longing to transcend themselves if only for a few moments, is and has always been one of the principal appetites of the soul."[17] Arguing for the inevitability of drug use, Andrew Weil wrote, "Like the fantasy that drugs can be made to go away, the idea that people who want drugs can be discouraged from using them is an impossible dream that gets us nowhere except in worse trouble."[18] A more convincing argument of a proper place in society for drugs might promote their medical use. For example, in his well-known study of heroin use, Arnold Trebach suggested that heroin has an important role to play in "the treatment of the organically ill," especially as a painkiller.[19] Similarly, criminologist Edwin Schur asked, "Why are we continuing to treat the addict as a criminal when he is in need of our help?"[20] More recently, Lynn Zimmer and John Morgan reviewed the research on marijuana and concluded, "Marijuana's therapeutic uses are well documented in the modern scientific literature."[21]

In any case, whether you accept drug use as a proper means of relieving the pressure of everyday life or as practice with medical worth, it is not so obvious that we should call drug use a form of crime. Nonetheless, over the past century, we in the United States have done so. The question is how and why.

It has been suggested that the way we have defined drugs and drug users reflects the symbolic meanings and cultural tensions of the twentieth century.[22] According to Musto, "The energy that has given impetus to drug control and prohibition came from profound tensions among socio-economic groups, ethnic minorities, and generations—as well as the psychological attractions of certain drugs."[23] In a study of the legal and moral developments around drug use in the United States during this century, sociologist Troy Duster observed that in 1900 most drug addicts were middle-aged and middle-class white women, while in 1969 most were lower- and working-class young black males.[24] Using that as a context for understanding how we have come to view drug use as crime, he argued that "the point is simply that middle America's moral hostility comes faster and easier when directed toward a young, lower-class Negro male, than toward a middle-aged white female."[25]

Thus, the importance of social and cultural context for understanding how and why we have come to emphasize the violence over the health needs of drug users becomes clear. During the last years of the nineteenth century, when marijuana use was legal and socially acceptable, its users were middle class; during the 1920s and 1930s, when marijuana use was being demonized, it "had become visible among members of minority groups—blacks in the South and illegal alien Mexicans in the Southwest."[26] During the late 1960s and the 1970s, when cocaine was widely if reluctantly accepted as a recreational drug, it was associated with "the urban smart set" and was considered "the rich man's drug."[27] In the 1980s, when cocaine was increasingly being sold as crack and crack cocaine became the demon drug, its users were "the persistent poor."[28]

People who use drugs are a lot of different things. They are fathers and mothers, sons and daughters, friends and neighbors, students and teachers, employers and employees, tenants and landlords, and more. Being a drug user is only one of their many identities or statuses in society. Some social statuses, however, are what Everett Hughes called "master" statuses.[29] In social situations, master statuses tend to "override all other statuses and have a certain priority."[30] Such is the case with the status of drug user. For example, Howard Becker studied deviance and observed, "Though the effects of opiate use may not impair one's working ability, to be known as an addict will probably lead to losing one's job."[31] The problem for the drug user is compounded by the fact that master statuses typically have associated with them auxiliary traits.[32] Once drug using is defined as criminal, it is easy to attach to the drug users the trait of violence. This lesson even found its way into the official record of federal government proceedings. Speaking on behalf of the U.S. Senate Judiciary Committee in 1990, Senator Joseph R. Biden, Jr., stated, "And of course, the more drugs these people consume, the more violent they will become—even when there is no economic motivation for such violence."[33]

The following sections of this chapter show how and why we have repeatedly constructed throughout this century the image of the drug user as a violent criminal. Specifically, they tell the stories of marijuana and crack cocaine users, and thereby the legend of the drug-crazed killer.

Anslinger and the Dangers of Marijuana Use

Just before the passage of the federal Marijuana Tax Act in 1937, Harry Anslinger was quoted in the *American Magazine* as saying, "How many murders, suicides, robberies, criminal assaults, hold-ups, burglaries, and deeds of maniacal insanity [marijuana] causes each year, especially among the young, can only be conjectured."[34] He was right about that. Given the state of scientific knowledge at that time, he really had no way of knowing to what extent, or even if, marijuana use caused crime or violence. But that did not deter Anslinger or his minions. They proceeded to tell their story and make their claims. Even decades later, John Kaplan wrote:

> In weighing the evidence on the connection between marijuana and aggression, one is struck by two things: one is the relatively large number of statements made by policy-making committees, medical societies, and public officials as compared with the relatively small number of studies that actually bear on this issue; the other is the even more striking fact that the studies and evidence relied on in these statements are of extremely weak probative value.[35]

Having served as narcotics commissioner in the United States for 32 years, Harry Anslinger was a master of the art of bureaucracy. John C. McWilliams demonstrates this point in his biography of Anslinger:

> [H]is longevity as an administrator becomes even more significant when one considers the intricacies of Washington politics. Institutional changes, social conditions, and philosophical shifts are commonplace. But Anslinger survived at the head of a small agency, whose average number of field agents from 1930 to 1962 was only 242, bringing stability and organization to a bureau that previously had been handicapped by ineffective and incompetent leadership. As vulnerable as he was to the whims of congressional and party politics, Anslinger almost always managed to obtain a budget increase over the preceding year, which he accomplished largely by cultivating congressmen who were members of appropriations committees.[36]

Anslinger combined his skill in government with his loathing of drugs and drug users. Ultimately, he used marijuana and the allegation that marijuana use causes crime and violence to build his agency and enhance his career.

An often-cited, short article appeared in the *New York Times* on July 6, 1927. Under the title "Mexican Family Go Insane," the article told in just a few paragraphs about a widow and her four young children in Mexico City who were found laughing hysterically after "eating the Marihuana plant." The seed was planted for the notion that marijuana use was a danger to society. In 1930, the Federal Bureau of Narcotics (FBN)was formed as an independent agency, and Harry Anslinger became its commissioner.[37] By the early 1930s, newspaper accounts and reports by local medical and law enforcement officials increasingly claimed that marijuana use was somehow connected to violent crime.[38] As head of a new agency that had yet to establish the respect and authority needed to do its job, Anslinger followed these accounts, accepted them as accurate, and embraced their conclusions as his own. By the late 1930s, he was authoring or coauthoring his own articles with titles such as "Marijuana: Assassin of Youth," "Youth Gone Loco," and "One More Peril for Youth."[39]

In 1936, *Reefer Madness* was released in movie theaters. The film opened with a notice to the audience that "incidents and characters portrayed in this motion picture are purely fictional." Then, the screen filled with an ominous warning that what viewers were about to see was based on "actual research" and could happen to "your" children. Viewers were cautioned that "events may startle you," but this is necessary to "sufficiently emphasize the frightful toll of the new drug menace which is destroying the youth of America in alarmingly increasing numbers. *Marijuana* is the drug—a violent narcotic—an unspeakable scourge—the *Real Public Enemy Number One!*"(emphasis is in the original). For about an hour, this film tells the story of Jimmy and his high school friends and how they are lured into becoming marijuana users, identifiable then by their unkempt hair and distant, maniacal stare. In the story, their marijuana use and hence behavior get out of control, and eventually a young girl is murdered. Of course, the actual research that demonstrates that marijuana use leads to "acts of shocking violence" was never revealed.

What was the evidence that marijuana use leads to madness and violence? At a conference called by the Treasury Department in Washington, D.C., on January 14, 1937, Commissioner Anslinger took the opportunity to address that question. After tiring of hearing from lawyers and scientists about the chemical and pharmacological uses of marijuana, he asked, "What are the proofs that the use of marijuana, in any of its forms, is habit-forming or addictive, and what are the indications and positive proofs that such addiction develops socially undesirable characteristics in the user?"[40] He answered his own question by producing what has since become known as his "gore file," including mostly unsubstantiated stories providing grisly and shocking accounts of what happened when people used marijuana. The following examples are from the file.[41]

- West Virginia: Negro raped a girl of 8 years of age. Two black men took a girl 14 years old and kept her for two days in a hut under the influence of marijuana. On recovery, she was found to be suffering from syphilis.
- In New Jersey in 1936, a particularly brutal murder occurred. One young man killed another, literally smashing his face and head to a pulp. One of the defenses was that the defendant's intellect was so prostrated from his smoking marijuana cigarettes that he did not know what he was doing. The fury of the murder was apparent. Not content with killing his friend, he tore out his tongue, his eyes, and so mutilated him that even the hardened coroner had to turn his eyes away from the gruesome sight.
- A young man in Baltimore was sentenced to be hanged for criminal assault on a 10-year-old girl. In his plea of not guilty, he testified that he was temporarily insane from smoking marijuana cigarettes.

- A citizen of Alamosa, Colorado, stated that there had been scores of cases of violent and petty crimes and insanity in southern Colorado in recent years incited by the use of marijuana. Local officials there had been seriously aroused about the problem.

In presenting these examples from the file, Anslinger reportedly "disclaimed full responsibility for the accuracy of the information" in that the bureau did not actually possess all the details of all of the cases described.[42]

Shortly thereafter, in1937,congressional hearings were held on a bill entitled Taxation of Marihuana. Like the Harrison Act before it, the bill may have been written as a revenue measure, but its real purpose was to gain federal control of marijuana and marijuana users.[43] The bill was passed and became law thanks in no small part to the efforts of Harry Anslinger. As usual, his inability to substantiate the evidence he presented during his testimony was outweighed by the horror he instilled in his listeners.

Hearings on H.R. 6385, Taxation of Marihuana, were held before the U.S. House Committee on Ways and Means on April 27 to 30, and May 4, 1937. As commissioner of narcotics, Department of the Treasury, Anslinger was the first to testify on April 27. As part of his testimony, he told a few stories from his gore file about the violence caused by marijuana (from page 22 of the report on the House hearings):

> *Mr. Anslinger:*   I will give you gentlemen just a few outstanding evidences of crimes that have been committed as a result of the use of marihuana.
>
> *Mr. [Daniel A.] Reed* [Rep. from New York]:   The testimony before the committee of which I was formerly chairman in reference to heroin said in reference to the effect of it that it made men feel fearless, and that a great majority of the crimes of great violence that were committed were committed by addicts, and one man stated that it would make a rabbit fight a bulldog. Does this drug [marihuana] have a similar effect?
>
> *Mr. Anslinger:*   Here is a gang of seven young men, all seven of them, young men under 21 years of age. They terrorized central Ohio for more than two months, and they were responsible for 38 stick-ups. They all boast they did these crimes while under the influence of marihuana.
>
> *Mr. [David J.] Lewis* [Rep. from Maryland]:   Was that an excuse, or a defense?
>
> *Mr. Anslinger:*   No, sir.
>
> *Mr. Lewis:*   Does it strengthen the criminal will; does it operate as whisky might, to provoke recklessness?
>
> *Mr. Anslinger:*   I think it makes them irresponsible. A man does not know what he is doing. It has not been recognized as a defense by the courts, although it has been used as a defense.
>
> *Mr. Lewis:*   Probably the word "excuse" or "mitigation" would be better than defense, I think.

> *Mr. Anslinger:*   Here is one of the worst cases I have seen. The district at-
> torney told me the defendant in this case pleaded that he was under the
> influence of marihuana when he committed that crime, but that has not
> been recognized. We have several cases of that kind. There was one town
> in Ohio where a young man went into a hotel and held up the clerk and
> killed him, and his defense was that he had been affected by the use of
> marihuana.

The questions and the accounts continued, and Anslinger did leave the
members of the committee with written copies of stories from his file.
However, nowhere did he provide firm evidence that these stories were
true. And even if they were, nowhere did he provide evidence that demonstrated how he could be certain that the violence he was describing was really an outcome of the use of marijuana. Nonetheless, in 1937, only four years
after the repeal of Prohibition, H.R. 6385 became law in the United States.

On March 7, 1996, a headline in the Baltimore *Sun* read, "The drug war
gets a general." Four-star Army General Barry R. McCaffrey was appointed
by President Bill Clinton to be director of the Office of National Drug
Control Policy (ONDCP), the first military leader to head the nation's war
on drugs. The Drug Policy Foundation (DPF), a Washington, D.C.–based
organization dedicated to the reform of drug policy, responded with an article in its newsletter to show how the influence of Harry Anslinger had
endured. The article was called "The First Drug Czar." Its subheading was
"Harry Anslinger set the tone and direction of American drug policy for
over 30 years. Some would say he still does."[44] Describing the life and times
of Harry Anslinger, the article concluded, "He has reflected an embedded
American distaste toward people who have grown ill because of seeming
lack of will, and he has struck a responsive chord within both Congress and
the public."[45]

Crack-Crazed Killers

By the end of the 1980s, newspapers around the United States, especially in
its largest cities, routinely told how the country was experiencing an epidemic or plague of crack cocaine that was "literally destroying the nation."[46]
Violence in the form of killing and even child abuse were being linked to the
use of this deadly drug. For example, on January 16, 1989, Larry Martz and
his associates wrote an article for *Newsweek* called "A Tide of Drug Killing"
in which they called crack a "uniquely evil" drug.[47] Under the subtitle, "The
crack plague spurs more inner-city murder," they wrote, "And as the police
and criminologists all but unanimously see it, the prime cause [of the
increasing homicide rate] has been the violence that goes with drugs—particularly the drug called crack, or rock cocaine."[48] They were not alone in

their claim. Examples of other news stories telling readers that crack use caused violence included the following:

- On April 21, 1988, an article in the *New York Times,* "Drug Violence Undermining Queens Hopes," told how crack had "fueled" a 25 percent increase in the homicide rate in Queens, New York City's "most middle-class borough."
- On December 30, 1988, an article in the New York *Daily News* reported on the rising homicide rate in the city and announced, "Crack whips killing toll."
- An editorial in the *New York Times* on May 28, 1989, simply called "Crack," told readers that crack cocaine "destroy[s] the quality of life, and life itself."
- A headline in the *Times Union* of Albany, New York, on March 17, 1990, read, "'Crack' gives birth to new horror of abused young."

These stories were consistent with the stories being told throughout the United States and with claims being made by government officials.

Early in the twentieth century, it was Harry Anslinger who led the charge to demonize drug use in America. His legacy was a massive body of federal and state legislation that made the use of certain drugs (though not all) criminal. After his death and after the federal government mobilized its criminal justice resources to face the "challenge of crime in a free society,"[49] Richard Nixon assumed the presidency of the United States. In 1972 he formally declared war on drugs.[50] Still, despite the creation of a few new federal agencies and a fair amount of rhetoric, Nixon did not make a serious commitment to his war.[51] The war began in earnest after Ronald Reagan reprised the declaration and then his successor as president, George Bush, rallied the troops. With the support of Congress and the passage of the Anti-Drug Abuse Act of 1988, President Bush created the ONDCP and appointed William Bennett to serve as the first "drug czar" of the United States.[52] Crack was his first target.

The initial charge of the new drug czar was to prepare a national drug control strategy. In the first ONDCP report in 1989, crack was blamed for perhaps all of the world's troubles. Its introduction asserted:

> Crack is responsible for the fact that vast patches of the American urban landscape are rapidly deteriorating beyond effective control by civil authorities. Crack is responsible for the explosion in recent drug-related emergencies—a 28–fold increase in hospital admissions involving cocaine smoked since 1984. Crack use is increasingly responsible for the continued marketing success enjoyed by a huge international cocaine trafficking industry, with all its consequential evils. And crack is spreading—like a plague.[53]

All that from a product that was introduced to the market fewer than five years before the report was published.

In the end, research and experience would show that crack did have a particularly damaging impact on life in America. However, that impact would be different for different people and for different communities, and the havoc wreaked by crack would be related to the social and economic circumstances of the communities where it was used rather than to the character of the people who used it.[54] Just a decade later these lessons were obvious even to the federal government and the media. On July 12, 1998, a headline in the Baltimore *Sun* read, "Study finds drug use varies by region and age, requiring local strategies." The article told how in response to research findings reported by the National Institute of Justice (NIJ), President Clinton was "releasing $32 million in federal grants" to local governments to "devise strategies tailored for their communities." Whatever the truth, in the middle of the 1980s, no one really knew much about crack or what it would do to people or communities.

A lack of knowledge and understanding of the problem did not deter the federal government from passing legislation that singled out people who were involved with crack for especially harsh treatment. Under the 1986 Narcotics Penalties and Enforcement Act, to receive the same sentence as a convicted crack dealer who sold 5 grams of product, a powder cocaine dealer would have to be convicted of selling 500 grams. While the legislation specifically was directed at dealers, in part it was designed to respond to what was believed about crack users. For example, according to Republican Representative Bill McCollum of Florida, the bill was appropriate because "crack is more addictive than powder cocaine."[55]

In fairness, making policy in the face of moral panic is perhaps more common than making policy in response to knowledge and reason. Policy, programs, and practices designed and developed in response to the crack hysteria were a classic example of this on the state as well as the federal level.[56] For example, consider what happened during the summer of 1986 in New York, when I was working in an office of a state agency responsible for informing the governor's Director of Criminal Justice about criminal justice issues. Crack cocaine was first observed in New York City in 1983 or 1984, and in May 1986, the state division of Substance Abuse Services reported to the governor that 70 percent of a sample of 214 drug users in the city claimed to have tried crack.[57] It was a year of congressional elections, so political pressure was mounting to do something about this new menace.[58] The media were attracted to the story and began reporting that crack was responsible for the growing level of violence in the city.[59] Faced with this pressure, the state government had to do something about crack.

At the request of the Governor's Office and the state legislature, countless memoranda, briefing notes, and short reports were prepared by state employees at various state agencies about crack and its potential impact, particularly its relation to violence. Proposals for new laws, new policies, and new programs proliferated. But crack was a new drug and a new problem, so little was known about it. In fact, the systems and procedures for measuring the extent of crack use, for demonstrating the link between crack and violence, and for assessing the extent and nature of the problem were not yet in place. For example, in 1986 Paul Goldstein and I were working on a study of drugs and homicide in New York State.[60] That study involved collecting data about every homicide reported under the Uniform Crime Reports (UCR) program in New York in 1984. It quickly became clear that police departments in the middle of the 1980s in New York State were not maintaining records that could help them or anyone to establish the drug relatedness of homicides or any other crime.

Given the pressure to do something even in the absence of knowledge, state government officials began to make proposals. On June 17, 1986, Governor Mario M. Cuomo issued a press release that promised $10 million for "new and expanded programs to prevent and treat crack and other drugs" in order to "meet the urgent need to alert the public fully to the severe physical and mental dangers of crack." On July 18, 1986, the governor testified before the U.S. House Select Committee on Narcotics Abuse and Control. In arguing for a national drug strategy, he said to the committee members, "And what is the lure of crack? It appears to amount to an initial blast of false self-confidence, power, exhilaration—maybe for seven minutes. That's it—that's the kick. But then the depression, paranoia, and sometimes violence or suicide." I'm not sure how he knew that.

Over the years, law enforcement and public health experience with the drug and research findings demonstrated that using crack did not necessarily make people violent. In the midst of the crack hysteria in New York City in 1988, I was conducting a study with Paul Goldstein and Pat Ryan collecting data during active police investigation about the drug relatedness of 414 homicides from 17 police precincts around the city. We found that almost 1 of every 3 of those homicides in some way involved crack.[61] However, we found that while 85 percent of those homicides were related to crack in that they involved disputes over crack market dealings, only 5 of the 414 killings could be explained as the result of someone having used crack, and two of those also involved another drug as well.

Crack made drugs the number one concern of the government in New York state during the late 1980s. In January 1989, Governor Cuomo announced in his annual message to the state legislature that the three most serious problems facing the state were "drugs, drugs, and drugs." On October 1, 1989, the governor issued Executive Order Number 120, establishing a Statewide Anti-Drug Abuse Council. In an analysis of arrest statistics in New York City comparing 1986 to 1989, Steven Belenko found that "[s]oon after the anti-crack enforcement began in the spring of 1986, arrests for crack possession or sales were exceeding 1,400 per month. By 1989, crack arrests were averaging 3,600 per month, an increase of 157%."[62] So before anyone really knew much about the drug or what it was actually doing to people and their communities, crack became the demon drug, and programs and policies were made to respond to it.

The Relationship between Drug Use and Violence

To say that the media, government officials, academics, and others have been telling stories about drug use and violence and using those stories to support a claim that drug users are crazed killers is not the same as saying that there is no relationship between drug use and violence. A great deal of research conducted during the later decades of the twentieth century has demonstrated that, to some extent, there is. Notably, this research has tended to focus on drug or alcohol use by victims of violence rather than violent offenders, and on homicide rather than other forms of violence. Given the relative availability of toxicological data on homicide victims, this is not surprising.

For an early study of data collected from the homicide squad files of the Philadelphia Police Department, Marvin Wolfgang and Rolf Strohm analyzed data for 588 homicides committed between January 1948 and December 1952.[63] They found that in 64 percent of the cases, the victim had consumed an alcoholic beverage immediately prior to having been killed.[64] They concluded that alcohol plays either a causal or complicating role in lethal violence. Years later, in a follow-up to that study, John Hepburn and Harwin Voss found noticeable patterns of intoxicant use by homicide victims in both Philadelphia and Chicago.[65]

Other studies have considered the use of drugs besides alcohol by homicide victims. In a study of homicide in Philadelphia, Margaret Zahn and Marc Bencivengo found that homicide was the leading cause of death among drug users and that drug users accounted for about 31 percent of all homicide victims in the city in 1972.[66] More recently, Zahn with Marc Riedel and Lois Mock conducted a nationwide study of homicide and found that in those cases in which drugs were found in the body of the victim after death, alcohol and narcotics were the most commonly found drugs.[67] They did note, however, that, in general, drugs were not detectable in the bodies of victims after death.[68]

Using autopsy and toxicological data for a New York City study of the bodies of people "thought to have died unnaturally," Paul Haberman and Michael Baden concluded, "Apart from substance abuse, homicide was the leading cause of death of narcotics abusers, alcoholics, and those with both conditions."[69] Conversely, in a study of blood alcohol levels of victims of homicide in Los Angeles from 1970 to 1979, Richard Goodman and his associates found that alcohol consumption had been common among the people in their sample.[70] Using data from autopsy records from 1981 from the Office of the Medical Examiner in New York City, Kenneth Tardiff and Elliott Gross studied the circumstances of cases involving homicide victims and concluded that "victims of drug-related homicides were more likely to have only drugs present in their blood, victims of robberies were more likely to have neither alcohol nor drugs, and victims of disputes had alcohol either with or without drugs."[71]

A study of homicide victims by Robert Budd during the middle 1980s, when crack cocaine was moving into the largest of American cities, looked specifically for a link between cocaine and violence. Based on a sample of 114 homicide victims from Los Angeles County, Budd noted, "In 1987, more than one out of every five homicide victims in the county were found to have cocaine and/or its major metabolite benzoylecgonine present in their blood and/or body tissues, indicating use of cocaine a short time prior to death."[72] Looking at the data over several years, he found, "In the last seven years, cocaine has gone from a rarely detected drug [in homicide victims] to the second most frequently detected drug (second only to alcohol)."[73]

While most of the attention has gone to their victims, some studies have looked instead at the drug use of homicide offenders. During the middle 1980s, Lawrence Gary studied homicide data from various cities around the United States and found, at least among black males, a strong relationship between the commission of homicide and the use of alcohol.[74] Around the same time, William Wieczorek and his associates looked at data for 1,887 incarcerated homicide offenders interviewed for the U.S. Census Bureau surveys of inmates in 1981 and 1983. They found that 56 percent reported having been under the influence of a drug, most often alcohol, at the time of their offense.[75] Patricia Ladoceur and Mark Temple in 1985 studied rapists from the 1979 prisoner inmate survey and—finding that "less than half" of offenders studied were "under the influence of drugs" and that "a large proportion of offenders were also not under the influence of alcohol" at the time of the offense—they concluded, "If there are connections between substance abuse and crime, the links are probably not as direct as has been previously thought."[76]

Throughout the later decades of the twentieth century, a number of other studies similarly established the concomitance of drug use and violence.[77] One interesting development in recent years has been the finding that where there are gangs, there is also drug use and violence.[78] However, whether the observed drug use is in any way responsible for the violence in which gang members participate is not clear.

In 1990, Jeffrey Fagan published findings of an extensive review of the research on drugs, alcohol, and aggression and determined that "intoxication does not consistently lead to aggressive behavior."[79] He wrote,

"Although intoxication is widely found to be associated with aggressive conduct, the association is far from consistent and the reasons are diverse and poorly understood."[80] Similarly, Jan and Marcia Chaiken reviewed studies of drugs and crime and concluded that "the [u]se of illicit drugs does not appear to be strongly related to onset and participation in predatory crime."[81]

In summary, by 1990, we knew that violent situations often involve people who are using alcohol or other drugs. We also knew that it is not reasonable to conclude that violence is a direct result of alcohol or drug use. When someone who is using alcohol or other drugs does something violent, it cannot necessarily be concluded that their use of violence is a consequence of their use of alcohol or other drugs. Observation and research have shown that where there is violence there is likely to be drug or alcohol use,[82] but they have not shown that where there is alcohol or other drug use there is likely to be violence. In any case, concomitance or even covariation are not the same thing as causality.

Knowing that, at best, the current state of knowledge could not support an argument for a causal link between drug or alcohol use and violence did not stop the federal government from developing programs to routinely measure the relationship between illicit drug use and crime and violence. Early in the century, Harry Anslinger understood that government agencies compete with one another for resources. That was very clear to me as an employee in New York participating in the annual budget process of the state government. Proposals for new programs (and sometimes even for continuation of existing ones) were submitted first to the office director, then to the agency commissioner, then to the governor's Office of the Budget, and then to the state legislature. At each step, our proposals were in direct competition with other proposals for a share of the limited resources of the government. More sophisticated bureaucrats understand not only that there is a competition but also how to win that competition. One way in the so-called information age of the late twentieth century is to have a program that produces an annual statistical report. It shows not only that you are doing something but also that there is a problem that you need to do something about.

Consider the Federal Bureau of Investigation's UCR. Just as there is probably no criminologist who has not criticized the UCR, there is probably no criminologist who, at one time or another, has not cited UCR statistics. No matter how flawed they are, UCR statistics are the official crime statistics, and the UCR program has been supported continuously for most of the century. In the early 1970s, the Bureau of Justice Statistics (BJS) developed the National Crime Victimization Survey (NCVS), and, for better or worse, that program also has become a mainstay of the federal criminal justice budget. In the 1980s, NIJ recognized the need for its own statistical program, and Drug Use Forecasting (DUF)was born.

NIJ began the DUF program in 1987 and, since then, has regularly produced reports using DUF data.[83] A note from the NIJ Director James K. Stewart in the first report informed readers that "DUF information is based on the objective results of anonymous urine testing of samples of arrestees in 22 cities in all parts of the country, augmented by information from voluntary interviews."[84] Urine samples are collected and interviews conducted quarterly in a central booking location at each of the sites. Throughout the years, DUF data have shown that large proportions of people arrested in various places for various crimes test positive for a variety of drugs. One of the problems of DUF data is that testing positive for one or another drug at the time of arrest tells us little or nothing about the use of drugs at time of offense. Still, if used properly, DUF data can have some value. For example, they can show trends in the popularity of particular drugs in particular communities among particular samples of arrestees in those communities.

By the late 1990s it became apparent that if DUF was to survive as a program, competing with other federal programs for funding and resources, it needed to be representative of something. The FBI's UCR program, though not always successful at doing so, is set up to collect data on all crimes known to the police in every U.S. jurisdiction. BJS's NCVS program collects data from a national sample of respondents. How competitive is a program that tells us about drug using trends among small samples of people in a variety of communities that were not even systematically selected for participation in the program? So DUF began to evolve, and the Arrestee Drug Abuse Monitoring program (ADAM) was invented to take its place. According to the letter from NIJ Director Jeremy Travis introducing the 1996 DUF Annual Report, "Since this Report was last published, the President has submitted a budget request to Congress to reengineer DUF into the Arrestee Drug Abuse Monitoring (ADAM) program. ADAM will build on DUF's success by more than tripling in size to conduct quarterly data collection in 75 urban areas."[85]

If ADAM succeeds, it will be interesting and perhaps useful to know what drugs people arrested in communities around the United States are using. Unfortunately, however, such data will not necessarily help us understand the relationship between drugs and crime or violence. Nor, then, can it help us respond appropriately to problems that are derivative of that nexus. The DUF program and hence the ADAM program do not question the assumption of a relationship between drugs and crime or violence. Unless we know that drug using contributes to crime or violence, why do we need to invest our resources in knowing what drugs criminal or violent offenders are using? How will it help us to know whether drug using contributes to violence?

A young man I interviewed in a modern maximum security prison near Woodbourne, New York, offered his own explanation for why violence and drug using are so often found together.[86] We sat alone in a drab and dusky room off a corridor not far from the prison cell blocks.

This man told me how a "cheap competition" had turned into fatal gun play. He, a friend, and a girl they knew were walking down a street in their neighborhood when they saw two guys walking toward them. The guys, he said, started "sweatin'" his friend. The guys came from another neighborhood, but he recognized them as members of another "group." (When I asked him if he meant "gang," he became philosophical and asked me, "What is a gang? These were friends. Let's just say that.") When he asked them what they were doing in his neighborhood, they ignored him. Friends stick together. They stand tall for each other, he told me. So when these guys continued to "sweat" and "dis" his friend, he became angry. When a fight started, he put a gun to the face of one of the other guys and told him to stop bothering his friend. As he recounts the story, when they would not, the gun went off in the guy's face.

Just before this chance encounter on the street, the man I was speaking to remembers having been snorting cocaine. Earlier that morning he had about .5 grams by himself. About 15 minutes before the encounter, he had shared about 1.5 grams with a few friends. So he was high at the time, but he was emphatic when he told me that his drug consumption had nothing to do with the outcome. As he described it, it was an outgrowth of environment. There's peer pressure, he told me. There's image. There's messed-up education. There's "too much flashed in our faces without us being able to get it." What he called "the cake," he told me, is made up of more than one ingredient. The cocaine, the drugs, are just one of the ingredients. He did not need to be using drugs, he said, for the shooting to have happened.

Conclusion

A legend is a story that is handed down over time and accepted as historical truth despite the absence of empirical verification. From the tolerance of drugs during the late nineteenth century, through Harry Anslinger's attacks on marijuana users in the 1930s, to the contemporary assault on crack users, the evidence that people who use drugs become a source of social violence has never been consistent with the claims. While policy makers have been ignorant of or have chosen to ignore research findings and the lessons of history and experience, political and personal agendas have been promoted on the basis of anecdotal evidence and media accounts. In this way, the story of the drug-crazed killer has become an American legend of the twentieth century.

Throughout the twentieth century in the United States, our criminal justice system has focused its attention on drugs and drug users. For example, in New York City, from 1984 to 1989, the period when crack cocaine and its users were being demonized, data from the New York State Division of Criminal Justice Services show that the number of felony arrests for violent offenses increased by 19.8 percent, while the number of felony arrests for drug offenses increased by 142.7 percent. Similarly, the number of felony prosecutions for violent offenses increased by 3.7 percent, while the number of felony prosecutions for drug offenses increased by 372.6 percent. Why were drugs and the people who used them considered worthy of so much attention? By focusing on drug users, which was accomplished by defining them as violent, it was possible to create a massive criminal justice system that devoted more resources to arresting drug users than it did to arresting people actually charged with violent offenses. There are both rational and nonrational reasons for this.

First, drug users are an easy and plentiful target. For that reason, they can serve as fodder for a criminal justice industry that was intent on expanding rapidly and dramatically, especially at the end of the twentieth century.[87] Only so many people are killed in any given year, and therefore only so many murderers can be brought to justice. According to UCR statistics, in 1996 there were 18,108 homicide offenders throughout the United States.[88] On the other hand, despite recognizing the difficulty of really knowing how many people use illicit drugs during any given year, the ONDCP in its 1998 drug control strategy estimated that there were about 13 million illicit drug users in 1996 in the United States.[89] Any person or agency that wants to show that they are tough on crime can do a lot more with 13 million drug users than they can with 18,000 murderers.

Our moral and cultural tendency to equate drugs with evil has also contributed to our willingness, if not our desire, to demonize drug users. As numerous historians and social scientists have observed, throughout the twentieth century there have been in the United States a series of drug scares accompanied in each case with some measure of hysteria about drug users.[90] Craig Reinarman and Harry Levine have suggested that these moral panics are the result of "pharmacological determinism."

> Citizens and scientists alike have been inculcated with the notion that illicit drugs are inherently dangerous like contagious diseases. But drugs, unlike viruses, are not active agents; they are inert substances. They do not jump out of their containers and into people's bodies without the people in those bodies actively deciding to ingest them. Many Americans understand that drug abuse is more likely among some types of people and under some circumstances than others. Yet, because of our history, American culture lacks a vocabulary with which people can speak about drugs in this more complicated, qualified way.[91]

Rather than try to understand and appreciate the complex role that drugs do or could play in our lives and our culture, it is easier to think of drugs as one thing and drug users as one type of person.

Toward the end of July 1998 a wave of steaming hot weather swept across the southeastern United States from Texas and settled on the mid-Atlantic coast. In that sweltering heat, Representative Elijah E. Cummings led about a dozen members of the Congressional Black Caucus the short distance from Washington, D.C., to Baltimore, Maryland, where local government officials routinely claim that 55,000 of its approximately 650,000 citizens are drug addicts. On July 21 in the Baltimore *Sun*, Peter Hermann wrote about this visit in an article called "A 'human face' for addiction." He noted that Baltimore was to be the "first stop for the caucus, whose members plan a nationwide tour of urban and rural America to promote a series of bills to make drug addiction a priority in Congress." No legislative proposals were offered, but after six hours the visitors acknowledged that drug addiction is "more of a health issue than a law enforcement problem." That would suggest an emphasis on treatment over arrest. On the day of the visit, Baltimore—where Mayor Kurt L. Schmoke has repeatedly expressed his willingness to at least study drug legalization, where Police Commissioner Thomas C. Frazier has repeatedly said that the police "can't arrest its way out of the drug problem," where a needle-exchange program was established with minimal controversy, and where local researchers were taken seriously when they proposed a study "in which heroin would be distributed to hard-core addicts in an effort to reduce crime"—had only 7,500 treatment slots available for its estimated 55,000 drug addicts, and a waiting list of 30 days.

One man who watched but did not get to meet the visitors from Congress was 52-year-old James Burley. Burley, according to the *Sun*, was a drug addict for 30 years and throughout his life was arrested 41 times, "mostly for stealing to get drug money." After being released from prison the last time, he sought treatment and claims to have faked a suicide at a hospital emergency room to be considered eligible. He told the *Sun* reporter, "All the times that I got arrested, no one ever saw fit to offer me any treatment. I had to beg and ask a judge for some help, and he sent me to jail and said I had to work my way into treatment. It was hard to convince someone that I was worth saving."

Endnotes

1. Kaplan, J. (1971). *Marijuana—The New Prohibition*. New York: Pocket Books.
2. Kaplan 1971:91ff. See also Inciardi, J. (1992). *The War on Drugs II*. Mountain View, CA: Mayfield. McWilliams, J. C. (1990) *The Protectors: Harry J. Anslinger and the Federal Bureau of Narcotics*. Newark: University of Delaware.
3. DREIM # 236.
4. Roth, J. A. (1994b). *Psychoactive Substances and Violence. Research in Brief*. February. Washington, DC: National Institute of Justice.
5. See Currie, E. (1993). *Reckoning—Drugs, the Cities, and the American Future*. New York: Hill and Wang, pp.170–71. Inciardi 1992:160.

6. Nurco, D. N., Hanlon, T. F., Balter, M. B., Kinlock, T. W., Slaght, E. (1991). "A Classification of Narcotics Addicts Based on Type, Amount, and Severity of Crime." *Journal of Drug Issues* 21:429–48.

7. Inciardi 1992:3.

8. Inciardi 1992:4–8.

9. Inciardi 1992:5, 6–7, 9.

10. Musto, D. (1997). "Opium, Cocaine and Marijuana in American History." In L. K. Gaines and P. B. Kraska (eds.), *Drugs, Crime, and Justice—Contemporary Perspectives.* Prospect Heights, IL: Waveland, p. 23.

11. Inciardi 1992:15.

12. Inciardi 1992:17.

13. Inciardi 1992:17.

14. Inciardi 1992:15.

15. Inciardi 1992. Kaplan 1971; Musto 1997; Smith, M. A. (1988). "The Drug Problem—Is There an Answer?" *Federal Probation* 52:3–6.

16. Falco, M. (1989). *Winning the War on Drugs—A National Strategy.* New York: Priority Press. Smith 1988.

17. Huxley, A. (1954). *Doors of Perception.* New York: Harper and Row, p. 62.

18. Weil, A. (1972). *The Natural Mind—An Investigation of Drugs and Higher Consciousness.* Boston: Houghton Mifflin, p. 189.

19. Trebach, A. S. (1982). *The Heroin Solution.* New Haven: Yale University Press, p. 22.

20. Schur, E. (1962). *Narcotic Addiction in Britain and America—The Impact of Public Policy.* Bloomington: Indiana University Press, p. 186.

21. Zimmer, L. and Morgan, J. P. (1997). *Marijuana Myths, Marijuana Facts—A Review of Scientific Evidence.* New York: Lindesmith Center, p. 17.

22. Bakalar, J. B. and Grinspoon, L. (1984). *Drug Control in a Free Society.* Cambridge: Cambridge University Press, p. 69.

23. Musto, D. (1973). *The American Disease.* New Haven: Yale University Press.

24. Duster, T. (1970). *The Legislation of Morality—Law, Drugs, and Moral Judgment.* New York: The Free Press, pp. 20–21.

25. Duster 1970:21.

26. Inciardi 1992:21. See also Sloman, L. (1979), *Reefer Madness—Marijuana in America.* New York: Grove. Zimmer and Morgan 1997.

27. Inciardi 1992:82.

28. Williams, T. (1992). *Crackhouse—Notes from the End of the Line.* New York: Penguin Books.

29. Hughes, E.C. (1945). "Dilemmas and Contradictions of Status." *American Journal of Sociology* 50:353–59.

30. Becker, H.S. (1963). *The Outsiders—Studies in the Sociology of Deviance.* New York: The Free Press, p. 33.

31. Becker 1963:34.

32. Hughes 1945.

33. Biden, J. R., Jr. (1990). *Fighting Drug Abuse: A National Strategy.* Washington, DC: Prepared by the Majority Staffs of the Senate Judiciary Committee and the International Narcotics Control Caucus, January, p. 5.

34. Cited in Kaplan 1971:92.

35. Kaplan 1971:92.

36. McWilliams 1990:13–14.

37. McWilliams 1990:46.

38. See Inciardi 1992; McWilliams 1990; Sloman 1979.

39. McWilliams 1990:50.

40. Sloman 1979:57.

41. Sloman 1979:58–60; Kaplan 1971:93–96.

42. Kaplan 1971:93.

43. Brownstein, H. H. 1992. "Making Peace in the War on Drugs. *Humanity and Society* 16:217–35. Inciardi 1992; Musto 1973; Smith 1988.

44. Meisler, S. (1996). "The First Drug Czar." *The Drug Policy Letter* 29:13–17. The article was a reprint and originally appeared in *The Nation* on February 20, 1962, not too long before Anslinger retired in May 1962.

45. Meisler 1996:17.

46. Reinarman, C. and Levine, H. (1989). "Crack in Context: Politics and Media in the Making of a Drug Scare." *Contemporary Drug Problems* 16:536.

47. Martz, L. et al. (1989). "The Tide of Drug Killing." *Newsweek* January 16:44.

48. Martz 1989:44.

49. President's Commission on Law Enforcement and Administration of Justice. (1968). *The Challenge of Crime in a Free Society—The Complete Official Report*. New York: Avon Books.

50. Inciardi 1992: 156

51. Inciardi 1992:156.

52. Inciardi 1992:270–1.

53. Office of National Drug Control Policy. (1989). *National Drug Control Strategy*. September. Washington, DC: Executive Office of the President.

54. See the various articles included in Reinarman, C. and Levine, H. G. (1997a). *Crack in America—Demon Drugs and Social Justice*. Berkeley: University of California Press. See also Reuter, P. H. and Ebener, P. A. (1992). *Cocaine: The First Decade*. RAND Drug Policy Research Center Issue Paper. April. Santa Monica, CA: The RAND Drug Policy Research Center.

55. Quoted in Morley, J. (1996). "White Grams' Burden." *The Drug Policy Letter*. Winter:17.

56. Brownstein, H. H. (1998). "The Drugs-Violence Connection: Constructing Policy from Research Findings." Pp. 59–70 in E. L. Jensen and J. Gerber (eds.), *The New War on Drugs: Symbolic Politics and Criminal Justice Policy*. Cincinnati: Anderson. Brownstein, H. H. (1996). *The Rise and Fall of a Violent Crime Wave: Crack Cocaine and the Social Construction of a Crime Problem*. Guilderland, NY: Harrow and Heston. Reinarman and Levine 1989.

57. Division of Substance Abuse Services. (1986). *Study of Crack Smokers*. Albany, NY: NYS Division of Substance Abuse Services.

58. Reinarman and Levine 1989.

59. Brownstein, H. H. (1991). "The Media and the Construction of Random Drug Violence." *Social Justice* 18:85–103.

60. The study was conducted through NDRI (then Narcotic and Drug Research, later National Development and Research Institutes) and funded by the National Institute of Justice.

61. Goldstein, P. J., Brownstein, H. H., Ryan, P. J., Bellucci, P. A. (1989). "Crack and Homicide in New York City, 1988: A Conceptually-Based Event Analysis." *Contemporary Drug Problems* 16:651–87.

62. Belenko, S. R. (1993). *Crack and the Evolution of Anti-Drug Policy*. Westport, CT: Greenwood, p. 117.

63. Wolfgang, M. E. and Strohm, R. B. (1956). "The Relationship between Alcohol and Criminal Homicide." *Quarterly Journal of Studies on Alcohol* 17:411–25.

64. Wolfgang and Strohm 1956:416.

65. Hepburn, J. and Voss, H. L. (1970). "Patterns of Criminal Homicide—A Comparison of Chicago and Philadelphia." *Criminology* 8:21–45.

66. Zahn, M. A. and Bencivengo, M. (1974). "Violent Death: A Comparison between Drug Users and Nondrug Users." *Addictive Diseases* 1:283–96.

67. Riedel, M., Zahn, M. A. and Mock, L. (1985). *The Nature and Patterns of American Homicide*. Washington, DC: National Institute of Justice.

68. Riedel, Zahn and Mock 1985:19.

69. Haberman, P. W. and Baden, M. M. (1978). *Alcohol, Other Drugs and Violent Death*. New York: Oxford University Press, p. 8.

70. Goodman, R. A. Mercy, J. A., Loya, F., Rosenberg, M. L., Smith, J.C., Allen, N. H., Vargas, L. and Kolts, R. (1986). "Alcohol Use and Interpersonal Violence: Alcohol Detected in Homicide Victims." *American Journal of Public Health* 76:144–49.

71. Tardiff, K. and Gross, E. M. (1986). "Homicide in New York City." *Bulletin of the New York Academy of Medicine* 62: 413–26.

72. Budd, R. D. (1989). "Cocaine Abuse and Violent Death." *American Journal of Drug and Alcohol Abuse* 14:375.

73. Budd 1989:377.

74. Gary, L. E. (1986). "Drinking, Homicide, and the Black Male." *Journal of Black Studies* 17:15–31.

75. Wieczorek, W F., Welte, J. W., and Abel, E. L. (1990). "Alcohol, Drugs, and Murder: A Study of Convicted Homicide Offenders." *Journal of Criminal Justice* 18:220.

76. Ladoceur, P. and Temple, M. (1985). "Substance Use among Rapists: A Comparison with Other Serious Felons." *Crime and Delinquency* 31:288.

77. Altschuler, D. M. and Brounstein, P. J. (1991). "Patterns of Drug Use, Drug Trafficking, and Other Delinquency Among Inner-City Adolescent Males in Washington, D.C." *Criminology* 29:589–621. Ball, J.C., Schaeffer, J.W., and Nurco, D.N. (1983). "The Day-to-Day Criminality of Heroin Addicts in Baltimore—A Study in the Continuity of Offense Rates." *Drug and Alcohol Dependence* 12:119–42. Dembo, R.L. et al. (1990). "The Relationship between Cocaine Use, Drug Sales, and Other Delinquency among a Cohort of High Risk Youths Over Time." Pp. 112–35 in M. De La Rosa, E. Y. Lambert, and B. Gropper (eds.), *Drugs and Violence: Causes, Correlates, and Consequences*, NIDA Research Monograph No. 103. Rockville, MD: National Institute on Drug Abuse. Fendrich, M. et al. (1995). "Substance Involvement among Juvenile Murderers: Comparisons with Older Offenders Based on Prison Inmates." *The International Journal of the Addictions* 30:1363–82; Spunt, B. et al. (1995). "Drug Use by Homicide Offenders." *Journal of Psychoactive Drugs* 27:125–34.

78. De La Rosa, M. and Soriano, F. I. (1992). "Understanding Criminal Activity and Use of Alcohol and Cocaine Derivatives by Multi-Ethnic Gang Members." Pp. 24–42 in R. Cervantes (ed.), Substance Abuse and Gang Violence. Newbury Park, CA: Sage. Fagan, J. (1989). "The Social Organization of Drug Use and Drug Dealing Among Urban Gangs." *Criminology* 27:633–667; Fagan, J. and Chin, K. L. (1990). "Violence as Regulation and Social Control in the Distribution of Crack." Pp. 8–43 in M. De La Rosa, E. Y. Lambert, and B. Gropper (eds.), *Drugs and Violence: Causes, Correlates, and Consequences*. Washington, DC: National Institute on Drug Abuse. Klein, M., Maxson, C. L., and Cunningham, L. C. (1991). "'Crack,' Street Gangs, and Violence." *Criminology* 29:701–17.

79. Fagan, J. (1990). "Intoxication and Aggression." Pp. 241–320 in M. Tonry and J. Q. Wilson (eds.), *Drugs and Crime*. Chicago: University of Chicago Press, p. 243.

80. Fagan 1990: 243–4.

81. Chaiken, J. M. and Chaiken, M. R. (1990). "Drugs and Predatory Crime." Pp. 203–39 in M. Tonry and J. Q. Wilson (eds.), *Drugs and Crime*. Chicago: University of Chicago Press, p. 243.

82. Kaplan, H. B. (1995). *Drugs, Crime, and Other Deviant Adaptations—Longitudinal Studies*. New York: Plenum.

83. National Institute of Justice. (1990). *DUF—1988 Drug Use Forecasting Annual Report— Drugs and Crime in America*. Research in Action. March. Washington, DC: U.S. Department of Justice.

84. NIJ 1990:2.

85. National Institute of Justice. (1997). *1996 Drug Use Forecasting—Annual Report on Adult and Juvenile Arrestees*. June. Washington, DC: U.S. Department of Justice.

86. DREIM # 039.

87. Gordon, D. R. (1990). *The Justice Juggernaut—Fighting Street Crime, Controlling Citizens*. New Brunswick, NJ: Rutgers University Press.

88. Federal Bureau of Investigation. (1997). *Crime in the United States, 1996*. Washington, DC: U.S. Government Printing Office.

89. Office of National Drug Control Policy. (1998). *The National Drug Control Strategy, 1998—A Ten Year Plan*. Washington, DC: Executive Office of the President.

90. Inciardi 1992; Jensen, E. L. and Gerber, .J (1998). *The New War on Drugs: Symbolic Politics and Criminal Justice Policy*. Cincinnati: Anderson. Musto 1973. Reinarman and Levine 1989.

91. Reinarman, C. and Levine, H. G. (1997b). "Crack in Context—America's Latest Demon Drug." Pp. 1–17 in C. Reinarman and H. G. Levine (eds.), *Crack in America—Demon Drugs and Social Justice*. Berkeley: University of California Press.

3

The Yarn of the Malevolent Drug Dealer

As we sat across the table from each other in an office near the counseling area of Woodbourne Prison in New York, I told the man facing me that I was doing research and wanted to talk to him about the homicide for which he had been sentenced.[1] He smiled and told me he had been acquitted of that homicide. He was in prison for an assault. But, he interrupted before I could end our meeting, he had indeed committed the homicide and would be happy to tell me about it.

It was a winter day near the end of 1984, and he was 21 years old. He and a close friend were heavily involved in dealing cocaine. Every other day they would meet their supplier, who would give them $800 worth of cocaine for $400. (They were good customers, so it was given to them on consignment.) They would cut the cocaine into smaller weights and place it into foil packets for sale on the street. Then they went around the block to their usual corner, where they sold the cocaine to regular customers whom, he told me, knew them for their personal honesty and high-quality product. They both carried guns, serving as their own enforcer. Sometimes their mothers, who were also friends, would act as steerers for them, bringing customers with money to the boys. Their mothers, however, also did this for rival dealers, including some of the many Rastafarian dealers in the neighborhood. The boys did not like this, so sometimes they shortchanged their mothers.

The morning of the killing, he sat in the car while his friend went into the building where their supplier lived. He was tired. The night before, he had driven to another state to see his girlfriend, and at 7:00 A.M. he and his partner met for an early breakfast. After breakfast, they sniffed cocaine and shared a pint of Southern Comfort. Then they went to see their supplier. After 30 minutes of waiting for his friend to come back to the car, he decided to go inside and see what was happening. In the first floor hallway, he saw his friend against the wall with a gun pointed at his head. Holding the gun was a local Rastafarian drug dealer with whom they had been feuding ever since he accused them of stealing his customers. Suddenly, the Rastafarian dealer turned the gun toward him and fired. The bullet flew over his head. Instantly, he raised his hands, which were still in his coat pockets holding his guns, and fired back. One bullet hit the rival dealer in the mouth, killing him. He took the dead man's drugs, money, and gun, grabbed his friend, and ran outside shooting wildly all the time. They jumped into their car and drove away.

Throughout the twentieth century, we have been regaled with stories of the violent adventures of drug dealers, of drug dealers as adventurous heroes. In this chapter, those stories are considered in the context of government reports, media accounts, and research findings to address the question of how drug trafficking and drug markets are related to violence and how we as a society view that relationship. Emphasis is on how drug dealers came to be viewed as the purveyors of violence, with particular attention to what happened in the crack markets of big cities in the United States in the 1980s. The significance of placing drug markets outside of the legitimate methods and procedures of dispute resolution is considered. From my own research, specific case descriptions of drug market activity, taken from interviews with individuals involved in the illicit drug markets in New York City in the late twentieth century, are included.

The Relationship between Drug Markets and Violence

Against the black cover of the August 19, 1991, edition of *U.S. News & World Report* was a picture of several small, clear vials with pink plastic tops, each containing a gritty white substance. The headline on the cover read, "The Men Who Created Crack." The story, by Gordon Witkin, ran for ten pages. In ten "chapters," it told the story of "how crack infiltrated America." It was presented as "a cautionary tale about what happens when hopelessness grips whole communities—how it lays them open to the allure of easy money and unspeakable violence." Along with the text, photographs, and a map showing the routes by which crack presumably traveled to and through the United States, each page of the article had a single column with the story of someone who allegedly played an important role in the establishment of the crack trade in American cities. For example, there were the Chambers brothers who ran 200 crack houses employing 500 people in Detroit. Their employees worked long hours and followed strict rules. According to the article, "Quality-control managers posed as crack buyers to keep an eye on the product. Rule breakers were referred to the so-called wrecking crew, which, officials say, exacted discipline by tossing violators out a window."[2] In Miami, there was Vivian Blake and Lester Coke, reportedly leaders of a Jamaican drug trafficking organization called the Shower posse. "The Showers took their name from the fierce gun battles they initiated: They 'showered' the area with blood and body parts."[3] To put the adventures of these violent drug outlaws in context, the column on the last page of the article was about Chicago and had a picture of the legendary Al Capone, an adventurous drug dealer from another era of American history.

While most of the research exploring the link between drugs and violence has focused on drug *use*, there have been attempts to uncover and understand how violence may be related to drug *trafficking*. In a historical review of homicide statistics in the United States during the twentieth century, Margaret Zahn observed a temporal relationship between overall homicide rates and the establishment of markets for illegal goods.[4] Her research demonstrated that, for the period of the twentieth century through 1980, homicide rates peaked in the 1920s and 1930s when control of the illegal alcohol market was being disputed, declined after the end of Prohibition, leveled off before beginning to rise again in 1965, and finally peaked again in 1974 when competition ensued for control of the illegal heroin and cocaine markets. She wrote, "It seems possible, if not likely, that establishing and maintaining a market for illegal goods (booze in the 1920s and early 1930s; heroin and cocaine in the late 1960s and early 1970s) may involve controlling and/or reducing competition, solving disputes between alternate suppliers or eliminating dissatisfied customers."[5]

A number of studies in the 1980s supported Zahn's contention that there was a link between violence and illicit markets. Ronald Heffernan and his associates studied homicides in one police precinct in New York City in 1981 and found that 42 percent of the killings in their sample in some way involved illegal drug trafficking.[6] In her study of marijuana growing in California, Patricia Adler described the danger and violence associated with the business, noting how growers were "required [to carry] and occasionally [use] shotguns, handguns, and rifles."[7] Then, toward the end of the decade, Jeffrey Fagan studied gangs, drug dealing, and violence and concluded that while "involvement in drug trafficking may be higher in gangs than among other urban youth,"[8] at the same time it can be argued that "[s]erious crime and violence occur regardless of the prevalence of drug dealing within the gang."[9] Just as Zahn had earlier suggested that the violence associated with illicit markets was most pronounced when those markets were unstable, Fagan reminded us that violence by people involved in drug dealing also occurs independent of their drug market activity.

In a pioneering epidemiological study of heroin addicts in Chicago in the 1970s, Patrick Hughes and his colleagues observed that heroin dealers routinely used violence in their daily lives.

[H]eroin dealers must have a reputation for violence, otherwise addicts and other deviants would simply take their drugs and their money. In the communities we studied, most dealers either carried, or had easy access to, guns and knives. By working in pairs or small groups they could beat or injure anyone who caused trouble.[10]

That is, Hughes believed that the violence of the heroin dealers was a matter of necessity, with the dealers needing to use it to survive in a world in which social relationships were governed by violence. He observed that "dealers were not the only source of violence. Deviants of all sorts frequented the addicts' street hangouts, and in these high-crime neighborhoods there was always the risk of confrontation by a drunk, or by members of a delinquent gang who wanted to take away an addict's freshly stolen television set."[11]

From his early work in Chicago, Hughes had uncovered what he viewed as an "addict subculture, outside the law, [that] governed itself by violence."[12] Others have likewise argued that there are subcultures of violence,[13] and social scientists have long known that culture and social structure are inextricably related.[14] So, to the extent that violence is inherent in the values and way of life of any group or subgroup of people, violence is also then a product of their routine patterns of social relationship. That would explain, at least in part, the violence Paul Goldstein and I found in our study of homicide in New York City in 1988,[15] a time of newly emerging and unstable crack cocaine markets and exceptionally high recorded levels of violent crime.[16]

Crack does not exist in nature. It had to be thought up and then manufactured by people. In his article for *U.S. News* about the establishment of crack markets in the United States, Witkin wrote, "Crack was not invented; it was created by a sharp crowd of sinister geniuses who took a simple production technique to make a packaged, ready-to-consume form of the product [otherwise expensive cocaine] with a low unit price to entice massive numbers of consumers."[17] So crack was not only a new drug, but also what Craig Reinarman and Harry Levine called "a marketing innovation."[18] In sum, crack was so popular because as a product it was easy to manufacture, could be packaged in low-priced units for sale, and had high addiction potential.[19] So, as an economic market, crack had both high sales volumes and high profit margins.[20]

As a new product, crack was introduced in U.S. cities without an existing consumer base. That was not a problem. In fact, given the glut of cocaine entering the United States during the early 1980s,[21] that was the point of crack cocaine. As Terry Williams observed in his ethnographic study of crack dealing in New York City in the late 1980s, in that it was a low-priced form of a high-priced product with a high addiction potential, "Crack offered a chance to expand sales [of cocaine] in ways never possible before because it was packaged in small quantities that sold for as little as two to five dollars. This allowed dealers to attract a new class of consumer: the persistent poor."[22] In addition, as a new product in a new market, there was no established hierarchy of power and authority to regulate or control the manufacture, distribution, sale, or purchasing of crack. Similarly, as an illicit product it was not subject to legal constraints or controls. So, anyone with a little initiative and enough money for a small amount of cocaine had the opportunity to go into business for him- or herself. Operating outside of both the legitimate and the illegitimate economies, these crack dealing entrepreneurs commonly used violence to resolve disputes, such as those between dealers over market share or between dealers and their customers over product quality.[23]

In the 1990s, violent crime rates began to decline throughout most of the United States at the same time that researchers in large cities began to observe that crack markets were becoming more stable and less violent.[24] By the late 1990s, a series of reports by the National Institute of Justice (NIJ) looked closely at the relationship between drugs (particularly crack) and violence. As part of an attempt to understand the decline in officially measured violent crime in the United States during the 1990s, these reports looked at the crack–violence nexus in the broader context of national and regional demographic patterns, changes in criminal justice and specifically law enforcement policies and practices, and changes in economic and social conditions.[25] While they naturally showed that violence in a community is related to a variety of factors, these reports did support the conclusion that the violence in the United States during the late 1980s could at least in part be explained in terms of drug market instability.[26]

Systemic Drug-Related Violence

When I first met Paul Goldstein in the middle of the 1980s, he had just written an article about his idea that drugs could be related to violence in three different ways.[27] Beyond the notion that drug ingestion or the compulsive need to get money for drugs could drive a person to violence, what intrigued me most about his framework was what he called the systemic type of drug-related violence. As Paul defined it, drug-related violence was systemic when the violence was a product of the traditionally aggressive patterns of interaction within any system of drug use and distribution. In that sense, violence might occur when rival drug dealers disagreed about the boundaries of their sales territory, or when drug workers needed to be admonished for misappropriating drugs or money that rightfully belonged to their boss. Similarly, drug dealers might have to be chided by customers to whom they sold adulterated or phony drugs, and customers who bought good drugs might have to be reprimanded for not paying the dealers from whom they purchased those drugs. What was so fascinating was that these problems could occur in any business, but in legitimate businesses, there are mechanisms for resolving them that do not involve violence.

When Paul and I, with the help of Pat Ryan, studied homicides during active police investigations in New York City in 1988, a year when crack markets in the city were at their most violent, we did find that more than half of the homicides we studied were related to drugs and about 75 percent of those were systemic.[28] Of the systemic cases, 65 percent involved crack cocaine.[29] Of the known offenders in the drug-related cases, we found that more than 50 percent did have an official record in New York State for prior criminal offending.[30] In fact, among the almost 500 offenders who carried out those homicides, we found a few who did fit the popular image of the drug dealer as a malevolent and violent individual. One, perhaps the most notable, was involved in at least three separate homicides, the last one being his own.[31]

As we heard it from the detectives who were working the cases, the story began when a young man was approached by a stranger. The man was standing at a telephone booth with a woman he knew. The stranger, a man just a few years his senior, walked up to him and without question fired three shots from a semiautomatic handgun into his head. The police determined that the man was killed on the orders of local drug dealers. The man was an employee of the dealers and apparently was trying to go into business for himself. Unfortunately for him, he was trying to do so in their territory without their permission. Besides, he owed his employers money, and they were tired of waiting for him to pay them back.

A few months later, a 30-year-old woman from Jamaica walked into a hotel room where she was supposed to meet someone she knew. Instead she was greeted by a stranger who choked her, stabbed her, and beat her to death. The woman was known to the police as a high-level drug dealer, specifically a drug courier. It was not clear what she had done, but whatever it was it had not made her bosses happy. The stranger who killed her was the same man who earlier killed the man at the phone booth.

The man who committed the two murders was known to the police to be a hired killer for a number of drug dealers. He charged from $200 to $400 per killing. His specialty was intimidating dealers who encroached on the territories of his employers. He was so good at it that his reputation had inspired local legend. In one story, he was walking down a street with his arm around his girlfriend when, for no apparent reason, he took out a handgun and, without releasing his embrace, shot her in the head. Next, he was supposed to have dragged her body to a park and dropped it under some bushes. He was so cool about it he was given the nickname "Ice." He was also supposed to have been smart. For example, he never used the same weapon twice, instead disposing of it after use and buying a new one for the next job.

Local hero or not, he was not that smart. Within months of the second killing, he was shot in the head at a drug sales location. It appears that he was not satisfied with his income as an enforcer for other drug dealers and started his own business robbing those same drug dealers. As a contract employee for so many dealers, he knew a great deal about the local business community and used that knowledge to select robbery victims. The dealers who were hiring him to kill their business rivals and recalcitrant employees grew tired of his interference in their street-level trade. He was the victim of a contract with another enforcer in retaliation for robbing the employees of the people for whom he worked.

It would be hard to argue against the pure malevolence of this man. A closer look at his violence as it relates specifically to the drug market, however, suggests something else. In each instance, his violence was directed at someone who participated in the drug market or someone, such as his girlfriend, who associated with other people who did. It was not random or aimless, but rather deliberate and focused. It was not necessarily or even primarily used to cause harm or pain or to dominate people he did not know, but rather for the purpose of doing business—the drug business. Of the homicides we studied in New York that were related to the drug market, more than one-third involved disputes between rival dealers over territory, about one-fifth involved the robbery of a drug dealer, about one-seventh involved assaults to collect drug-related debts, and the remainder involved things such as disputes over bad drugs, disputes over the theft of drugs, and the punishment of drug workers.[32] None involved a drug dealer or drug worker or drug customer chasing after people not involved in the trade. Further, we found that of those offenders and victims of these killings who were known to the police, more than half of the offenders and about two-thirds of the victims were known to the local police to have been drug traffickers, and almost as many had official prior criminal histories for drug sales or possession.[33] That is, systemic drug-related violence is almost always aimed at people involved in the drug markets. When it does affect other people, they are likely to be people who are unfortunate enough to reside or be present in an area where drug markets operate.

Remember the story of how crack markets were opened and evolved in American cities? In the 1991 *U.S. News & World Report* article on the growth and violence of crack markets, Witkin wrote, "What turned crack into a craze was mass marketing that would have made McDonald's proud."[34] But while dealing in crack or other drugs may be a business, it is not a business like your neighborhood supermarket or your local gas station. Drug dealers are businesspeople who work in a domain where their business operations and exchanges are not governed by law or other formal or traditional means of social control. In a legitimate business, disputes over who has what rights to what share of the market or whether the quality of a product or service meets established standards, for example, are settled through institutionalized legal means. For drug dealers, this is not an option. Instead, violence is used to resolve business disputes over market share and product quality. Thus, it can be argued that drug dealers are not necessarily evil people who engage in violence for its own sake or demons who direct violence at innocent people, but rather are businesspeople who are trying to preserve or enhance their share of the market or the quality of their product.

Battling over Market Share

Whatever drug is being bought and sold, a drug market is an economic market. There are differences in terms of things such as the characteristics of sellers and buyers, the level of demand for the product, the organization of the business, and the size and frequency of purchases.[35] But the underlying dynamic of any drug market is economic. There are buyers and sellers, supply and demand, and competition.

A distinctive characteristic of any drug market as an economic market is the nature of the risks faced by market participants. These risks have been identified as "arrest, possibly leading to conviction and incarceration; loss of the gains from their criminal activity, as a result of law-enforcement actions or theft by competitors, suppliers, customers, or deceptive collaborators; and injury or death caused by these other market participants."[36] If a legitimate business is the victim of theft, it can seek reparation through law enforcement, and, if that is unsuccessful, through an insurance claim or other legal action. If a legitimate business has its legally established market share unfairly threatened by a competitor, it can seek to have the intrusive operations of that competitor halted by the courts. Drug operations do not have refuge in the law and must respond to threats to their business directly and with their own resources.

Similarly, theft by employees can be damaging in any business. In a legitimate business, the dishonest employee can be fired or even turned over to law enforcement authorities. Drug dealers do not have those options and need to deal with such problems on their own. The killing of two young men in New York City, as described by detectives for the 1988 homicide study, demonstrates how this can operate.[37]

Three young men, all in their early 20s, were selling crack for a local drug dealer. It appears that they saw an opportunity to increase their income and were caught having "messed up the money." That is, they stole from their employer. The employer was unhappy and went with a business associate to rob the men of their drugs and money and to murder them. The robbery was designed to serve as a cover for the murder. Fortunately for the police, the drug dealer employer was a cousin of one of the murdered employees. When they received word that the dealer would be attending a wedding of a mutual relative, they waited for him outside the restaurant and arrested him when he walked outside for a cigarette. He asked for one last drink and was then taken to jail wearing his tuxedo.

In those instances when drug dealers disagree about their rights in a particular market, it is not always clear whose claim is legitimate, or at least justifiable. Since their business operates outside of the law, there are no legal standards, and the courts have no jurisdiction in the commercial dispute. In a story told us by a New York City detective about a 1988 homicide, my colleagues and I heard about a 36-year-old man from the Dominican Republic who was shot several times in the head and neck.[38] He was a low-level crack dealer operating in an area claimed by other dealers whose ancestry went back to Puerto Rico. Apparently, he was told that if he intended to sell drugs in the area he would have to purchase his product from a particular Puerto Rican supplier. He refused and instead began to expand his own sales in the market they claimed as theirs. He was sitting in his car when two men walked up to him and shot him.

On the bottom corner of the front page of the *Washington Post* on Sunday, April 28, 1996, was an article called "The Drug Fiefdom of Northern Mexico." Arguing that "Northern Mexico's slide toward becoming a new Latin fiefdom for the movement of drugs is a major problem for the United States," the subtitle was "Cartels' Billions Distort Economy of Booming Industrial Region." Besides the text, the pictures of people and cars crossing the border from Mexico to the United States, and a map showing where the crossings were taking place, there were pictures of the smiling faces of cartel "leaders." There was Caro Quintero of the Sonora Cartel, known for being one of the "first Mexican organizations to transport drugs for the Colombian kingpins." There was Carrillo Fuentes of the Juarez Cartel, who "pioneered the use of Boeing 727s for bulk shipments of as much as 15 tons of cocaine between South America and Northern Mexico." And there was Garcia Abrego of the Gulf Cartel, which was at one time "the undisputed champ of the Mexican organizations." Brilliant businessmen all, they might have been showcased in the *Wall Street Journal* rather than the *Washington Post* except for one thing—their use of violence to resolve disputes over market share. As Molly Moore and John Ward Anderson wrote, "Shootouts between rival groups often occur along the border; in some major cities, drug assassinations are nearly a daily occurrence. The victims' bodies are found with the telltale mafia signatures—hands tied and a single bullet in the head."

Managing Product Quality

Success in business depends on the quality of the product or service being sold. The drug business is no exception. One way to use quality to maximize sales is to convince customers and potential customers that your service or product is of the highest quality. Quality control measures are necessary to assure that standards of quality are maintained by everyone involved in the manufacture or distribution of what you sell. Drug dealers mark their products with name brands or other markings, for example, to make sure that they are distinguishable from the supposedly lesser-quality products of others.[39]

Such a marketing plan was described by a youngster who was interviewed for the study my colleagues and I did of young people under custody in New York for violent offending.[40] As this young man told the interviewer, back in the community where he lived before his custody he had been involved in a very organized crack selling business. An older supplier would bring the raw product, cocaine, from other parts of the region. He and his friends were responsible for preparing it for sale as crack: cooking, cutting, and weighing. Then it would be sold at a crack spot. To distinguish their product from others, they would use purple tops on their vials. Every selling organization had its own color. According to the boy being interviewed, "The crackheads would come for the purple tops, 'cause it was the best."

If someone were to use your markings to sell a lesser-quality product, it would reflect on your product and probably have an adverse impact on your sales—clearly an unacceptable situation. While sanctions in legitimate businesses are typically legal in nature, in the drug business, they are most often violent.

The story of what happened to the young man called Soapy is an example of how this works.[41] My colleagues and I heard this story from New York City Police Department detectives as part of our study of homicide in New York City in 1988. Soapy got his name from his practice of mixing little chunks of soap in vials that were supposed to contain only crack cocaine. He took these vials to a spot that belonged to another dealer and sold them as if they were real. The dealer who "owned" the spot knew Soapy's trickery would reflect badly on him, so he warned Soapy to stay away or face retaliation in the form of death. Soapy disregarded the warning and was killed on the spot.

Of course, not all drug dealers are equally intelligent. Sometimes they do foolish things that, despite their best efforts, can hurt their own business. Such was the case with the man who killed Soapy. The police received a tip from an informer about the automobile owned by the drug dealer who killed Soapy. They found the car and took it and the man who was sitting in it at the time to the police station. When Soapy's killer heard on the street that his car had been impounded by the police, he became angry. He believed the car had been taken illegally and rushed to the police station to demand his constitutional right to his car. The police were happy to see him and immediately arrested him for Soapy's murder.

Declaring War on Drug Dealers

Given the evidence from research and statistics and the observations of people in the field of law enforcement, it would be difficult to argue that drug dealers do not use violence. They do. However, whether they are violent people who use violence without restraint is another question. The evidence that they use violence in their business dealings is irrefutable. Plus, there are reasonable claims being made by reasonable people suggesting that violence engendered in drug markets spreads or disperses to other areas of social life.[42] Nonetheless, the conclusion that drug dealers are all congenitally violent people who use violence gratuitously is not so easily sustained. Of course, that has not stopped us as a society from declaring war on drug dealers.

While the Harrison Act of 1914 and the Marijuana Tax Act of 1937 technically were both federal government revenue bills, their real intention was not to regulate drug traffic but to control drug use.[43] Attention did not shift to drug dealers until the later decades of the twentieth century when Richard Nixon in 1971, and then Ronald Reagan in 1982, declared war on drugs.[44] This agenda was crystallized under George Bush when he established the Office of National Drug Control Policy (ONDCP) and named William Bennett as its first director. In the first ONDCP report, issued in September 1989, Bennett was given his mandate to coordinate the antidrug effort of the United States.[45] The 1989 report was presented as the blueprint from which future plans would be drawn, and it made clear that drug dealers would be the leading enemy (though not the only one) in the war on drugs. In the introduction, Bennett wrote:

> In the teeth of a crisis—especially one which for so long appeared to spiral wildly out of control—we naturally look for villains. We need not look far; there are plenty of them. Anyone who sells drugs—and (to a great if poorly understood extent) anyone who uses them—is involved in an international criminal enterprise that is killing thousands of Americans each year. For the worst and most brutal drug gangsters, the death penalty is an appropriate sentence of honest justice.[46]

Thus the executive office of the president of the United States countered the claim that drug dealers are adventurous heroes and made the claim that drug dealers are evil villains.

The first ONDCP report was prepared in only six months, and Bennett and his staff reportedly did consult members of Congress. So, it was not surprising that when Congress issued its own report making its own claims, those claims were fairly consistent with the ones being made in the name of the president.[47] Similarly, a report issued around that time by the attorney general's office supported the claim that traffickers were the problem, indicating that in support of the president's initiative "the U.S. Department of Justice has established as its highest law enforcement priorities the identification and elimination of criminal drug trafficking organizations and the forfeiture of their ill-gotten gains."[48]

Not everyone agreed with the emphasis on drug dealers, what was being called a "supply side" approach.[49] On November 15, 1989, before the U.S. House Select Committee on Narcotics Abuse and Control, Lynn Curtis, the president of the Milton Eisenhower Foundation, testified that

> the present policy needs to be balanced more with the lesson that, especially in the inner city, demand creates supply. . . . We need to explore a variety of innovative ways to link prevention, treatment, intensive outreach and aftercare, youth enterprise development, remedial education, extended family discipline, mentoring, peer counseling, employment and job placement.[50]

Such claims did not deter the ONDCP. When the second ONDCP report was issued in January 1990, Bennett formally established the nation's war on drug dealers with the words "It is the policy of the United States to disrupt, dismantle, and ultimately destroy the illegal market for drugs."[51]

Policy makers in state governments followed a similar path. In 1973, for example, under New York's Governor Nelson Rockefeller, the state government shifted its drug policy from what it was in the 1960s (trying to get low-level drug users to enter drug treatment and reserving criminal penalties for high-level drug traffickers) to a policy that "sought to frighten drug users out of their habit and drug dealers out of their trade, and thus to reduce illegal drug use, or at least contain its spread."[52] In 1995, Governor George Pataki, responding to evidence that could no longer be ignored, discussed proposals to change the so-called Rockefeller drug laws. On March 5, 1995, an article called "Minor Players, Major Penalties" appeared in the *New York Times*. It began, "The [Rockefeller] laws were meant to destroy the trade by burying the drug lords. But experts and law-enforcement officials say the drug business has hardly missed a beat and that most of the bosses are still doing well or are comfortably retired."

Earlier, when violence was widely being used to open crack markets in New York City in the middle of the 1980s, the failure of the Rockefeller drug laws to "destroy the drug trade" did not deter Governor Mario Cuomo from declaring war on drug dealers. In the summer of 1986, I was working in a New York State office directly responsible to the governor's director of criminal justice. I remember the confusion and excitement that summer as we, along with other state workers in other relevant state agencies, scrambled to learn as much as we could about crack cocaine, a drug that was first observed in the city around 1983.[53] Reams of paper were used to prepare memos and internal reports in response to questions by policy makers in the executive and legislative branches of the state government in response to media accounts and statistics showing rising levels of violent crime. Unfortunately, the drug was so new that our knowledge of it was not really sufficient for making informed policy. Nonetheless, given the media and corresponding public outcry, something had to be done.

On August 14, 1986, the press office of the governor of New York issued a press release announcing "three new State law enforcement initiatives to aid in New York's battle against the cocaine derivative 'crack' and the abuse of other illegal drugs in the State." There was the formation of a Statewide Drug Enforcement Task Force, support for legislation "that would substantively increase the penalties for the sale of crack," and support for legislation "to criminalize the laundering of monies obtained from illegal drug sales." Clearly, the focus was on crack and crack dealers. In the release was a quote attributed to the governor in which he said, "We will accept nothing less than the toughest penalties for those who sell this addictive, destructive drug to our children."

One of the responsibilities of the new task force was to prepare an annual Anti-Drug Abuse Strategy Report. Staff from the relevant state agencies were "temporarily" assigned to work for the task force. Its first report was issued in November 1989 and repeatedly called for a comprehensive approach to the problem of substance abuse, with a balance of programs including prevention, criminal justice, and treatment initiatives. It could be argued that the comprehensive, balanced approach was proposed in response to the fact that by 1989 much more was known about crack. That was not the case. The real reason for the broad focus was stated in the executive summary of the first New York State report:

> While there has been much recent discussion of supply and demand issues, particularly in respect to illegal drug trafficking and abuse, we must recognize that most of the control of the supply side of the equation is out of the reach of states and localities; it is a federal responsibility. Moreover, if the federal government is serious about its war on drugs, it must substantially increase financial support to the state and local governments on the front lines.[54]

So, the state government in New York was not saying that drug dealers were not the main villain, but only that they were a villain out of the reach of the states. New York would focus on the problem in ways through which it could more easily show success (such as arresting large numbers of drug users) or in ways through which success would be so hard to measure that victory could be declared due to lack of evidence to the contrary (such as through education or prevention programs). And it was asking the federal government for more money to do this job.

Conclusion

A yarn is an elaborate narrative telling of a real or imagined adventure. Throughout the twentieth century, yarns have been told, and hence claims have been made, about people who deal in illicit drugs. There are some stories in which drug dealers are violent adventurers, others in which they are evil and violence personified, and others still in which they are astute entrepreneurs who use violence to survive and succeed in a lucrative and unregulated area of commerce. There may be some truth in each of these typifications, but by themselves they are broad simplifications. Some drug dealers probably do lead exciting lives, maybe people like the drug lords from Mexico, Caro Quintero and Carrillo Fuentes. Some drug dealers probably enjoy violence for the sake of violence, perhaps people like the drug enforcer from New York City known as Ice. Others probably are brilliant in business, such as the men or women who invented crack and the strategy for marketing it.

The difference between drug dealing and most other things people do for a living is that drug dealing is illegal, and drug dealers are apt to use violence where others are likely to use the law. Yet, in the end, the mix of people who engage in drug dealing are probably more alike than different from the mix of people who engage in any other occupational endeavor. Like other workers, they vary in terms of personal qualities and in terms of how they do their job and how well they do it. In any field, some workers are successful at their job, others are not. Some workers adhere to ethical practices, others do not. Some get rich from what they do, others barely earn enough to support themselves. Some find their job exciting and rewarding, others find it tedious and predictable. Read the various ethnographic accounts by researchers who invested themselves in learning about the lives of particular drug dealers, observing them as people, and this conclusion becomes obvious.[55] Why, then, have claims makers in the United States in the later years of the twentieth century vilified drug dealers as violent, evil people?

By all measures, the world of drug dealing and trafficking is violent. But that violence is as much a part of the circumstances of that world as it is the character of the people who inhabit it. And the violence of that world is largely directed at those inhabitants, not at outsiders. Still, drug dealers make an easy target for policy makers. If illicit drugs are identified with pain and suffering, then the people who are held responsible for the manufacture and distribution of those drugs are surely themselves the source of that pain and suffering. To target and vilify those dealers is to target those people responsible for the pain and suffering. Plus, drug dealing is so widespread in so many communities that it's easy to arrest and prosecute as many drug dealers as you like. More arrests, more prosecutions, and more commitments to jail and prison can be taken as a sign of doing something. The level of violence in a community may not decline, but at least the bad guys are being punished.

An article in the *Washington Post* on July 17, 1998, announced the plans of a candidate for mayor of Washington, D.C. "Mayoral candidate Jack Evans yesterday pledged to sweep the District's open-air drug markets, vowing to move more than 1,000 uniformed police officers from administrative work and special units to street duty in an effort to lower crime." Evans's proposal involved "a program to use a special task force to crack down on organized drug trafficking." The reporter went on to say that Evans was not the first local politician to propose fighting crime by using transferred police officers to disrupt the local drug trade. Owners of stores in the communities where drugs are sold have also heard it before. One store owner observed that when he has called the police in the past they have come and chased the drug dealers away, but after "the police move them out, they come right back." If we are going to address the problem of violence associated with drug markets in our communities in a meaningful way, simplistic solutions will not be sufficient. Pointing to drug dealers as the source of the problem will not be enough.

Endnotes

1. DREIM #049.

2. Witkin, G. (1991). "The Men Who Crated Crack." *U.S. News & World Report* August 19:47.

3. Witkin 1991:50.

4. Zahn, M. (1980). "Homicide in the Twentieth Century United States." In J. A. Inciardi and C. E. Faupel (eds.), *History and Crime*. Beverly Hills: Sage.

5. Zahn 1980:128.

6. Heffernan, R., Martin, J. M. and Romano, A. T. (1982). "Homicide Related to Drug Trafficking." *Federal Probation* 46:3–7.

7. Adler, P. (1985). *Wheeling and Dealing: An Ethnography of an Upper-Level Dealing and Smuggling Community*. New York: Columbia University Press, p. 55.

8. Fagan, J. (1989). "The Social Organization of Drug Use and Drug Dealing among Urban Gangs." *Criminology* 27:635.

9. Fagan 1989:630.

10. Hughes, P. (1977). *Behind the Wall of Respect—Community Experiments in Heroin Addiction*. Chicago: University of Chicago, p. 31.

11. Hughes 1977:31.

12. Hughes 1977:31.

13. Wolfgang, M. E. and Ferracuti, F. (1975). *The Subculture of Violence: Towards an Integrated Theory of Criminology*. London: Tavistock.

14. Gordon, M. M. (1964). *Assimilation in American Life—The Role of Race, Religion, and National Origins*. New York: Oxford University Press.

15. Brownstein, H. H., Baxi, H. H. R. S., Goldstein, P. J., and Ryan, P. J. (1992). "The Relationship of Drugs, Drug Trafficking, and Drug Traffickers to Homicide." *Journal of Crime and Justice* 15:25–44. Goldstein, P. J., Brownstein, H. H., Ryan, P. J. and Bellucci, P. A. (1989).

"Crack and Homicide in New York City, 1988: A Conceptually-Based Event Analysis." *Contemporary Drug Problems* 16:651–87.

16. Brownstein, H. H. et al. (1993). *1992 Crime and Justice Annual Report.* Albany, NY: NYS Division of Criminal Justice Services.

17. Witkin 1991:44. See also Williams, T. (1992). *Crackhouse—Notes from the End of the Line.* New York: Penguin Books.

18. Reinarman, C. and H. G. Levine. (1997). "Crack in Context—America's Latest Demon Drug." Pp. 1–17 in C. Reinarman and H. G. Levine (eds.), *Crack in America—Demon Drugs and Social Justice.* Berkeley: University of California Press, p. 2.

19. Inciardi, J. A., Lockwood, D., and Pottieger, A. E. (1993). *Women and Crack Cocaine.* New York: Macmillan. Johnson, B. D., Hamid, A., and Sanabria, H. (1992). "Emerging Models of Crack Distribution." In T. Mieczkowski (ed.), *Drugs, Crime, and Social Policy: Research, Issues, and Concerns.* Boston: Allyn and Bacon, pp. 56–78.

20. Belenko, S. (1990). "The Impact of Drug Offenders on the Criminal Justice System." In R. Weisheit (ed.), *Drugs, Crime and the Criminal Justice System.* Cincinnati: Anderson, pp. 27–78. Falco, M. (1989). *Winning the Drug War: A National Strategy.* New York: Priority. Inciardi, J. A. (1989). "Beyond Cocaine: Basuco, Crack, and Other Cocaine Products." *Contemporary Drug Problems* 14:461–92. Massing, M. (1989). "Crack's Destructive Sprint across America." *New York Times Magazine* October 1:38, 40–41, 58, 60, 62. Office of the Attorney General. (1989). *Drug Trafficking: A Report to the President of the United States.* Washington, DC: U.S. Department of Justice., Reuter, P., MacCoun, R. and Murphy, P. (1990). *Money from Crime: A Study of the Economics of Drug Dealing in Washington, D.C.* Santa Monica, CA: RAND.

21. Office of the Attorney General 1989:7. Office of National Drug Control Policy. (1989). *National Drug Control Strategy.* Washington, DC: Executive Office of the President, p. 62.

22. Williams 1992:9.

23. Belenko 1990; Brownstein et al. 1992; Fagan, J. and Chin, K. L. (1990). "Violence as Regulation and Social Control in the Distribution of Crack." In M. De La Rosa, E. Y. Lambert, and B. Gropper (eds.), *Drugs and Violence: Causes, Correlates, and Consequences.* Washington, DC: National Institute on Drug Abuse. Goldstein et al. 1989; Mieczkowski, T. 1990. "Crack Distribution in Detroit." *Contemporary Drug Problems* 17:9–29; Office of the Attorney General 1989.

24. Brownstein, H. H. (1996). *The Rise and Fall of a Violent Crime Wave—Crack Cocaine and the Social Construction of a Crime Problem.* Guilderland, NY: Harrow and Heston. Johnson et al. 1992; Smith, M. E., Sviridoff, M., Sadd, S., Curtis, R., and Grinc, R. (1992). *The Neighborhood Effects of Street-Level Drug Enforcement—Tactical Narcotics Teams in New York—AN Evaluation of TNT.* New York: The Vera Institute of Justice.

25. Golub, A. and Johnson, B. D. (1997). *Crack's Decline: Some Surprises Across U.S. Cities.* National Institute of Justice Research in Brief. Washington, DC: U.S. Department of Justice. Lattimore, P. K., Trudeau, J., Riley, J. K., Leiter, J. and Edwards, S. (1997). *Homicide in Eight U.S. Cities: Trends, Context, and Policy Implications—An Intramural Research Project.* Washington, DC: National Institute of Justice. Riley, K. J. (1997). *Crack, Powder Cocaine, and Heroin: Drug Purchase and Use Patterns in Six U.S. Cities.* Washington, DC: National Institute of Justice.

26. Lattimore et al. 1997:87–92.

27. Goldstein, P. J. (1985) "The Drugs/Violence Nexus: A Tripartite Conceptual Framework." *Journal of Drug Issues* 15:493–506.

28. Brownstein et al. 1992; Goldstein et al. 1989.

29. Goldstein et al. 1989:668.

30. Brownstein et al. 1992:39.

31. DRCAH2 # 008, 141, 330.

32. Brownstein et al. 1992:34.

33. Brownstein et al. 1992:38,39.

34. Witkin 1991:44.

35. Reuter et al. 1990.

36. Reuter et al. 1990:20.

37. DRCAH2 # 296.

38. DRCAH2 # 147.

39. Goldstein, P. J., et al. (1984). "The Marketing of Street Heroin in New York City." *Journal of Drug Issues* 14:553–66.

40. LAVIDA # 205.

41. DRCAH2 # 035.

42. Blumstein, A. (1995). "Violence by Young People: Why the Deadly Nexus." *National Institute of Justice Journal*. August. Washington, DC: U.S. Department of Justice, pp. 2–9; Fagan 1989; Hughes 1977.

43. Brownstein, H. H. (1992). "Making Peace in the War on Drugs." *Humanity and Society* 6:217–35. Inciardi, J. A. (1992). *The War on Drugs II—The Continuing Epic of Heroin, Cocaine, Crack, Crime, AIDS, and Public Policy*. Mountain View, CA: Mayfield. Musto, D. F. (1973). *The American Disease*. New Haven: Yale University Press; Smith, M. (1988). "The Drug Problem— Is There an Answer?" *Federal Probation* 52:3–6; Trebach, A. S. (1982). *The Heroin Solution*. New Haven: Yale University Press.

44. Inciardi 1992. Weisheit, R. A. (1990). "Civil War on Drugs." Pp. 1–10 in R. A. Weisheit (ed.), *Drugs, Crime and the Criminal Justice System*. Cincinnati: Anderson. Wisotsky, S. (1986). *Breaking the Impasse in the War on Drugs*. New York: Greenwood.

45. Office of National Drug Control Policy (1989). *National Drug Control Strategy*. January. Washington, DC: Executive Office of the President, p. 3.

46. Office of National Drug Control Policy 1989:7.

47. Biden, J. R., Jr. (1990). *Fighting Drug Abuse: A National Strategy*. Prepared by the Majority Staffs of the Senate Judiciary Committee and the International Narcotics Control Caucus, January.

48. Office of the Attorney General. (1989). *Drug Trafficking—A Report to the President of the United States*. August 3. Washington, DC: U.S. Department of Justice.

49. Walker, S. (1994). *Sense and Nonsense about Crime and Drugs—A Policy Guide*. Third Edition. Belmont, CA: Wadsworth, pp. 258–59.

50. Curtis, L. A. (1989). *The National Drug Control Strategy and Inner City Policy*. Testimony Before the Select Committee on Narcotics Abuse and Control, U.S. House of Representatives, November 15, 1989. Washington, DC: Milton Eisenhower Foundation, p. 1.

51. Office of National Drug Control Policy. (1990). *National Drug Control Strategy*. January. Washington, DC: Executive Office of the President, p. 1.

52. Joint Committee on New York Drug Law Evaluation. (1977). *The Nation's Toughest Drug Law: Evaluation of the New York Experience*. Final Report. New York: The Association of the Bar of the City of New York, p. 3.

53. Governor's Office of Employee Relations. (1986). "Crack—The Deadliest Cocaine of All." *GOER News*. September. Albany, NY: GOER, pp. 11–12.

54. Governor's Statewide Anti-Drug Abuse Council. (1989). *State of New York Anti-Drug Abuse Strategy Report*. Albany, NY: Governor's Statewide Anti-Drug Abuse Council, p. ii.

55. See, for example, Adler, P. A. (1985). *Wheeling and Dealing: An Ethnography of an Upper-Level Drug Dealing and Smuggling Community*. New York: Columbia University Press. Baskin, D. R. and Sommers, I. B. (1998). *Casualties of Community Disorder—Women's Careers in Violent Crime*. Boulder, CO: Westview. Bourgois, P. (1995). *In Search of Respect—Selling Crack in El Barrio*. Cambridge: Cambridge University Press; Simon, D. and Burns, E. (1997). *The Corner—A Year in the Life of an Inner-City Neighborhood*. New York: Broadway Books. Waldorf, D., Reinarman, C., and Murphy, S. (1991). *Cocaine Changes—The Experience of Using and Quitting*. Philadelphia: Temple University; Williams, T. (1992). *Crackhouse—Notes from the End of the Line*. New York: Penguin. Williams, T. (1989). *Cocaine Kids—The Inside Story of a Teenage Drug Ring*. Reading, MA: Addison-Wesley.

4

The Allegory of the Innocent Bystander

Just about the time that the stories of the danger of using and selling crack cocaine were becoming old, the news media began to tell another story about New York City. In this story the epidemic of crack spreads from the inner city to the outer boroughs and the suburbs, and innocent people become the victims of the violence that inevitably accompanies the drug. Early in 1989, in an article in *New York* magazine, Eric Pooley wrote:

> Although there are a few parts of town where people still think of the crack epidemic as something distant and alien—the area around Gracie Mansion [the mayor's home] would seem to be one—most neighborhoods in the city by now have been forced to deal with either crack or its foul byproducts; if not crack houses and street dealers or users, then crackhead crimes such as purse snatchings, car break-ins, burglaries, knife-point robberies, muggings, and murders.[1]

Later that year, in a *Time* magazine article called "The Decline of New York," Joelle Attinger wrote, "A growing sense of vulnerability has been deepened by the belief that deadly violence, once mostly confined to crime-ridden ghetto neighborhoods that the police once wrote off as free-fire zones, is now lashing out randomly at anyone, even in areas once considered relatively safe."[2]

Over time, the story was personalized and expanded from crack-related violence to violence in general. On September 4, 1990, the headline of the *New York Post* read, "Tourist Slain Protecting Mom." The story that followed was one that always frightens the people of New York City. Not only does it raise the question of their own vulnerability as human beings, it affirms one of the worst stereotypes about their city. The story told readers that New York, an exciting place to visit, was not necessarily a safe place for visitors.

According to the account in the *Post*, a young man visiting New York with his family was killed as he "tried to protect his mother from the blood-thirsty bunch stalking the 7th Avenue IND station at 53rd Street." The family had come to the city to attend a sporting event. They were on a subway platform when a group of youngsters tried to rob them. The young man ran after them and, for his effort, was stabbed to death.

Unfortunately for the people of New York City, the media virtually had proclaimed 1990 the year of the innocent bystander.[3] In the months before the killing of the tourist, several other people were likewise innocent victims of the city's growing homicide count. On August 5, 1990, the New York *Daily News* told of two such victims. Beginning on the cover of its Sunday edition, the paper told first of a young man who was standing on a corner in the Greenwich Village section of the city making a telephone call when he was shot to death. Apparently, he was the victim of what the paper called "a botched robbery." Then there was the baby boy, only 9 months old, wandering in his walker near the entrance to his home when bullets meant for his uncle came through the door and killed him.

Throughout the summer of 1990, newspaper headlines told the story of innocent bystander killings. A headline in the New York *Daily News* on August 5 bemoaned, "Innocent is slain by the damned." On August 12, a headline in the *New York Times* proclaimed, "Bystander Deaths Reshape City Lives." The story received national attention on July 31 when a headline in *USA Today* read, "New NYC fear: Stray bullets."

Not long after, the news media reported that the danger of innocent people being caught in the rising tide of violence had spread from New York to other American cities. In the summer of 1991, an article from the Knight-Ridder wire service appeared near the end of the first section of the Baltimore *Sun* announcing, "Bystander shooting rate mushrooms." Noting that neither the FBI nor local police departments routinely maintained statistics on incidents of violence against bystanders, the article referred to findings from a study by Lawrence Sherman, a professor at the University of Maryland. Specifically, "From 1986 to 1988, Sherman's research showed: Bystanders were killed by gunshots in Los Angeles 33 times; in New York, 32 times; in Washington and Philadelphia four times; and in Boston, twice. An additional 200 bystanders were wounded nationwide."[4]

In the years that followed, the idea that anyone could be the victim of violence was so frightening that the belief that good people could be its victims always remained a public concern. When a small boy was killed during a gun battle between drug dealers in New Orleans in 1992, an Associated Press story on October 27 quoted a 5-year-old girl who said, "They was shooting all over us and it turned out it was Eric that got dead." In a commentary published in the *Sun* of Baltimore on September 23, 1992, Claude Lewis called car jacking (a rare but at that time a frequently reported form of urban violence in which an armed stranger walks up to your car and demands your car or your life), "[o]ur new terrorism." On November 19, 1993, an article in the *Sun* offered advice on which type of "defense mechanism" citizens should carry, whether a can of pepper spray is better than a personal siren. On August 20, 1995, writers for the same newspaper described Baltimore as being at "war," with citizens living in fear and despair of the "carnage."

Good news came early in 1997. On January 30, an article by Peter Hermann of the Baltimore *Sun* reported on the findings of a new study done in the city of Baltimore. The headline ended with the words "Random attacks rarer in Baltimore, study finds." The study by researchers at Johns Hopkins University examined hospital reports of shootings in the city for three years and found "more shooting victims are hit multiple times from a closer distance and suffer head wounds, leading experts to conclude that gunmen have moved from spraying street corners and are carefully targeting their victims and making sure they are dead." The article quoted Police Commissioner Thomas C. Frazier as saying, "Drive-bys are out, executions are in."

The number of innocent people caught in the crossfires of the urban violence of the late-twentieth-century United States was never very great. For law enforcement agencies, federal and local, the numbers were never large enough to warrant the allocation of resources necessary even to count them. Obvious and poignant examples were reported in newspapers when they occurred, as were reports on findings of studies that were done. Still, the problem was never widespread. Nonetheless, the innocent bystander stands for virtue, the person who is victimized by violent crime through no fault of his or her own. So the story became an allegory, the problem seemed real, and the concern contributed to the redistribution of criminal justice resources toward policies and programs favoring more law enforcement and less rehabilitation and treatment of offenders.

This story of the innocent bystander actually has two parts. The first is about the innocent bystander as a social type. It tells of the good people who unwittingly and through no fault of their own become the victims of violence as it spreads from cities, to suburbs, to rural areas. Despite the claims of the media and others, their number is always small, though an actual account is not really attainable given its dependence on what *innocent* and *bystander* mean. The second part of the story is about violence against strangers, people who at least arguably are both innocent and bystanders in the sense that they are not known to their assailant. While recent homicide statistics have been used to support claims about the growing number of people being killed by strangers, a closer look at those statistics and at research in the area shows that the extent to which violence against strangers is a problem really depends on how the word *stranger* is defined and on how the number of strangers involved in violence is measured. This chapter discusses the meanings of these terms and demonstrates how the notion of innocent bystanders has been used to construct a sense of danger in U.S. communities that is not consistent with the actual risk of violent victimization faced by most people.

Who Is an Innocent Bystander?

Sometimes innocent people truly are the victims of violence that is not intended for them. When Paul Goldstein, Pat Ryan, and I asked detectives from the New York City Police Department to provide us with details about homicides they were investigating over an eight-month period in 1988, a few such cases did occur. For example, there was a 19-year-old girl who was killed because she forgot to take her keys to school.[5] She came home one evening and tried to get into her house. When she realized she did not have her house key, she rang the doorbell. No one answered. So she walked to the corner to use the telephone there to call her mother. At the same time, two men known by the police to have been drug dealers were driving through the neighborhood. They became embroiled in an argument. Driving by the corner where the girl was talking on the telephone, they exchanged pistol fire. One stray bullet hit the girl in the back.

The girl was killed simply because she lived near a corner where drugs were sold. But not all innocent bystanders are equally innocent, nor are they all equally bystanders. In another killing described by the detectives in New York, a middle-aged woman was killed by a bullet that was fired through the window of her home.[6] She was shot in the back while standing and holding an infant. As far as police could tell, she neither used nor sold drugs. But it was not a stray bullet. The four men who drove by her home and shot through her window were low-level drug dealers. A few days earlier, in the first hours of the morning, a friend of her son had been kidnapped by some of these men and physically harassed while being driven around the neighborhood. He was released, and two days later he retaliated; that evening, about a dozen bullets were fired through the window of the home of the sister of one of the men who had kidnapped him. The four men were sustaining the rhythm of retaliation when they fired the shots that killed the woman at the window. Her son was known to the police as a major drug dealer. Had she known that, she would have known that, despite her own lack of involvement in the drug trade, she was a potential target of rival dealers. According to the police, "[She] had to know that her son was dealing drugs. He was unemployed yet was driving around in two Mercedes sedans." Maybe she was an innocent victim, but not in the same way as the girl who was trying to get home to her mother.

Studies of violence victims who are truly innocent bystanders show that they are few in number. For our 1988 study of homicide events in New York City, my colleagues and I specifically asked the police detectives which cases involved innocent bystanders.[7] Of 414 homicide events in our sample, at least one victim could be identified by the police as an innocent bystander in only five cases.[8]

In a study mentioned earlier in this chapter, Lawrence Sherman and his associates examined random shootings of bystanders from 1977 to 1988 in four United States cities: New York, Los Angeles, Boston, and Washington, D.C. They reviewed published news accounts from one major newspaper in each of these cities. Assuming that newspapers are a reasonable source of information about such events, they concluded that "bystander shootings are increasing rapidly in at least four cities, and probably more."[9] Yet, in the article's summary abstract, if not in its conclusion, they pointed out that, while they were prepared to report the existence of increasing trends, the "base rate was quite low, and total bystander deaths appear to comprise less than 1% of all homicides in these cities."[10] In fact, for 1988, when their data showed the greatest number of bystander shootings, they found for all four cities a total of 37 innocent bystanders killed and 98 wounded. Of course, each shooting was a personal tragedy, but together they represented a total of only 135 people in cities with a combined residential population of close to 12 million.

Perhaps of even greater interest in the research by Sherman and his associates, however, is the complexity of their definition of *innocent bystanders*, or what they called *mushrooms* ("slang for an innocent bystander who 'pops up' in the path of fire, catching a bullet intended for someone else"). Conceptually, for example, they considered the relationship of the victim to the offender, they contrasted "bystander murders" from murders involving " 'totally innocent' victims," and they wondered aloud about the significance of the medical condition of the victim and the relative safety of the location of the occurrence. Ultimately, they concluded, "Bystander deaths violate the routine assumptions necessary for conducting daily life,"[11] whatever those conditions may be. Then they equated bystander shootings with "random murders of bystanders" and defined them as

> *shootings of persons with bullets not intended for them as individuals*—either with bullets aimed at someone else in particular, with bullets aimed at no one (as in bullets fired in the air), or with bullets aimed at a crowd of persons or stream of automobile traffic without individual targets. We can further define them as by-products of shooting as a routine activity, rather than a single event in the lifetime of the murderer.[12] [Italics in the original.]

Given this definition, they examined the news accounts they had collected and concluded not only that bystander shootings were increasing, but specifically that "the nature of the increase clearly varies, with crowd shootings predominating in New York and Los Angeles, and stray bullets hitting lone 'mushrooms' in Boston and Washington D.C."[13] All this from a limited number of newspaper accounts.

The official government programs for measuring crime and victimization do not routinely collect or maintain data or report statistics on the number or people who are the innocent victims of crime. That is, there is no official record of the number of innocent bystanders who are victims of any crime, let alone violent crime. The Federal Bureau of Investigation (FBI) does not collect or maintain such data for its imperfect but official Uniform Crime Reports (UCR) program and does not report such statistics in its annual report, *Crime in the United States*. The Bureau of Justice Statistics (BJS) does not collect or maintain such data through its imperfect but official victimization survey, nor does it report such statistics through its National Crime Victimization (NCVS) Survey reports. Individual police departments on occasion may report statistics on the number of innocent bystanders of violence in their own jurisdiction,[14] but those reports are neither routine nor systematic, in that they typically do not reflect uniform standards of data collection and do not necessarily define innocent bystanders in ways that make them comparable to findings in other jurisdictions. Consequently, it is not possible to say with confidence how many people are innocent victims of violence. Given that, it is not reasonable to claim that violence against innocent bystanders is a social problem.

As noted earlier, another way to consider violence against innocent people is to look at violence against strangers. Like innocent bystanders, strangers are not known to their assailant. So, it may reasonably be claimed that they are not intended targets and therefore are not only innocent but also unwilling participants in the violence that besets them. Unfortunately, trying to measure and understand violence against strangers is fraught with its own difficulties.

When a Stranger Is Not a Stranger

A story that caught and held the attention of New Yorkers for most of 1989 told of an innocent victim of violence who was directly targeted by people she did not know for reasons she could not explain. In April of that year, when winter was over and spring was calling the people of the city back to its parks, a 28-year-old woman was running through Central Park. Alone, she was attacked, raped, and "savagely beaten" by a large group of youths that local officials described as a "wolf pack."[15] According to an article in the *New York Times* on April 25, 1989, "Police quoted some of the youths questioned in the case, all of whom live in Harlem near the park, as saying that the rampage grew out of a plan to attack joggers and bicyclists in the park for fun." Through the media, people of the city expressed anger at the attackers and concern for the young investment banker who was left in critical condition. A new word was coined, *wilding*, which referred to "random, apparently motiveless" violent rampages by groups of kids against an unsuspecting stranger.[16] While the word was new, the media suggested that the activity was not. Peter Reinharz, chief prosecutor for the Family Court Division of New York City's Law Department, equated wilding with two other types of crime: "wolf-pack" or multioffender robberies and "jostling" or pickpocketing by groups of kids. Together, he called these "wolf-pack cases" and noted that there were 622 such crimes in the city in 1988. Considering the Central Park attack, he did acknowledge that there was a difference between the attack on the jogger and groups of kids running up to a stranger, grabbing whatever was easily accessible, and running away. He was quoted as saying that "things have gotten a lot rougher."

Without doubt, sometimes people really do violent things to people they do not know. The following story is from the study my colleagues and I conducted of homicides in New York City in 1988.[17] A man was driving his Mercedes Benz through the streets of New York. When he stopped for a red light, a man he did not know walked up to the car and began washing its windows. The driver asked him to stop. When the other man did not stop, a dispute arose. The driver calmly got out of the car, hit the window washer on the back of his head with a baseball bat, put the bat in the trunk of the car, and drove away. Neither man had ever met nor had ever seen the other before. They were strangers, but not all strangers who engage in violence are really strangers.

According to Georg Simmel, "To be a stranger is naturally a very positive relation; it is a specific form of interaction."[18] In this sense, a stranger is not necessarily someone whose being is totally alien to us. We might not know a particular person, but in the context of our social world, it would be possible for us to know of that person. The distinction between a stranger and an acquaintance, then, would be a matter of degree rather than a matter of relationship.

Marc Riedel applied Simmel's notion of the stranger to stranger violence. He suggested that two types of stranger relationships exist that depend on the character of the social contact. Spontaneous stranger relationships "have an unrehearsed, immediate character about them."[19] An example would be the window washer and the driver who killed him. Anyone could be the victim of such offhand and impetuous behavior. Selective stranger relationships, on the other hand, "[seem] to take on a one-sided nature."[20] The case of the jogger in Central Park would be an example since she did not know her assailants and was unknown to them but was purposely selected by them because she was running alone in the park.

Noting that encounters with strangers are common though rarely violent in contemporary society, Riedel then suggested that violence between strangers does not occur without reason. So, in addition to his two types of stranger relationships, he posited two types of encounter that he associated with stranger violence. He suggested that violence between strangers occurs when there is an alteration of "conventional stranger relationships to achieve a deviant purpose."[21] The deviant purpose may be exploitative or confrontational. According to Riedel, "[W]hile exploitation refers to the covert use of settings or relationships, confrontation refers to the defiant facing of another stranger to achieve deviant ends."[22] Given these distinctions, he concluded that most violence between strangers, particularly lethal violence, is most likely to occur when strangers meet spontaneously in confrontational situations.[23] Robbery, on the other hand, would be more likely when one person selects someone that he or she does not know for exploitation.

A story my colleagues and I heard from a detective during our study of homicides in New York City in 1988 involved a case of a stranger selected by others for violent victimization because of the car he was driving.[24] A young male, age 25, rented a nice car to drive from upstate New York to visit friends in the city. While the car was parked near his friend's house, it was noticed by a couple of younger males, ages 20 and 17. They watched the car for about a week and decided they wanted it. So, one day, they kidnapped the man from upstate when he got into the car. They shot him eight times in the head. When asked by detectives why they killed him, one said, "[B]ecause if you kill the owner of the car, he can't report it stolen."

The imprecise nature of stranger relationships in violent events was further revealed in an analysis I did of interview data from a study Barry Spunt and I did with Susan Crimmins of women incarcerated in New York State for homicide. Of 215 women who were interviewed, 34 told stories of intentionally having killed someone whom they clearly did not know.[25] Most of these women said they had killed or participated in the killing of a stranger during a robbery or a dispute, usually involving money or drugs. One woman told us how her friends goaded her into participating in a robbery they had planned.[26] She claimed that she had not even participated in the selection of the victim. Nonetheless, she was in prison because the man was found dead after they had tied him up and left him alone in a room with another participant in the robbery.

The extent to which a stranger is really a stranger became confused in some of the other stories the interviewed women told. One woman told of a night when after selling drugs all day she was getting high with a girl she knew.[27] They needed a ride and so got into a car with a man they did not know. The woman sat in the front with the driver, and her friend sat in the back. During the drive, the man repeatedly propositioned her until she finally said, "Yeah, yeah, I'll go out with you." But when they arrived at their destination, she refused. The way she described it, "He was like every other typical man. He wanted to buy some sex. But it got out of hand." The woman looked at her friend, whom she knew was holding a knife. She gave her a signal, and they pulled the knife on the man. In the fight that followed, he was killed. When they got into the car with him, he was clearly a stranger. By the time they killed him, they knew him well enough to want him dead.

Muddling the definition of a stranger even further were the 11 women who said they had known the person they killed in a business context but not necessarily as a person, or as someone they considered a new or recent acquaintance. Many of the relationships described in these cases were not very different from that described by the woman above, the woman who killed a man she had just met. Six of the 11 women said they had killed a "john" or a "trick" whom they may or may not ever have seen before.[28] Another woman said she and her boyfriend had killed the girlfriend of someone to whom they sold drugs, having known of the victim only through her relationship to their customer.[29] One woman simply said she killed a guy she knew from the streets.[30] The difference between a stranger and a casual acquaintance, then, is not always clear.

Despite this lack of clarity, for almost a decade the news media have been drawing attention to stranger violence as a growing problem in America. For example, on October 23, 1995, the headline on a front-page article in the *Washington Post* announced "The New Face of Murder in America." Citing statistics from the Justice Department, the article noted that "the proportion of people slain by family members has declined sharply, while the number of people killed in robberies and by unknown persons has grown in the 1990s."

Official crime and victimization statistics both shed some light on this subject and themselves have been used to make additional claims about stranger violence. *Crime in the United States*, the FBI's annual report on Uniform Crime Reports (UCR) statistics, had a special section in 1993 on "Homicide Patterns: Past and Present."[31] The section was justified with the following statement:

> Murder has always been regarded as the most serious of all crimes. Today, the prevailing public perception is that homicides, in general, are more vicious and senseless than ever before. In an effort to address this issue, the following study examines the changing nature of murder from 1965 to 1992.[32]

In support of the public perception, the special section used 13 tables of statistics from the Supplementary Homicide Reports (SHR) to reach the alarming conclusion that "[e]very American now has a realistic chance of murder victimization in view of the random nature the crime has assumed."[33] Statistically, this conclusion is arguable; politically, it is explosive; and realistically, it is questionable.[34]

The special section of the 1993 UCR report included a table showing that the proportion of murders involving one family member killed by another had declined dramatically since 1965, from 31 percent in 1965 to only 12 percent in 1992.[35] Because fewer people are killed by family members, however, does not necessarily mean more people are killed by strangers. Under the SHR reporting program, besides considering murders by a variety of family members, victims also could be reported as having been killed by acquaintances, friends, boyfriends, girlfriends, or neighbors as well as by people they do not know. In addition, it is possible for police departments reporting murders to the FBI to report that the person who killed the victim is not known, as in cases when no arrest has been made.

According to UCR statistics, from the middle of the 1980s to the middle of the 1990s, the clearance rate for homicides throughout the United States declined from 70 percent to 65 percent. (By UCR reckoning, that percentage represents the ratio of the total number of arrests made during a given year [no matter what year the crime for which the arrest is made took place] to all crimes reported as known to the police that year.) A smaller proportion of arrests made should mean a higher proportion of unknown offenders and hence a higher proportion of unknown relationships between homicide victims and their killers, and it did. In the middle of the 1980s about 30 percent of relationships between homicide victims and offenders were reported to the FBI as unknown, and in the middle of the 1990s that proportion jumped to almost 40 percent. Interestingly, the proportion of victims reported as having been killed by a stranger during this period apparently also increased but only slightly, to the extent it did so at all. In the middle of the 1980s, around 13 percent of all homicide victims were reported as having been killed by a stranger, compared to the same 13 percent in 1994 and 15 percent in 1995.

The NCVS similarly has supported the claim that violence by strangers is on the rise in the United States. But BJS began making that claim in the early 1980s. Compared to the aggregate police reports that are tabulated for the UCR, the NCVS involves an annual national survey of a sample of households and persons ages 12 and older and collects data about all incidents of victimization those households and people experienced during the past year.[36] In 1982 BJS released a report called *Violent Crime by Strangers.*[37] Based on data collected from 1973 to 1979, the report opened with the words "Three of every five violent crimes are committed by persons who are strangers to their victims."[38]

The question of what is meant by a violent crime was answered without difficulty in the BJS report. The violent crimes the report referred to included rape, robbery, aggravated assault, and simple assault. Homicide was not included since murder victims cannot respond to survey questions. For the NCVS, the question "who is a stranger" is not so simple to answer. According to the report, "Victims identify their offender, when known, by one of a series of relationships ranging from that of stranger to specified relative."[39] The report provided great detail about the characteristics of known offenders, victims, and incidents, but said no more about the issue of offenders not known. It did note, however, "Evidence and logic both suggest that a victim is more likely to report a crime to an interviewer if the offender is a total stranger and less likely to do so if the offender is a close relative."[40] That said, the report went on to say that "the proportion of crimes committed by strangers may be somewhat overstated."[41] Then, that issue was dropped, and its significance left unstated. For example, the report did not discuss the potential impact on the statistics as a measure of violent victimization if all the unreported family violence in surveyed households had, in fact, been reported.

Five years later, BJS issued another report on stranger violence, *Violent Crime by Strangers and Nonstrangers*.[42] On the cover of that report was a box with a message from the agency director, Steven R. Schlesinger: "It is often said that the fear of crime is largely a fear of strangers. As this Special Report indicates, while almost half of all violent crimes are committed by total strangers, almost 40% occur among friends, acquaintances, or relatives, including spouses or ex-spouses."[43] Using NCVS data from 1982 to 1984, this report was essentially an update of the earlier BJS report, but this time with seven rather than four pages of material. The emphasis was again on characteristics of known victims, offenders, and incidents. However, this time the note about the underreporting of violence by nonstrangers was accompanied by the following footnote in tiny print: "A 1971 reverse records check in San Jose found that known victims of violent crime by a relative reported the incident to a survey interviewer only 22% of the time. Crimes by acquaintances were reported 58% of the time; crimes by strangers, 75% of the time."[44] The statement also was followed by an acknowledgment from the federal agency that "some victims of domestic violence may not perceive these acts as criminal."[45]

Perhaps in recognition of the shortcomings of its measure, more recent reports by the BJS on victimization have not emphasized the relationship between the offender and victim of violent offenses. In 1994, after two decades of NCVS reports, BJS published *Criminal Victimization in the United States: 1973–92 Trends*.[46] The 136-page report, mostly tables, included much about the characteristics of known victims, offenders, and incidents of a variety of personal and property offenses, but nothing about the extent to which the victims of violence were victims of strangers. A 10-page update in 1997, *Criminal Victimization 1996—Changes 1995–96 with Trends 1993–96*, included a small table and one paragraph on page 6 with the words, "Among categories of violent crime included in the NCVS, the greatest likelihood of the victim's knowing the offender occurred with rape—68% of the rape victims. The least likelihood was robbery; 23% of robbery victims knew the offender."[47] Note that for 1996, NCVS survey respondents reported 363,000 rapes or sexual assaults and 1,171,000 robberies.[48]

Innocent Victims and Public Policy

While we do know that every instance of violence is tragic for all individuals involved, we have no way of knowing how many people are really victims of violence. Available statistics do suggest that the number of people victimized by violence, fortunately, is relatively small. In 1993, when the UCR recorded the highest number of homicides in recent years, for every 100,000 people living in the United States fewer than 10 were murdered.[49] In its examination of victimization trends from 1973 to 1992, BJS found that in 1992 about 32 of every 1,000 people age 12 or older living in the United States reported having been the victim of a violent crime, slightly fewer than had reported violent victimization in 1973.[50] Over this 20-year period, the number of people reporting having been the victim of violence ranged from a low of about 28 per 1,000 in 1986 to a high of about 35 per 1,000 in 1981.[51] Further, when the bureau issued its update showing trends through 1996,[52] it accompanied the publication with a press release announcing, "Violent Victimization Fell 10 Percent Last Year." Thus, by NCVS accounting, it is likely that, in any given year, 965 of every 1,000 people will *not* be the victim of a reported violent crime.

Remember the footnotes in the victimization survey reports of recent decades, the ones that indicated that the number of violent victimizations by family members is probably underreported, the number of violent victimizations by strangers is probably overstated, and that sometimes when people are the victims of violence in their families they do not consider it a reportable offense.[53] So, even if we accept the official statistics as reasonable measures of violent crime or violent victimization, at best they underreport the level of violence among people who know each other and overreport the level of violence among strangers.

Beyond the statistical observation that people who engage in violence are likely to know each other, research in this area has found that it is not uncommon for the offenders and the victims of violence to be the same people. From her clinical analyses, Deborah Prothrow-Stith concluded, "We know this, too—that growing up in violence places young people and their communities at terrible jeopardy. For the fact is, those who are the witnesses and victims of violence often become its perpetrators."[54] Similarly, from her well-known series of studies of the intergenerational transmission of violence, Cathy Spatz Widom observed that childhood victimization often leads to adult victimizing.[55]

Since the time almost four decades ago that Marvin Wolfgang introduced the notion of "victim precipitation" in his classic study of homicide, our ability to distinguish the victim from the offender in an instance of violence has become more difficult. From his study of homicide in Philadelphia from 1948 to 1952, Wolfgang concluded, "In many crimes, especially in criminal homicide, the victim is often a major contributor to the criminal act."[56] For 588 homicides in Wolfgang's sample, he found that no fewer than 26 percent involved victim precipitation. Victim precipitation and the way it confounds the distinction between victims and offenders was illustrated to me in during an interview I conducted with a young man in a New York State prison.[57]

After losing his job and his car on the same Tuesday morning in 1984, the young man ran into a friend and decided to go out drinking. The plan was to spend the evening getting drunk. Standing outside a neighborhood liquor store, they got into an argument about a drink the young man did not like. His friend was angry not only because he had recommended it but also because the young man poured it out instead of giving it to him when he no longer wanted it. They yelled at each other, said they were no longer friends, and threatened to call the police on each other. Later in the evening, they made up and went for a walk in a nearby woods. Once they were where no one else could hear or see them, the friend began saying things about the young man's sister and how she would look "with no clothes on." The young man became angry and told his friend to stop. But he continued and even hit the young man when he bent over to light a cigarette. Then the friend took out a knife and said, "It's time to meet your maker." They were both very high. They started to run. In a clearing, the young man found a cement block. He hid behind a tree. When he saw his friend, he either tripped or hit him with the block. In any case, his friend fell to the ground. The young man started to run away; then went back and set fire to the body of his friend, to make sure he was dead. The young man ended up in prison; his friend ended up dead. The young man was guilty, but his friend was not innocent.

Combine the evidence of available statistics with what we know from research findings and it becomes clear that despite media and government claims, violence against innocent bystanders and violence against strangers is not now and is not becoming the predominant type of interpersonal violence. Violence among people who know each other, including unreported family violence, is a more common problem than is violence among people who do not. The question, then, is why the media, the government, and even an occasional academic researcher repeatedly have made the claim that violence, as the FBI suggested in its special report on homicide,[58] has become increasingly random.

Given the nature of how public policy is made and government programs are developed, problems need to be simple and their solutions need to be measurable. If I learned anything in my years of government service, I learned that those who make policy and those who design programs are responsive principally to the requirements of a succession of civic elections and annual budgets and the demands of social crises that are perceived as real, whether or not they are.[59] Ultimately, this is true for the elected officials who must satisfy those citizens who are needed to keep them into office, and for the executives of government who must satisfy the legislators who vote for or against their proposals. It is true for the political appointees who must satisfy the people who appointed them to their jobs, and for the bureaucrats who must satisfy their politically appointed bosses. It is true for the local project managers who must satisfy the bureaucrats and elected officials who pass funding and other goodies along to them to keep their programs operative, and for the news reporters who must satisfy the people who provide access to the information they need to write their stories.

In this environment, violence against innocent people is a better problem than is violence directed by one family member against another or violence that is focused in some communities of people and not others. Violence against innocent people is simple. The good guys are clearly defined and so are the bad guys. How to allocate your resources and where to spend your dollars is obvious. Help the good guys; get the bad guys. Helping the good guys may be a worthy objective, but its impact is not immediately apparent and therefore does not readily satisfy the needs of policy makers and program developers. In a study of victims and victim services, Robert Elias found, ultimately, that "[r]ather than offering real improvements, most victim policies still leave people victimized: by crime, criminal justice, and the political process."[60] The difficulty lies in figuring out how to measure the impact of helping victims and then trying to link helping victims with reducing violence. The better problem for public policy makers and program managers is getting the bad guys. Getting bad guys can be measured easily with arrest statistics, and linking more arrests with reduced violence is an idea that sounds reasonable enough to satisfy the public that something is being done, even if the evidence of research cannot confirm that it is.

Unfortunately, because something seems simple or sounds reasonable does not necessarily mean its impact or outcome will be real. The notion that witnesses to and victims of violence come from the same pool of people who commit violence belies the notion that violence increasingly involves strangers and innocent bystanders. If victims and offenders are even potentially the same people, then the good guys cannot be distinguished easily from the bad guys. Making policy and developing programs becomes a more complicated and difficult process, just as violence becomes a more intractable problem. This makes life more difficult for policy makers, program developers, and even for the news media.

Conclusion

An allegory is a symbolic story that makes its point by embodying its characters with moral qualities. It "undertakes to make a doctrine or thesis interesting and persuasive by converting it into a narrative in which the agents, and sometimes the setting as well, represent general concepts, moral qualities, or other abstractions."[61] By broadly granting all victims of violent crime the moral quality of innocence, they become not only interesting but also an easily identifiable and agreeable symbol for any effort to address the problem of violence. That focus may simplify the task of those who must make decisions about how to allocate resources that are necessary to address the problem of violence, but it does not necessarily address the problem in a way that will make a meaningful difference in the lives of people who experience violence.

When my colleagues and I interviewed youngsters detained in youth facilities around New York State for one of a variety of violent offenses, I was struck by how often these kids who had done violence to someone else themselves had been the victims of violence, in the homes where they lived with their families and on the streets where they grew up with their friends. The evidence is not equivocal. Most people who are victims of violence are not innocent bystanders. Most people who are victims of violence are not unknown to the people who victimize them. Sometimes the victims of violence even contribute to their own victimization. More important, the people who victimize others likely have been victimized themselves.

None of this is meant to suggest that violence is not tragic or that victims of violence are not good people. The point is that whether they are good or bad by any standard of society is not relevant to the tragedy of their victimization. Viewing them as good or bad—through the construction of a social type such as the innocent bystander, for example—oversimplifies the problem. This itself becomes a problem in that, by focusing on the innocence of victims of violence, we are distracted from the circumstances and conditions that envelop all people who are enmeshed in a web of violence. Untangling that web, and solving the problems that have created it, is very difficult. Distinguishing good people from bad people and using resources to eliminate the bad people is much easier to do. Not better, just easier.

Endnotes

1. Pooley, E. (1989). "Fighting Back against Crack." *New York* January 23:32.

2. Attinger, J. (1989) "The Decline of New York." *Time* September 17:38.

3. Brownstein, H. H.(1991). "The Media and the Construction of Random Drug Violence." *Social Justice* 18:85–103.

4. Knight-Ridder. (1991). "Bystander shooting rate mushrooms." *The Sun* (Baltimore) August 8:A23. See also Sherman, L. W., Steele, L., Laufersweiler, D., Hoffer, N., and Julian, S. A. (1989). "Stray Bullets and 'Mushrooms': Random Shootings of Bystanders in Four Cities, 1977–1988." *Journal of Quantitative Criminology* 5:297–316.

5. DRCAH2 # 009.

6. DRCAH2 # 259.

7. Brownstein, H. H., Baxi, H. R. S., Goldstein, P. J., and Ryan, P. J. (1992). "The Relationship of Drugs, Drug Trafficking, and Drug Traffickers to Homicide." *Journal of Crime and Justice* 15:25–44. Goldstein, P. J., Brownstein, H. H., Ryan, P. J., and Bellucci, P. A. (1989). "Crack and Homicide in New York City, 1988: A Conceptually Based Event Analysis." *Contemporary Drug Problems* 16:651–87. Goldstein, P. J., Brownstein, H. H., and Ryan, P. J. (1992). "Drug-Related Homicide in New York: 1984 and 1988." *Crime and Delinquency* 38:459–76.

8. Brownstein et al. 1992:35.

9. Sherman et al. 1989:314.

10. Sherman et al. 1989:297.

11. Sherman et al. 1989:299.

12. Sherman et al. 1989:301–2.

13. Sherman et al. 1989:314.

14. Brownstein 1991:95.

15. Pitt, D. E. (1989). "Gang Attack: Unusual for its Viciousness." *The New York Times* April 25:B1.

16. Pitt 1989: See also Derber, C. (1996). *The Wilding of America—How Greed and Violence Are Eroding Our Nation's Character*. New York: St. Martin's.

17. DRCAH2 # 057.

18. Simmel, G. (1950). *The Sociology of Georg Simmel*. Tr., ed., and with an introduction by K. H. Wolff. New York: Free Press.

19. Riedel, M. (1993). *Stranger Violence: A Theoretical Inquiry*. New York: Garland, p. 118.

20. Riedel 1993:118.

21. Riedel 1993:130.

22. Riedel 1993:130.

23. Riedel 1993:160.

24. DRCAH2 # 130.

25. Brownstein, H. H., Langley, S., Crimmins, S., and Spunt, B. (1995). "Women Who Kill Strangers." Paper presented at the annual meeting of the American Society of Criminology, Boston, November.

26. FEMDREIM # 198.

27. FEMDREIM # 004.

28. FEMDREIM # 021, 131, 228, 231, 438, 450.

29. FEMDREIM # 045.

30. FEMDREIM # 462.

31. Federal Bureau of Investigation. (1994). *Crime in the United States, 1993*. Washington, DC: U.S. Government Printing Office.

32. Federal Bureau of Investigation 1994:283.

33. Federal Bureau of Investigation 1994:287.

34. Compare Riedel, M. (1998). "Counting Stranger Homicides—A Case Study of Statistical Prestidigitation." *Homicide Studies* 2:206–19.

35. Reidel 1998:285.

36. Bureau of Justice Statistics. (1994). *Criminal Victimization in the United States: 1973–92 Trends*. July. Washington, DC: U.S. Department of Justice.

37. Rand, M. R. (1982). *Violent Crime by Strangers*. Bureau of Justice Statistics Bulletin. Washington, DC: Bureau of Justice Statistics.

38. Rand 1982:1.

39. Rand 1982:1.

40. Rand 1982:1.

41. Rand 1982:1.

42. Timrots, A. D. and Rand, M. R. (1987). *Violent Crime by Strangers and Nonstrangers*. Bureau of Justice Statistics Special Report. January. Washington, DC: Bureau of Justice Statistics.

43. Timrots and Rand 1987:1.

44. Timrots and Rand 1987:1.

45. Timrots and Rand 1987:1.

46. Bureau of Justice Statistics. (1994). *Criminal Victimization in the United States: 1973–92*. July. Washington, DC: U.S. Department of Justice.

47. Ringel, C. (1997). *Criminal Victimization 1996—Changes 1995–96 with Trends 1993–96*. November. Washington, DC: Bureau of Justice Statistics, p. 6.

48. Ringel 1997:3.

49. Federal Bureau of Investigation 1994:13.

50. Bureau of Justice Statistics 1994:9.

51. Bureau of Justice Statistics 1994:9.

52. Ringel 1997.

53. Bureau of Justice Statistics 1994; Rand 1982; Timrots and Rand 1987.

54. Prothrow-Stith, D. (with M. Weissman). (1991). *Deadly Consequences*. New York: HarperCollins, p. 64.

55. Widom, C. S. (1992). *The Cycle of Violence*. NIJ Research in Brief. October. Washington, DC: National Institute of Justice, p. 5. See also Widom C. S. (1996). *The Cycle of Violence Revisited*. NIJ Research Preview. Washington, DC: National Institute of Justice.

56. Wolfgang, M. E. (1958). *Patterns in Criminal Homicide*. Philadelphia: University of Pennsylvania, p. 245.

57. DREIM # 019.

58. Federal Bureau of Investigation 1994.

59. Brownstein, H. H. (1998). "The Drugs-Violence Connection: Constructing Policy from Research Findings." In E. L. Jensen and J. Gerger (eds.), *The New War on Drugs—Symbolic Politics and Criminal Justice Policy*. Cincinnati:Anderson. Brownstein, H. H. (1996). *The Rise and Fall of a Violent Crime Wave*. Guilderland, NY: Harrow and Heston. Brownstein, H. H. (1995). "The Social Construction of Crime Problems: Insiders and the Use of Official Statistics." *Journal of Crime and Justice* 18:17–30. Brownstein, H. H. and Goldstein, P. J. (1990). "Research and the Development of Public Policy: The Case of Drugs and Violent Crime." *Journal of Applied Sociology* 7:77–92.

60. Elias, R. (1993). *Victims Still—The Political Manipulation of Crime Victims*. Newbury Park, CA: Sage, p. 3.

61. Abrams, M. H. (1957). *A Glossary of Literary Terms*. New York: Holt, Rinehart and Winston, p. 2.

5

The Family in the United States:
A Romantic Tragedy

When I met him in the prison he was then calling home, five years had passed since the day he had killed his son. His youthful face and demeanor suggested that he could have been the boyish but caring father of a television comedy family. The story he told made it clear that he was not.[1]

It was a summer day in 1984 in a suburban community outside of New York City. He was 25 years old, living in an attached house with his wife, a 2-year-old son, and a newborn daughter. He worked as a mechanic but was home that morning. His wife was out, leaving him alone with their two children. He loved his children, he told me, but he lacked maturity and experience as a father.

After his wife left the house, his infant daughter began to cry. Thinking she might be wet, he changed her diaper. She continued to cry. When her crying turned to screaming, he became upset, not knowing what to do next. His son was sitting on the sofa, and he sat down next to him. What happened next is not clear. He asked his son a question, whether he wanted something. When the answer did not satisfy him, he began hitting the 2-year-old boy.

This was not the first time he had hit his son. The beatings started when the boy was just 6 months old. In the past, he had ended each attack by leaving the house and trying to calm himself. For the same reason, he began most mornings by smoking marijuana. The morning of the fatal beating he had not smoked his usual joint, but he had taken his prescription medicines. He was taking three kinds of medication for a recent ulcer, something for a vein that had collapsed in his arm when he was in the hospital, and a pain medicine for the inflammation in his ribs. He could not name any of the prescriptions, nor did he know how any of them affected him.

As soon as his wife returned, he told her how he had beaten their son. He thought maybe they should take the boy to the hospital, but his wife said no. She felt that the child looked okay. She also feared they would lose their son if they told the authorities about the beatings. For the next few days, the boy seemed fine. When they finally did take him to the hospital on the third day, he was dead. The boy died from internal bleeding, and the father was arrested for murder.

The story he told about his own childhood suggested how violence might have found its way into his relations with his wife and children, a domestic arrangement that otherwise had the trappings of a peaceful family life. The oldest of six children, he became the target of his mother's anger when his father abandoned their family. As he recalled, he was only 7 years old when his mother turned to drinking, and then to burning and cutting him. When school officials asked about the marks on his body, his mother told them he was hyperactive and fell a lot. When he was 15 years old, he ran away after his mother's boyfriend warned him that she had threatened to kill him. He spent his days on the streets and his nights looking for his father in the bars where he had heard his father was working as a bookie. He eventually found his father, and they began hanging out and drinking together. He soon left his father and at various times added diet pills and cocaine to his repertoire of self-medications. There were several arrests, mostly for breaking and entering, some time in prison, and years of treatment for his drug problems. He did eventually earn a high school equivalency diploma. From a rough start, he seemed to have found the path to a normal family life.

When I sat across the table from him, I saw him as a decent person. He was polite and reserved. The family life he described sounded fairly conventional, until he told me what had happened to his son. On the surface, the picture he drew of his everyday life with his wife and children could be likened to the image of the family that Americans watched on television, the Cleavers in the 1950s or the Cosbys in the 1980s, for example. When he started talking about his relationship with his son, the theme of his story changed from love and caring to frustration and violence.

As observers and analysts of culture, anthropologists traditionally have viewed the family as a building block or social unit serving the needs of a community of people for procreation, socialization, and economic well-being.[2] As observers and analysts of social life and social relationships, various sociologists have described the family in terms of its structure and function.[3] Ultimately, many mid-twentieth-century students of the family saw it as a place of love and caring, what Christopher Lasch called a "haven in a heartless world."[4] In describing the origins of the family, Kathleen Gough wrote, "The family was essential to the dawn of civilization, allowing a vast leap forward in cooperation, knowledge, love, and creativeness."[5] Similarly, in their sociology textbook, Peter and Brigitte Berger wrote, "For almost everyone, the family is, as it were, the *home port* from which the individual starts out on his lifelong journey through society" (emphasis in original).[6]

The theoretical ideal of the family as a place of refuge for people living in a world otherwise fraught with risk and danger may have been attractive to social scientists during the middle of the twentieth century, but even then not everyone viewed it that way, either in real life or in fiction. The imperfection of this ideal was nicely voiced by Antonia Fraser in her mystery novel *The Wild Island*. Jemima Shore, the main character of the story, goes to an isolated island to escape the pressure and routine of her everyday life as a celebrity. Her plans go awry, and she is compelled to solve a mystery involving an island family with much violence in its history. Help in sorting out the mystery comes in the form of a letter from an old teacher, Mother Agnes of the Convent of the Blessed Eleanor. In the letter, Mother Agnes tells Jemima, "At its best [the family is] an incarnation of the highest principles of human conduct, a source of wonderful comfort. Yet isn't it distressing how the Devil will never leave even the most sacred institutions alone?"[7]

After years of studying family and intimate violence, by the 1990s Richard Gelles wondered aloud how we had ever come to characterize the family as "warm, intimate, stress reducing, and the place that people flee for safety."[8] His research had shown that the family was one of society's most violent institutions in that people were "more likely to be killed, physically assaulted, hit, beat up, slapped, or spanked in their own homes by other family members than anywhere else, or by anyone else."[9]

This chapter is about the stories we tell and the claims we make about the social institution of the family. In that sense, it is different from the other chapters in this book, which focus on social claims about individuals and their behavior. During the middle years of the twentieth century, the stories being told by social scientists and the media about the family in the United States emphasized the family in modern society as a refuge or sanctuary for its members. In the last decades of the century, violence in families was recognized and acknowledged, and new stories and claims about the family emerged.[10] The media gave attention to the most notorious and lurid incidents of violence among family members, and social scientists with government support seriously studied family violence. In response to the new social reality, programs and policies were developed from uncertain and even controversial research findings. This chapter incorporates official statistics, findings from research, and media images of family life to show how the family was *socially reconstructed* during the latter half of the twentieth century from a social institution providing safety and security to one of potential violence and abuse. The implications of that shift are also discussed.

The "Normal" U.S. Family

Early in the twentieth century, radio replaced the kitchen stove or the fireplace as the family hearth, and around the middle of the century, television replaced radio. Programs about families were a staple both of radio and television. The image of television families over the years—from the Cleavers and the Andersons in the 1950s to the Conners and the Simpsons in the 1990s—has undergone considerable change, though the change has been more subtle than dramatic. Throughout the years, the image of the family on television generally was that of a haven. However, by the 1980s and 1990s, the situations in which families were placed were more likely to reflect contemporary issues and concerns.

Since 1979, Tim Brooks and Earle Marsh have edited and updated a directory of television programming, prime time and cable, from 1946 to the present.[11] The following are examples from their 1995 edition about popular television shows, particularly situation comedies about families. Often adapted from radio, the first such shows in the late 1940s and 1950s were specifically about loving families.

- *Mama.* 1949–1956. "*Mama* was one of the best-loved of the early family comedies, and was in many ways the prototype of the 'growing family' series which later proliferated on television. . . . There were no cheap gags or bumbling parents in *Mama*, but rather a warmhearted, humorous, true-to-life account of a Norwegian-American family of five making their way in turn-of-the-century San Francisco." (p. 631)

From the 1950s to the 1960s, situation comedies about families were particularly popular. A family crisis, often minor, would be resolved in the end (for better or worse) by sensible, wise, and always loving family members.

- *Father Knows Best.* 1954–1963. "It was set in the typical Midwestern community of Springfield, where Jim Anderson was an agent for the General Insurance Company. Every evening he would come home from work, take off his sports jacket, put on his comfortable sweater, and deal with the everyday problems of a growing family. . . . When a family crisis arose, Jim would calm the waters with a warm smile and some sensible advise." (p. 346)
- *The Danny Thomas Show.* 1953–1971. "*Make Room for Daddy*, as it was originally called [during] its first three seasons, was a reflection of Danny's own life as an entertainer and the problems created by his frequent absences from his children. The title came from a phrase used in the real-life Thomas household: whenever Danny returned home from a tour, his children had to shift bedrooms, to 'make room for Daddy.' In the series, Danny played nightclub entertainer Danny Williams, a sometimes loud but ultimately soft-

hearted lord of the household, who was constantly being upstaged by his bratty but lovable kids." (p. 240)

In the 1960s and 1970s, family shows on television reflected the acceptance of variation in the shape of families but held on to the notion of the family as a loving refuge.

• *The Brady Bunch.* 1969–1974. "*The Brady Bunch* was one of the last of the old-style fun-around-the-house situation comedies, full of well-scrubbed children, trivial adventures, and relentlessly middle-class parents. The premise here was a kind of conglomerate family, formed by a widow with three daughters who married a widower with three sons. . . . Typical stories revolved around the children going steady, family camping trips, competition for the family telephone (at one point Dad installed a pay phone), and of course war in the bathroom." (p. 131)

• *My Three Sons.* 1960–1972. "The 'family' in this case was all-male. Steve Douglas, a consulting aviation engineer, lived with his children at 837 Mill St. in a medium-sized Midwestern city. A widower, he seemed to spend more time raising his three sons than he did at his job, what with the usual growing pains of boys just beginning to date, going on camping trips, and other 'adventures' of middle-class suburbia. Steve also spent a good deal of time fending off attractive women, who wanted to marry him and take over that lovable, ready-made family." (pp. 719–20)

The 1980s brought change, particularly in the nature of the problems faced by the television family. Still, in the end family members found comfort, if not solutions, in the caring domain of the family.

• *Family Ties.* 1982–1989. "The mellow 1960s clashed with the conservative 1980s in this generation-gap comedy, which in some ways reflected America's changing values in the Reagan era. . . . It was set in middle America—Columbus, Ohio—where one-time flower children Elyse and Steve Keaton still espoused the liberal values of the idealistic '60s, although they were now parents and professionals. . . . They were a loving family, though the kids could never understand those Bob Dylan records their parents kept playing." (p. 340)

• *The Cosby Show.* 1984–1992. "Most of the action took place at the Huxtable residence, a New York City brownstone where Cliff (an obstetrician) also maintained his office. He and his wife Clair (a legal aid attorney) tried to bring up the kids with a combination of love and parental firmness, while leading their own active professional lives. . . . *The Cosby Show* was criticized for its unrealistic portrayal of blacks as wealthy, well-educated professionals, and for its lack of attention to black-white relations. Others defended it as providing role models for what blacks could achieve, and lessons for all races in how to raise a family in a calm and loving manner." (p. 216)

- *Growing Pains.* 1985–1992. "If *Father Knows Best* had been revived in the 1980s, it would have been called *Growing Pains*. . . . In addition to the safe little stories of dates, first jobs, and fun around the house, *Growing Pains* periodically tackled more serious issues than *Father Knows Best* ever imagined, including drunk driving, teen suicide, racism, and peer pressure on [teenage son] Mike to use cocaine. As in the earlier series, however, a wise dad and mom saw their basically decent kids through it all." (p. 420)

As the 1980s became the 1990s, the situations became more raunchy and the characters more crude. But the love its members felt for each other still held the family together.

- *Married . . . With Children.* 1987–1995+. "Suburban Chicago was the setting for this domestic comedy that had all the warmth of a boa constrictor. The Bundys were not your typical family. Although they occasionally let it slip that they cared for each other, every member of the household seemed intent on belittling or putting down the others." (p. 646)
- *Roseanne.* 1988–1995+. "*Roseanne* . . . was the lineal descendant of blue-collar TV families stretching back to *All in the Family* and *The Honeymooners*, but like all great hits it introduced new elements to reflect its times: mom, not dad, was the center of the household; both were hefty people (and always in the kitchen), not TV-handsome; both worked; and when mom got home, she never failed to have a foul word for her kids. . . . One thing that didn't change, however, was the basic element of a loving family." (p. 886)
- *The Simpsons.* 1989–1995+. "Certain series defined how much 1990s television had changed (for better or worse, depending on your point of view) from the squeaky-clean days of the 1950s and 1960s. . . . Arguably, *The Simpsons* was the most subversive of them all. It got away with its anarchic message largely because it was a cartoon. . . . Although Homer (Simpson) and his wife Marge had their disagreements, they did love each other and their three kids." (p. 935)

Over time, television programs about families did change. Situations adapted to the times, the structure of the family became more diverse, relationships became more complex, and characters became less wholesome.[12] Still, in the end, whatever crises the family faced, whatever characters were assembled and called a family, whatever idiosyncrasies or flaws the characters had, the family was always there, Lasch's "haven in a heartless world."

Despite its roots in sociological theory,[13] the television image of the family from the middle of the twentieth century as a safe place could not withstand the mounting evidence of social research and clinical observation that not all families were loving and supportive of their members. A great deal of research and analysis showed that the family could be an institution that put its members at risk of violent victimization.[14] In the simplest terms possible, Deborah Prothrow-Stith wrote, "Violence is a problem that begins at home."[15] In words more explicit and graphic, James Gilligan, based on his experience as the medical director of a prison hospital and the clinical director of psychiatric services for a state prison system, wrote:

> The violent criminals I have known have been objects of violence from early childhood. They have seen their closest relatives—their fathers and mothers and sisters and brothers—murdered in front of their eyes, often by other family members. As children, these men were shot, axed, scalded, beaten, strangled, tortured, drugged, starved, suffocated, set on fire, thrown out of windows, raped, or prostituted by mothers who were their "pimps"; their bones have been broken; they have been locked in closets or attics for extended periods, and one man I know was deliberately locked by his parents in an empty icebox until he suffered brain damage from oxygen deprivation before he was let out.[16]

As early as 1965 the federal government released a report that addressed issues being raised about the U.S. family. Daniel Patrick Moynihan, who would one day be a U.S. senator from New York but who was then a sociologist serving as assistant secretary of labor and director of the Office of Policy Planning and Research for the Department of Labor, produced a report called *The Negro Family: The Case for National Action.*[17] Although it was a government report targeted at a small audience of policy makers, the Moynihan report nonetheless gained widespread notoriety and became a source of extensive public controversy.[18] At a time when new legislation made the dream of civil rights seem real and attainable, the Moynihan report argued that "[a]t the heart of the deterioration of the fabric of Negro society is the deterioration of the Negro family."[19]

Specifically, Moynihan argued that "[i]n essence, the Negro community has been forced into a matriarchal structure which, because it is so out of line with the rest of the American society, seriously retards the progress of the group as a whole and imposes a crushing burden on the Negro male and, in consequence, on a great many Negro women as well."[20] He then observed that what he called a pathological tangle of "poverty, failure, and isolation among Negro youth" inevitably resulted in a "disastrous delinquency and crime rate," most notably in the area of violent crimes including rape, murder, and aggravated assault.[21]

While the Moynihan report did place the family at the root of society's problems, it also pointed to race as the factor that distinguished families that worked well from those that did not. For example, suggesting that it was "probable" at that time that most violent offenses were "committed by Negroes," Moynihan implied that violence was the product of high rates of illegitimacy and dependency among black families.[22] The impact of the report was so great that it served as a focal point for much of the academic and policy debate about the U.S. family for many years to follow.[23] This was unfortunate because many social scientists and government officials already knew that the relationship between violence and families was complex and could not be explained by single factors such as race.[24] Fortunately, however, it did help bring attention to the problem of the relationship between family life and violence. Three decades later, Nijole Benokraitis could write without fear of contradiction in the opening pages of her popular introductory family text, "The home is one of the most physically and psychologically brutal settings in society, especially for women, teenage girls, and young children."[25]

When Families Don't Work

We may never be able to agree about what arrangement of people constitutes a family. Can a man and woman and their children alone be considered a family, or must a family include extended members? Must there be two and only two parents and, if so, can they be of the same gender? Must there be children, or can a childless couple also be a family? Nor may we ever agree about the proper role of a family. Is a family only a family if its parental members, and only its parental members, procreate? To what extent is a family responsible for the socialization of children? Can a family be a family if it is economically unstable?

Just as we may disagree about what a family is, we may also disagree about when a family is not working. Arguably, violence among family members is a good indicator that a family is not fulfilling its social role. Yet given the image of the family as a haven in a heartless world, it becomes difficult for us to recognize violence as an indication of a problem in a family. As Gelles wrote, "Our desire to idealize family life is partly responsible for a tendency either not to see family and intimate violence or to condone it as being a necessary and important part of raising children, relating to spouses, and conducting other family transactions."[26] The following story shows how violence can progress in a family while outsiders see the signs and try to respond but cannot forestall the violence.

Every day the *New York Times* runs a column called "News Summary," which is essentially an annotated index of the main news reports of the day. On November 3, 1987, under the "Regional" subheading of that column was a brief summary of an article that appeared on page B1. It read: "The parents of a badly beaten girl discovered by police who answered a call for medical help at the couple's Greenwich Village apartment were charged with the attempted murder of their 6-year-old daughter." The story was called "Couple Held In Beating of Daughter" and its subheading read "18-Month-Old Son Was Tied to Playpen." The article was mostly about who the couple was and what the police had found. He was identified as a lawyer and she as a former book editor. The children had been adopted with the help of a friend who was a gynecologist. The police found the boy "covered with his urine" and tied with a "$3\frac{1}{2}$ foot piece of twine around his waist" to his playpen. The girl was "in extremely critical condition" with "bleeding in the brain and bruises to her head and spine." Neither parent would make a statement. The mother had cuts and bruises and apparently had also been beaten.

The next day, the story moved to three short columns at the bottom of the first page of the *Times* before concluding on page B1. The girl, Lisa Steinberg, remained in critical condition, and there was not much new to report about what had happened. So "Officials Said to Ignore Pleas for Abused Girl" told more about the couple and their children. Apparently, Joel Barnet Steinberg and Hedda Nussbaum were not married but had lived together for seventeen years. Lisa and her brother Mitchell had both been adopted. The story quoted coworkers and neighbors who all said that for years they had repeatedly called authorities to report evidence of violence and repeatedly had been ignored. Neighbors called the police or abuse hotlines when they heard the screaming. Coworkers at the publishing house where Nussbaum worked called when she came to work bruised or battered. One neighbor was quoted as saying "There were authorities, people in power, who did nothing." The article also noted, "Undetermined amounts of cocaine and marijuana, $25,000 in cash and drug paraphernalia were found in the couple's apartment, the police said."

Between November 3, 1987, when Lisa Steinberg was found dying, to January 31, 1988, the day after Joel Steinberg was convicted of manslaughter for her death, a total of 456 days, the *Times* had at least one article about the story on each of 114 days. Mostly the stories offered new details, raised questions about the responsibility of Hedda Nussbaum (the mother, who herself apparently had been beaten by Joel Steinberg), or they raised questions about the nature of domestic violence and child abuse, about government policies with regard to abuse, and about the agencies and people who were supposed to serve the abused. For example, November 8, 1988, the first Sunday after the girl had been found, there was an article beginning on the bottom of the front page that reviewed the events of the past week, including Lisa's death and "the arrest of her adoptive parents for murder." It went on to cite and quote "experts" who psychoanalyzed the relationship between Steinberg and Nussbaum as fitting "a rough pattern of behavior characteristic among abusers and the abused." When the article continued on page 44, it was accompanied by a shorter, boxed piece telling readers how to identify child abuse and how to get help.

On October 27, 1988, as the trial for the murder of Lisa Steinberg was getting under way, the *New York Times* reported on page B3 that "Judge Dismisses Charge For Nussbaum." Legal authorities determined that

Nussbaum, because of her own physical and mental abuse at the hands of her lover, Joel Steinberg, was not "criminally responsible for Lisa's death." On January 31, 1989, the *Times* reported at the top of page 1 that "Steinberg Is Guilty of First-Degree Manslaughter." Joel Steinberg was not found guilty of murder, and Hedda Nussbaum was held legally guilty of nothing.

Despite the lesser sentence of the father and the exoneration of the mother, it is reasonable to conclude that as a family the Steinbergs did not work. A child died at the hands of her parents. It is also reasonable to conclude that society in this case did not work. Given our image at the time of what the family should be, officials with the authority to remove the child from a violent home were limited in their ability to do so. Still, during the last decades of the twentieth century, new statistics and stories about families like the Steinbergs did raise the question of violence in families and how we should respond to it.

The Birth of Family Violence

There are different ways that a family can give birth to violence. Sometimes violence is borne of family dysfunction, when members feel they cannot give to the family what they think they should or do not receive what they think they deserve. Maybe a parent cannot provide economic security, or maybe a child does not feel loved. Consider the family situation of the woman my colleagues and I interviewed who arranged for the murder of her parents after her mother threw her out of their home.[27] The young woman felt that her mother had been cheating her of what was rightfully hers. She believed that her mother was taking for herself things that her deceased grandmother had actually willed to her. One day, after a major battle, her mother told her to leave the house. The daughter was angry. She said to herself, "That's it. You just gotta do them. You just gotta do them both." She really only wanted her mother dead, but if her father lived she believed he eventually would come to blame her, so he too had to be killed. Through a drug dealer she knew, the woman arranged for three men to kill her parents. She was supposed to arrange for a garage door to remain open so the three men could enter her parent's house. When they arrived it was locked. In a way, she was relieved, feeling uncertain about her plan. She went to sleep at a girlfriend's house. Meanwhile, the three men decided to break into the house. They beat the mother and drowned the father. When the two were found dead the next day, a neighbor came to tell the daughter. She truly was surprised to hear this but not really disappointed.

Other times violence may be the heritage that one generation of a family passes on to the next. Consider the story of Garland Hampton as reported in the *New York Times* on December 12, 1994. Hampton was then 15 years old. He was also in County Jail in Milwaukee, Wisconsin, charged with murder. The killing of a fellow gang member culminated in five years of criminal activity including stealing bicycles, shooting and wounding gang rivals, carrying a gun, and possessing cocaine. The article began:

> Milwaukee, Dec. 11 – When other children were hearing fairy tales, Garland Hampton heard bedtime stories about the day Uncle Robert killed two Milwaukee police officers, or the time Grandma, with both barrels, blew away the father of two of her children back in '62. By the time he was 9, he had seen his mother kill her boyfriend.

By the time he was arrested for murder at age 15, Garland Hampton was already a father. In the story in the *Times*, called "When the Family Heirloom Is Homicide," the 15-year-old mother of his son is quoted as saying that she will be there for the little boy.

Other times, violence is the product of people trying to maintain stability, order, or even normalcy in their family. One of the men interviewed in prison for our study of homicide offenders told the following story.[28] He admitted that he had blown off another man's head with an automatic 12-gauge shotgun. The man, his brother-on-law, lived nearby with his wife's mother. Often the brother-in-law offered to care for his young daughters. About a year before the killing, he noticed the man touching his daughters in an odd way as he held them in his lap on a rocking chair. One day, the father found his daughter crying. She told him her uncle had molested her. After that, the brother-in-law more openly threatened to do things to the girls. Their mother, his sister, did not want her brother to go to jail. The man only knew he had to protect his daughters. One day, while the father was working on his fence with his daughters nearby, his brother-in-law walked over to him and started babbling about how he wanted "to break her in." Frightened, the man took his daughters, ran into the house, and locked the doors. He got and held onto his shotgun, constantly peeking out the windows. Somehow the other man got into the house. They faced each other and began to argue. "Don't come near me," he said, before shooting and killing his wife's brother.

Or violence can be the inadvertent result of family love. Among the stories my colleagues and I heard from the detectives who participated in our study of homicide in New York City in 1988 was the story of a boy who killed his mother.[29] The mother, only 34 years old at the time, was selling drugs. Her 17-year-old son was concerned for her safety. He knew that the drug business was a violent one, and he wanted to protect his mother, so he decided to purchase a gun. When he came home with a shotgun, his mother became upset and they argued. During the argument about whether he should keep a gun in the house for his mother's safety, the gun went off, and his mother was killed. Apparently, she died because he wanted to protect her.

These examples show the different ways that violence makes its way into a family. Clearly, sometimes the violence is intentional, and other times it is not. Sometimes family members mean to harm one another, other times they do not. In any case, in recent years, we are more apt to recognize and acknowledge that there can be violence in families.

Violence against Women and Children

Clearly, a family is not always a haven in a heartless world. Such is the case for many women living with an abusive spouse, often one they believe they cannot leave. Among the women my colleagues and I interviewed for a study of homicide by women were several women sentenced to prison for having killed a husband or lover. After listening to them speak of their lives with the man—and particularly of the occasion on which the woman finally lashed out and killed the abuser—I often felt like asking, "Why did you wait so long?" The things these women experienced were horrifying. But wait they did. Like so many other abused women, they never left the relationship. My colleagues and I often mused about finding the key, that moment or insight that told the woman who finally killed the abusive spouse that enough was enough. The literature on woman abuse speaks to this question, pointing to things such as fear and economic circumstances.[30] But the one thing that struck us was the importance of children. To take the abuse herself was one thing; to have it inflicted on her children was quite another.

One woman incarcerated for homicide believed that everything was fine until her husband started using drugs.[31] Before he started using alcohol, cocaine, and marijuana, she remembers them being happy. Then, as his drug use progressed, things changed. He became intoxicated and accused her of cheating on him. He threatened her and sometimes her children as well. On several occasions he assaulted her, choking her and pointing a gun at her. One night while she was sleeping, he pointed a large handgun at her head, woke her, and dragged her from the bed to examine a presumed lover's footprints in the carpet. When she said she would leave him, he threatened to kill her. The threats and abuse lasted for more than a year. She began to feel trapped. She was frightened but saw no way out. She prayed a lot.

One night, before he went out for the evening, her husband told her she was going to die that night. Then he would kill her kids. He had three guns in the house and had been snorting cocaine and drinking liquor that day, so she believed him. She told the interviewer, "He was irrational as it was and I wasn't sure whether he meant that was my last day to be on earth alive. It wasn't so bad that it was my last night, but now he wants to kill my kids, too? Come on! I think he just overstepped his boundaries there." She continued, "You know, I made my bed hard. I married this jerk, but my kids didn't do anything to him or anybody else." When he returned home from his night out, he continued talking about his plans to kill her and her kids. He was so drunk, though, he fell asleep. She considered her options: jumping out the window, running away. Then she took a gun and shot him.

Because a problem is real for an individual does not make it a problem for society. So once we acknowledge the existence of family violence, the next question is one of extent. How extensive is family violence, and to what extent does family violence affect not only individuals, but the social fabric as well? A report on "Violence by Intimates" released by the federal Bureau of Justice Statistics (BJS) suggests that there are six different sources of data by which to measure the incidence of violence among intimates.[32] Most of these are criminal justice sources, including the National Crime Victimization Survey (NCVS), the Uniform Crime Reports (UCR), the National Incident-Based Reporting System (NIBRS), the Supplementary Homicide Reports (SHR), and surveys of jail and prison inmates. The sixth is a public health source, the National Electronic Injury Surveillance System (NEISS) of the Consumer Product Safety Commission (CPSC), including counts of intentional injuries that result in admissions to hospital emergency departments.

Most of these data sources were discussed in the previous chapters. Briefly, the NCVS includes data about criminal victimization collected from an annual survey of a national sample of household respondents. The UCR is an aggregate count of particular crimes known to the police and, by itself, is not really a source of information about individual crimes or the relationship between victims and offenders. NIBRS is a program intended eventually to replace UCR by providing detailed data on particular incidents for 57 different types of crime. The SHR is a component of the UCR that collects some detail about incidents of homicide known to the police. The surveys of jail and prison inmates conducted by BJS include information provided by the offender about his or her relationship with the victim. Finally, NEISS hospital data include information provided by emergency staff and by persons admitted with injuries, identified by staff as intentional, of the characteristics of those injuries and the relationship of those persons to the person who inflicted the injury.

According to the BJS report, "On average each year from 1992 to 1996, there were more than 960,000 violent victimizations of women age 12 or older by an intimate (a current or former spouse, girlfriend, or boyfriend).[33]" This number is high, but the report continues that the violent victimization of women is more likely to occur at the hands of a stranger, friend, or acquaintance than at the hands of an intimate, and the extent of homicides involving intimates had declined over the past 20 years. Still, as the report also notes, females older than 12 years of age are eight times more likely than males to experience violent victimization at the hands of a current or former spouse, girlfriend, or boyfriend, and female homicide victims are much more likely than male victims of homicide to have been killed by an intimate.

State governments similarly have established systems for reporting statistics on violence against women at the hands of intimates. For example, in its annual report on statewide UCR statistics, New York State regularly includes one page on domestic violence.[34] At the top of the page is a sentence identifying the source of the data: "Domestic violence figures presented here represent offenses which have come to the attention of law enforcement officers, regardless of whether a formal complaint was filed or an arrest made." A table at the bottom of the page claims that there were 94,124 incidents of domestic violence in the state in 1996, and a graph at the top shows that that number represents an increase of 7.5 percent over 1995. Similarly, *1995 Crime and Delinquency in California* includes a page on domestic violence.[35] A small table shows the number of calls to police (246,315) and weapons used in domestic violence cases in California in 1995, and a column of text describes the state's legal definition of domestic violence and the legislative mandate to report it.

Family violence is not just about domestic violence involving spouses and other intimates. It also involves the abuse of children. In a national survey conducted during the late 1960s, when family violence was still not widely recognized as a social problem, David Gil found about 6,000 cases of physical child abuse and estimated that nationwide there were probably between 13 and 21 cases of child abuse for every 1,000 people living in the United States.[36] In the 1990s, the National Center for Child Abuse and Neglect commissioned a survey of community social service and law enforcement professionals in all 50 states who work with children to identify unreported cases of child abuse. From that survey, it was estimated that in 1996 more than 3 million children, or 43.5 for every child living in the United States, was the victim of child abuse.[37]

The federal and state attention to the problem suggests that during the last decades of the twentieth century, family violence is being taken more seriously than it was in earlier years. Trying to summarize our knowledge of family violence, Harvey Wallace notes that while the study of family violence is still a new field, our interest and concern in the problem was heightened in the early 1990s.[38] The remaining question is what have we done about it.

Responding to Family Violence

Under the State Justice Statistics program of BJS, the Justice Research and Statistics Association (JRSA) annually surveys official criminal justice researchers in each of 53 U.S. states and territories asking them about "the types of research, analytic activities, and publications in which they are involved."[39] For the period from January 1996 through September 1997, JRSA identified such activity among states in 41 different content areas. The area mentioned most often was drugs (by 47 states or territories), and the area mentioned second most often was domestic violence (by 40 states or territories). Much of this activity included straightforward reporting, as was the case of the New York and California reports mentioned earlier. There was also some new programming in this area. For example, in Iowa there was an evaluation of a program requiring persons convicted of domestic assault to attend an education program, and in Connecticut a group of government and academic researchers was impaneled to analyze 10 years of data from the state's family violence reporting program.[40] Alabama was working on an automated system to notify law enforcement officers of restraining orders on arrestees, and North Carolina provided local law enforcement officers with Polaroid cameras to develop photographic evidence in domestic violence cases.[41]

According to the JRSA report, to some extent the increased interest in family violence as an issue among state researchers came from the increased availability of funds for studies of domestic violence and sexual assault under the federal Violence Against Women Act in 1994.[42] That is, it did not so much reflect an interest in family violence as it did an interest in obtaining more funds for research departments. This is not surprising. Researchers are not supposed to embrace policy positions. Compared to policy makers whose job is to advocate for programs and policies that support a particular view of a problem, the role of the researcher is defined in terms of studying problems and offering objective information.[43] The question, then, is whether and how government policy makers responded to the evidence of violence within families or related to domestic settings.

After the courts in New York found Joel Steinberg responsible for the death of his adopted daughter, the *New York Times* in its February 1, 1989, edition had a story under the headline "Lisa's Legacy: Awareness Of Child Abuse and With It, Alarm." According to the reporter, "Fourteen months after she was beaten to death, 6-year-old Lisa Steinberg seems to have left as her legacy increased awareness of child abuse—and a new readiness to report cases in which abuse is suspected." In fact, according to statistics maintained by New York State, in 1990 in New York City, there were 44,617 reports of violence by one family member against another, a decrease of 14.6 percent when compared to the number of reports in 1989.[44] By 1996, the total number of such reports was down further to 42,308.[45] That is, while awareness was up, the number of reports was down.

Whether, as the newspaper claimed, any one incident resulted in increased awareness or reporting of violence in families, by the end of the twentieth century, federal, state, and local government policy makers had begun to take family violence more seriously. In New York, for example, the reason statistics about family violence were available was because on May

17,1979, Governor Hugh Carey had issued Executive Order Number 90 establishing the Governor's Task Force on Domestic Violence.[46] In fact, as described in a report prepared for the National Institute of Justice (NIJ) by Jeffrey Fagan, in the 1960s "society began paying attention to violence within families,"[47] and by the 1970s the federal government began criminalizing domestic violence through a reform process that "sought to increase the certainty and severity of legal responses" to cases of family violence, particularly those involving battered women.[48]

While research and evaluation efforts have lagged behind program and policy development in the area of family violence,[49] there has been some attempt to learn what efforts under the umbrella of criminalization work best to reduce violence among family members.[50] Notable was an experiment by Lawrence Sherman and his associates in Minneapolis that randomly assigned one of three police responses to calls for assistance in domestic violence cases: arrest of the alleged offender, asking the alleged offender to leave the scene, and offering advice to the disputants.[51] When the results showed the lowest rate of recidivism for those cases where an arrest had been made, mandatory or presumptive arrest in domestic assault calls quickly became popular among police departments throughout the nation.[52] However, the findings were subject to controversy, and, in the end, the impact of the research on law enforcement may have exceeded the definitude of its conclusions. Looking back at the study and its aftermath, Wallace wrote, "In retrospect, it may not matter whether the results of the study were accurate. Its greatest contribution may be that it generated an incredible amount of debate within academia and the law enforcement profession as to how to respond to domestic violence."[53] Thus, by the 1990s, family violence was acknowledged as a social problem and it was clear that something needed to be done. Just what needed to be done was not so clear.

Conclusion

Insofar as love is the central theme of family life, the story of the family is a romance. Unfortunately, for many people living in the United States today it is something other than that. There may be romance in the way people find each other and form families, but the romance increasingly turns into romantic tragedy. A tragedy is a story that ends in disaster, telling of "serious actions which turn out disastrously for the chief character."[54] While we cannot say with certainty that the family as a social institution has changed over time, we can see how the social portrayal of the family has changed from the mid-twentieth-century image of "a haven in a heartless world" to the late-twentieth-century image of an institution that places too many of its participants at risk of violent victimization.

During the 1992 spring television season, the lead character in a popular television program caught the attention of our nation's vice president. Murphy Brown, the character played by Candace Bergen on the show by the same name was the star of a television news program. The unmarried character became pregnant and decided that, instead of having an abortion, she would have the child on her own. Vice President Dan Quayle, while addressing the Commonwealth Club of San Francisco on May 19, 1992, made the following statement: "It doesn't help matters when prime-time TV has Murphy Brown, a character who supposedly epitomizes today's intelligent, highly paid, professional woman, mocking the importance of fathers by bearing a child alone and calling it just another lifestyle choice."[55] What he missed, aside from the fact that he was talking about a fictional character, is that the problem then and now is not how families were formed or how their members arranged themselves, but rather the presence of violence in so many households.

The explanations for the violence observed in families reflect the various theories about crime and delinquency in general.[56] We can talk about family violence as a reflection of violence in society, or about how children learn violence from their experiences with other people, or about how the strains of everyday life pressure people to act in violent ways in their homes, or even how some people find that the benefits of violence outweigh its costs. In the end, however, we cannot separate the violence within families from the institution of the family and, more generally, from the roles and values we assign to men and women in our society. In contemporary society, the family often is a battleground where men, women, and children struggle over power, control, and resources in a framework of love and caring. And despite the presence of love and caring, battles often result in violence.

Endnotes

1. DREIM # 120.

2. Downs, J. F. (1966). *The Two Worlds of the Washo—An Indian Tribe of California and Nevada*. New York: Holt, Rinehart and Winston. Ember, C. R. and Ember, M. (1977) *Cultural Anthropology*. Englewood Cliffs, NJ: Prentice-Hall. Friedl, E. (1962). *Vasilika—A Village in Modern Greece*. New York: Holt, Rinehart and Winston. Newman, P. L. (1965). *Knowing the Gururumba*. New York: Holt, Rinehart and Winston. Radcliffe-Brown, A. R. (1965). *Structure and Function in Primitive Society*. New York: The Free Press. Schusky, E. L. (1965). *Manual for Kinship Analysis*. New York: Holt, Rinehart and Winston.

3. Goode, W. J. (1964). *The Family*. Englewood Cliffs, NJ: Prentice-Hall. Parsons, T. and Bales, R. F. (1955). *Family, Socialization and Interaction Process*. New York: The Free Press. Skolnick, A. S. and Skolnick, J. H. (1971). *Family in Transition; Rethinking Marriage, Sexuality, Child Rearing, and Family Organization*. Boston: Little, Brown.

4. Lasch, C. (1977). *Haven in a Heartless World—The Family Beseiged*. New York: Basic Books.

5. Gough, K. (1975). "The Origin of the Family." Pp. 181–91 in D. H. Spain (ed.), *The Human Experience—Readings in Sociocultural Anthropology*. Homewood, IL: Dorsey Press, p. 191.

6. Berger, P. L. and Berger B. (1975). *Sociology—A Biographical Approach*. Second Expanded Edition. New York: Basic Books, p. 85.

7. From a letter written by Mother Agnes of the Convent of the Blessed Eleanor to Jemima Shore, characters in the novel *The Wild Island*, by Antonia Fraser, 1991, New York: Bantam Books Edition, p. 155. Originally published by W. W. Norton and Company, 1978.

8. Gelles, R. (1997). *Intimate Violence in Families*. Third Edition. Thousand Oaks, CA: Sage, p. 1.

9. Gelles 1997:1.

10. Compare Gelles 1997; Wallace, H. (1999). *Family Violence—Legal, Medical, and Social Perspectives*. Second Edition. Boston: Allyn and Bacon.

11. From *Complete Directory to Prime Time Network and Cable TV Shows* by Tim Brooks and Earle Marsh. Copyright © 1995 by Tim Brooks and Earle Marsh. Reprinted by permission of Ballantine Books, a Division of Random House Inc.

12. Compare Benokraitis, N. (1993). *Marriages and Families*. Englewood Cliffs, NJ: Prentice-Hall.

13. See Lasch 1977.

14. Asher, R. (1992). *Women with Alcoholic Husbands—Ambivalence and the Trap of Codependency*. Chapel Hill: University of North Carolina. Crowell, N. A. and Burgess, A. W. (eds.) (1996). *Understanding Violence against Women*. Washington, DC: National Academy Press. DeKeseredy, W. S. and Ellis, D. (1997). "Sibling Violence: A Review of Canadian Sociological Research and Suggestions for Further Empirical Research." *Humanity and Society* 21:397–411. Dobash, R. E. and Dobash, R. (1979). *Violence against Wives—A Case against the Patriarchy*. New York: The Free Press. Gelles 1997; Gondolf, E. W. (1989). *Man against Woman—What Every Woman Should Know about Violent Men*. Blue Ridge Summit, PA: Tab Books. Greenfeld, L. A. et al. (1998). *Violence by Intimates—Analysis of Data on Crimes by Current or Former Spouses, Boyfriends, and Girlfriends*. BJS Factbook. Washington, DC: U.S. Department of Justice; Hicks, R. A. and Gaughan, D. C. (1995). "Understanding Fatal Child Abuse." *Child Abuse and Neglect* 19:855–63. International Association of Chiefs of Police. (1997). *Family Violence in America—Breaking the Cycle for Children Who Witness*. Alexandria, VA: International Association of Chiefs of Police. Kelley, B. T., Thornberry, T. P. and Smith, C. A. (1997). *In the Wake of Childhood Maltreatment*. OJJDP Juvenile Justice Bulletin. Washington, DC: U.S. Department of Justice. Mohd, S. K. and Shafie, H. M. (1995). "Childhood Deaths from Physical Abuse." *Child Abuse and Neglect* 19:847–54. Steinmetz, S. K. and Straus, M. A. (eds.) (1974). *Violence in the Family*. New York: Dodd, Mead. Thornberry, T. P. (1994). *Violent Families and Youth Violence*. OJJDP Fact Sheet #21. Washington, DC: U.S. Department of Justice. Wallace 1999; Widom, C. S. (1992). *The Cycle of Violence*. NIJ Research in Brief. Washington, DC: U.S. Department of Justice. Widom, C. S. (1996). *The Cycle of Violence Revisited*. NIJ Research Preview. Washington, DC: U.S. Department of Justice. Zawitz, M. (1994). *Domestic Violence—Violence between Intimates*. Bureau of Justice Statistics Selected Findings. Washington, DC: U. S. Department of Justice.

15. Prothrow-Stith, D. (1991). *Deadly Consequences*. New York: The Free Press, p. 145.

16. Gilligan, J. (1996). *Violence—Our Deadly Epidemic and Its Causes*. New York: G. P. Putnam's Sons.

17. Office of Policy Planning and Research. (1965). *The Negro Family: The Case for National Action*. Washington, DC: U.S. Department of Labor.

18. Rainwater, L. and Yancey, W. L. (1967). *The Moynihan Report and the Politics of Controversy*. Cambridge: The M. I. T. Press.

19. Office of Policy Planning and Research 1965:5.

20. Office of Policy Planning and Research 1965:29.

21. Office of Policy Planning and Research 1965:38.

22. Office of Policy Planning and Research 1965.

23. Hutter, M. (1981). *The Changing Family—Comparative Perspectives*. New York: John Wiley. Rainwater and Yancey 1967.

24. Gelles 1997; Rainwater and Yancey 1967; Steinmetz and Straus 1974.

25. Benokraitis 1993:13.

26. Gelles 1997:1.

27. FEMDREIM # 208.

28. DREIM # 341.

29. DRCAH2 # 113.

30. See Asher 1992; Benokraitis 1993; DeKeseredy and Ellis 1997; Dobash and Dobash 1979; Gondolf 1989; Wallace 1999.

31. FEMDREIM # 457.

32. Greenfeld et al. 1998:vii.

33. Greenfeld et al. 1998:3–5.

34. Ely, R. E. et al. (1998). *1996 Crime and Justice Annual Report*. Albany, NY: NY State Division of Criminal Justice Services, p. 38.

35. Bureau of Criminal Information and Analysis. (n.d.) *1995 Crime and Delinquency in California*. Sacramento: California Department of Justice, p. 103.

36. Gil, D. (1970). *Violence against Children: Physical Child Abuse in the United States*. Cambridge: Harvard.

37. U.S. Department of Health and Human Services, Children's Bureau. (1998). *Child Maltreatment 1996: Reports from the States to the National Child Abuse and Neglect Data System*. Washington, DC: U.S. Government Printing Office, p. 3.

38. Wallace 1999:2.

39. Maline, K., Michel, N., Parisi, L., and Puryear, V. (1997). *Criminal Justice Issues in the States—1997 Directory*, Volume XIV. Washington, DC: Justice Research and Statistics Association, p. iv.

40. Maline et al. 1997:18 and 7.

41. Maline et al. 1997:2 and 37.

42. Maline et al. 1997:v.

43. Brownstein, H. H. and Goldstein, P. J. (1990) "Research and the Development of Public Policy: The Case of Drugs and Violent Crime." *Journal of Applied Sociology* 7:77–92. Bulmer, M. (1982). *The Uses of Social Research*. London: George Allen & Unwin. Mayer, R. R. and Greenwood, E. (1980). *The Design of Social Policy Research*. Englewood Cliffs, NJ: Prentice-Hall. Merton, R. K. and Moss, J. Z. (1985). "Basic Research and Its Potentials of Relevance." *The Mount Sinai Journal of Medicine* 52:679–84.

44. Rosen, R. A. (1991). *1990 Crime and Justice Annual Report*. Albany, NY: NYS Division of Criminal Justice Services, p. 104.

45. Ely 1998:38.

46. Rosen 1991:104.

47. Fagan, J. (1996). *The Criminalization of Domestic Violence: Promises and Limits*. National Institute of Justice Research Report. Washington, DC: U.S. Department of Justice, p. 7.

48. Fagan 1996:3.

49. Fagan 1996:5.

50. See Brookoff, D. (1997). *Drugs, Alcohol, and Domestic Violence in Memphis*. NIJ Research Preview. Washington, DC: U.S. Department of Justice. Fyfe, J. F., Klinger, D. A., and Flavin, J. A. (1997). "Differential Police Treatment of Male-On-Female Spousal Violence." *Criminology* 35:455–73. National Institute of Justice. (1995). Evaluation of Family Violence Programs. NIJ Research Preview. Washington, DC: U.S. Department of Justice. Orchowsky, S. (1998). "The Unique Nature of Domestic Violence in Rural Areas." *JRSA Forum* 16:1, 6–9. Sherman, L. W. (1992). *Policing Domestic Violence—Experiments and Dilemmas*. New York: Free Press.

51. Sherman, L. W, and Berk, R. (1984). "The Specific Deterrent Effects of Arrest for Domestic Assault." *American Sociological Review* 49:261–72.

52. See Gelles 1998; Wallace 1999.

53. Wallace 1999:217.

54. Abrams, M. H. (1957). *A Glossary of Literary Terms*. New York: Holt, Rinehart and Winston, p. 95.

55. Brooks and Marsh 1995:708.

56. Benokraitis 1993:409.

6

The Myth of the Liberated Woman

On a bright spring day just one month before the end of the school year, a fight broke out on a grassy area outside of Wilde Lake High School. According to a spokesperson for the school district, "The fight seems to have been caused by an 'ongoing dispute between the students—an interpersonal problem.'"[1] The disturbance at this suburban high school southwest of Baltimore would not have been noteworthy but for two things. First, a teacher died of a heart attack while trying to break up the fight. The death of a beloved teacher brought grief to the community and produced a sense of severity and urgency. Second, 9 of the 12 students involved in the fight were girls. The involvement of girls heightened local fears of spreading schoolgirl violence.

On May 16, 1997, two days after the fight and the death of the teacher, a small headline on the bottom corner of page 1 of the (Baltimore) *Sun* read, "Schoolgirl violence on rise in region." Accompanied by a picture of the teacher who died, the subheading of the article read, "Death of a teacher brings issue into focus." Focus, however, is not the same as perspective. While the article did open with a note about plans for a memorial service and the sadness felt by staff and students alike, most of what followed was a discussion of student violence, especially the increasing aggressiveness of girls. According to the article, "The death of a Columbia high school teacher after he broke up a schoolyard brawl has brought into sharp focus rising youth violence—particularly among girls—in Howard County and other suburban school systems."

This was not the first time the *Sun* had brought attention to the issue of schoolgirl violence. The previous summer an article by the same reporter, "Girls' crimes worry some officials," appeared in the Howard County section of the newspaper. The July 23, 1996, article used local crime statistics to demonstrate the growing involvement of girls in violence, for example, "the number of girls referred to the Howard County Juvenile Justice Department by police and citizens has more than doubled in six years—from 165 cases in fiscal 1990, to 390 in fiscal 1996." The news account did not say so, but while "the number of girls referred" increased by 136 percent, the county population increased by only 23 percent.[2]

Still, the case for an epidemic of violence by young girls was not that strong. In the *Sun* article written before the Wilde Lake fracas, the authors did cite a few local officials and regional experts who suggested that, like everyone else in our society, girls are getting more violent. But they also referred to national statistics showing that violent crime had not grown dramatically among girls and cited national authorities who believed that the argument that violence was and is increasing among girls is perhaps misleading. Meda Chesney-Lind, the director of women's studies at the University of Hawaii, was quoted as saying that the statistical change was, at least in part, due to the fact that "[w]e are paying more attention to [girls], and they are more likely to get arrested."

So the question remains as to whether girls and women in the United States have been and continue to become more violent as we approach the next millennium. Available statistics and research reports do not provide a definitive answer, leaving those with ideological and dogmatic convictions to reach conclusions that are based on values and beliefs rather than knowledge and information. With notions about women's "proper place" so deeply rooted in our history and culture, it is not surprising that the debate over women and violence has been grounded in the language of moral and political judgment. This chapter discusses the relationship between gender and violence, including claims made through official statistics, research reports, and media accounts. Special attention is given to theories proposed in the 1970s about the role of "women's liberation" in increasing the involvement of women in crime and violence, and later feminist theories that argue against that position. The chapter moves from Betty Friedan's call to arms in *The Feminine Mystique*, to Freda Adler's and Rita Simon's warnings of the consequences of liberating women, to contemporary notions of the increasing involvement of women in violent crime.

The Liberation of Women

During the fall of 1972, I was a graduate student at Temple University in Philadelphia, enrolled at the time in a seminar on the subject of sex role polarization. The seminar was taught by Betty Friedan, a visiting lecturer who had come to national attention and fame a decade earlier after the publication of her book *The Feminine Mystique*. There were about 20 students in the class, only 5 or so of whom were male. Over the course of 15 weekly sessions, Friedan taught us two things. From a broad range of sociological, psychological, and feminist readings, we learned that only through social, political, and economic liberation will women be able to fulfill their lives and be able to contribute in a world historically and culturally dominated by men. From a series of exercises that pitted the females in the class against the males, we learned that gender does matter. For example, given the same problem to solve, the men argued issues and never agreed on a solution; the women formed a circle, discussed the matter at hand, and reached consensus. A "male beauty contest," in which the women judged the men on the basis of their response to a question about their own masculinity, resulted in the men feeling angry and degraded and the women amused at the competitiveness of the men.

The Feminine Mystique was written to force women who did not even realize they were being denied equal treatment to face questions such as: "Who knows what women can be when they are finally free to become themselves? Who knows what women's intelligence will contribute when it can be nourished without denying love?"[3] Because the book was a call to arms, Friedan had to emphasize only one of the lessons she taught our class ten years later. She had to devote the book to making the case that women in the United States in the second half of the twentieth century had been subjugated by the patriarchal control of the institutions of society and were faced with a struggle that would have to be resolved if they were to become themselves and to make meaningful contributions to society. She wrote, "It is my thesis that as the Victorian culture did not permit women to accept or gratify their basic sexual needs, our culture does not permit women to accept or gratify their basic need to grow and fulfill their potentialities as human beings, a need which is not solely defined by their sexual role."[4]

As official U.S. crime statistics during the 1970s indicated increasing participation by women in crime, it was unfortunate that the women scholars who wrote about women and crime during the period had not participated in the seminar. That notwithstanding, they probably had read the book. In 1975, both Freda Adler and Rita Simon independently published books about women and crime that offered what might be called a liberationist or emancipation perspective.[5] Their general argument was that women will increasingly follow the criminal offending patterns of their male counterparts as they are liberated from their traditional and historical roles as women.[6]

Looking at the crime statistics of the period, Simon observed that women in greater numbers were participating in property crimes.[7] She concluded that greater participation of women in the workplace had resulted in more opportunities for women to participate in those property offenses that traditionally had been the province of men, such as fraud and embezzlement.[8]

For Adler, the expansion of women into the world of crime during the 1970s was more widespread and more diverse. When she looked at the crime statistics, she concluded, "By every indication available, female criminals appear to be surpassing males in the rate of increase for almost every major crime."[9] Nonetheless, like Simon, she related this changing pattern to the social and economic liberation of women, which both scholars suggested had made women more like men. "What is clear" she wrote, "is that as the position of women approximates the position of men, so does the frequency and type of their criminal activity."[10]

As the years have passed, the validity of this argument has been brought into question by other scholars. Some have agreed that the same forces that incite men to violence similarly impact on women, though suggesting that violence by both women and men can better be explained in terms of the impact of broader structural conditions.[11] Most, however, have taken the argument further, suggesting that the idea that given the same opportunity women will act the same as men is both naive and superficial in its understanding of the relationship between violence and gender.[12] For example, from a study of male and female robbers, Jody Miller concluded:

> Motivationally, then, it appears that women's participation in street violence can result from the same structural and cultural underpinnings that shape some of men's participation in these crimes, and that they receive rewards beyond protection for doing so. Yet gender remains a salient factor shaping their actions, as well as the actions of men.[13]

Notably, by 1991 even Rita Simon with Jean Landis wrote, "The fears raised in the late 1960s and 1970s that women's participation in crime would soon be commensurate with their representation in the population clearly were not realized."[14]

Nonetheless, at the time that Adler and Simon were writing in 1975, media accounts were readily accepting the notion that liberated women were more likely to engage in crime and violence. An article in *Newsweek* on January 6, 1975, spoke of the "new wave" of crime among women, using arrest statistics for the years 1960 to 1973 to demonstrate that "[t]he crime rate for women—especially for violent crimes—is maintaining a steady spiral upward."[15] While noting that not all criminologists agreed with this assessment, the article concluded, "The increase in crimes by women parallels women's exodus from the home to the outside world." Thus had been constructed the basis for the myth of the liberated woman as a violent social type.

Women and Violent Offending

Since, as was noted in the first chapter of this book, we do not and cannot have an adequate measure of the actual level of violence in society, we cannot know with certainty how much violence is committed by women as compared to men. Most available statistics about offenders are collected after they have been identified and processed by the criminal justice system. We have statistics about arrestees and prisoners, for example. Unfortunately, these statistics reflect not only the number of people who actually participate in violent offending, but also the efficiency, productivity, and even bias of the criminal justice system. That said, they are what we have, and if we use them with care and caution, they do tell us something.

According to the Uniform Crime Reports (UCR),[16] of 11,093,211 people reported by police agencies as having been arrested in 1996, not quite 21 percent were women. Notably, even that small proportion is reduced when only arrests for violent crimes are considered; only 15 percent of the 548,146 reported arrests for violent crimes involved women. The same source of statistics does suggest an increase in recent years in the number of women arrested for violent crime. From 1987 to 1996, the number of reports of women arrested for a violent crime increased by 53 percent, compared to an increase of 23 percent for men. From 1992 to 1996, the number of reports of women arrested for a violent crime increased by 23 percent, while declining by almost 5 percent for men. Still, in 1996 there were 465,222 men and only 82,924 women reported to have been arrested for a violent crime.

One statistic that does estimate the number of violent offenders *known to the police* rather than the number of offenders *arrested*, a conceptual though not necessarily an actual difference, is the count of persons identified as murderers through the Supplementary Homicide Reports (SHR) component of the UCR program. Using these statistics, the *Sourcebook for Criminal Justice Statistics* for 1996 includes a table showing the estimated rate of offenders who committed murder or nonnegligent manslaughter from 1976 to 1995.[17] It shows that the homicide offending rate for women in 1976 was 3.1 of every 100,000 women in the population, compared to 16.3 of every 100,000 men. By 1995, the rate for women had declined to 1.6, while the rate for men had increased to 17.2.

Perhaps women have been known to commit violence less often because of the way our society and culture have viewed and interpreted violence by women. After decades of studying gender and aggression, psychologist Anne Campbell concluded that for women "aggression is the *failure* of control" while for men it is "the *imposing* of control over others," thereby resulting in "separate styles of violent behavior" (emphasis in original).[18] That is, for men violence is instrumental, a means to enhanced social standing and a source of power. For women, it is internalized and a source of frustration. Consequently, violence by women not only has received less attention, historically it has been stigmatized as humorous or supercilious in the context of a society dominated by men.

Or perhaps women just do not do as much violence as men. When my colleagues and I sought to interview a sample of individuals incarcerated in

New York State for a homicide committed in 1984, we were quickly reminded that, in any given year, very few of those persons identified and
processed as homicide offenders are women. Among the women my colleagues and I interviewed for our later study of women incarcerated in New
York State for a homicide committed any year, many examples surfaced of
women whose actions and behavior were as violent as that of any man. That
is, their violence was aggressive rather than defensive and ruthless rather
than judicious.

One woman, for example, walked up to a man sitting in his car and,
without hesitation, shot and killed him.[19] When she was questioned by correctional officials, she told them he owed her money and she was only trying to frighten him. The gun, she said, had discharged accidentally. She told
the interviewer she was high on crack at the time and really could not
remember what happened, though she did not dispute the charge. The
police at the time produced three witnesses who all agreed that they saw her
walk over to the man and shoot him. It was 1986, she was 26 years old, and,
at the time of the killing, she had been selling crack for about a year. He
owed her money for drugs. "When [I was] using crack," she told the interviewer, "I was always into fighting over anything and with anybody, especially men."

Another woman we interviewed said she had "left more than ten people deceased out there," but had only been convicted and sentenced to
prison for killing two.[20] Those two were shot and killed during robberies
over two consecutive spring days in 1990. At the time, she was under parole
supervision. In both of the cases, she and her brother had been robbing drug
dealers. She described one of the killings to the interviewer as follows.

Late one night, just before midnight, the woman and her brother went
out to "do a robbery." At the time, she remembered, she was under the influence of alcohol and a little cocaine as well. Her brother did not want her to go
out in her condition, but she told him that, thanks to the alcohol, she felt like
she "could beat up the world." She "talked trash" and told him she could
beat him and anyone else. They argued, but finally he gave in, and she went
with him. When they got to the coke spot they had planned to rob, she remembered being "really hyped," thinking to herself, "I'm not a woman now,
I'm a man." As they stood with guns drawn facing the men they were robbing, she noticed that one of the men standing behind the scale was putting
his hand near his pocket. She told the interviewer, "I was always told, never
allow anybody to move after the specific orders were given. By me being
under the influence I did what I did because of the simple fact I didn't know
what [he] was going in [his] pocket for. Cause I knew he was told, 'Don't nobody move, nobody get hurt.'" So when the man behind the scale moved,
she swung at him with her pistol. The weapon discharged, and a bullet hit a
man standing next to the man she hit. She thought back, "Actually, the one I
took his life, it wasn't called for. The bullet wasn't meant for him." She really

had not intended to kill anyone. But, in her mind, she had done nothing wrong. She hit the man "to show when orders are given, don't do nothing but what you're supposed to do." She had not told anyone to move. "Why were they moving?" she wondered aloud.

These stories certainly demonstrate that women can be just as violent as men. But one or two or even dozens of stories do not necessarily suggest a pattern or a trend. Never more than a small proportion of any sample of violent offenders we interviewed were women. What such stories have done, however, is to lead researchers to drug involvement as a potentially fruitful area of inquiry for exploring the relationship between the social and economic liberation of women and the increasing involvement of women in violent crime in the latter years of the twentieth century.

From the liberationist perspective, it has been argued that the involvement or potential for involvement of women in the drug markets, particularly the violent crack cocaine markets of the late 1980s and early 1990s, provided an opportunity for greater involvement in violence as well.[21] Unlike the earlier heroin and cocaine markets, which were characterized by hierarchy and specialized roles, the "free-lance"[22] crack markets of this period provided an opportunity for young entrepreneurs with small amounts of cocaine to establish themselves as crack dealers. Theoretically, such opportunities would have been available to enterprising women as well as to men. In that violence was common in the emerging crack markets, the extent to which the crack markets did open opportunities not previously available to women, it also exposed them to a setting in which violence was commonly used as a means of social control.

This drug market opportunity thesis, which seemed to be theoretically promising as a paradigm for understanding the relationship between the liberation of women and their involvement in violence, was never empirically established.[23] A number of ethnographic studies of crack markets demonstrated that, in fact, the involvement of women in these markets was not comparable to that of men, and that new opportunities to participate in the violent drug trade were more likely to be made available to men than to women.[24] In a study of the involvement of women in the street economy of the Bushwick section of Brooklyn, Lisa Maher and Kathleen Daly found that not only did the opening of crack markets in the area not provide local women with new opportunities, it actually diminished income-earning opportunities that had traditionally been available to them, such as street-level sex work.[25]

Women and Violent Victimization

Whatever the extent to which violence by women is increasing, the number of women who are violent offenders pales in comparison to the number who are victims of violence. Just as we cannot adequately measure the actual extent of violent offending, neither can we measure the actual extent of violent victimization. Given that limitation, statistically the best criminal justice measure we have of violent victimization is the National Crime Victimization Survey (NCVS), produced by the Bureau of Justice Statistics (BJS). The results of that survey typically are used to make the case for the extent and nature of victimization in the United States. At the end of 1996, BJS published "Female Victims of Violent Crime." That report not only summarized the survey results involving women victims of violent crime in 1994, it also included some homicide numbers from the 1995 SHR and compared the contemporary statistics to those of earlier years to make the case that, from 1973 to 1994, "violent victimization rates of women and men converged."[26]

Toward the end of 1997, BJS published a sequel to its report on female victims of violence. In *Sex Differences in Violent Victimization, 1994*, Diane Craven used the NCVS statistics and reported that, in 1994, an estimated 5 million women and 6.6 million men reported having been the victim of violence.[27] Women, however, apparently were more likely than men to have been victimized by people they knew, to have been victimized in their own home or in the home of someone they knew, and to have been injured during an assault. Around that same time, BJS released a related report based on data from an "estimated 1.4 million hospital emergency department (ED) patients treated in 1994 for nonfatal injuries sustained in intentional or possibly intentional violence."[28] Supporting the conclusion that the violent victimization of women is more intimate than that of men, the hospital data report concluded, "A higher proportion of women than men were injured by someone with whom they shared an intimate relationship."[29] That same conclusion was supported by a report on female homicide victims in New York City during the early 1990s that used medical examiner data to show that most of the women homicide victims studied had been killed by an intimate partner or another family member.[30]

Over a year in the early 1990s, my colleagues and I interviewed more than 200 women incarcerated in New York State for homicide.[31] All of these women had been sentenced to prison for a most violent act, but through our interviews with them we learned that almost all had also been victims of and witnesses to violence, both as adults and as children. As children, 88 percent said they had experienced some type of harm, including 58 percent who said they had experienced serious physical harm (for example, being beaten up, threatened with a weapon, or hurt with a weapon), almost always by a family member. As adults, 95 percent said they had experienced some physical harm, including 79 percent who had experienced serious physical harm, almost always by an intimate partner.

Given the intimate nature of violence against women, the disparity in the level of violence *against* women compared to violence *by* women becomes even more pronounced when we consider that it is only recently that we as a nation have begun to recognize domestic violence as violence. Until late into the twentieth century, even in the United States, physical force was considered a legitimate means for a husband to control his wife, and domestic violence was considered a private matter.[32] In their analysis of the historical record of violence against wives, Rebecca and Russell Dobash wrote, "The use of physical violence against women in their position as wives is not the only means by which they are controlled and oppressed but it is one of the most brutal and explicit expressions of patriarchal domination."[33] During the 1970s, when women increasingly were organizing around issues of mutual concern, domestic violence became a matter of public rather than private safety.[34] In the years that followed, individual states enacted laws to criminalize domestic violence, and, in 1994, the federal government enacted the Violence Against Women Act. This act provided funds for programs, services, and research to help women who were the victims of violence and made possible federal prosecution of acts of violence against women because they were women.[35]

The criminalization of domestic violence did encourage policy makers to direct more attention and allocate more resources toward the problem of violence against women.[36] However, by criminalizing the problem, solutions were more likely to be in the form of criminal justice policies and programs directed at controlling criminal offenders, male and female, rather than public health solutions aimed at serving victims of crime and violence. According to the findings of a two-year study of criminal justice policy in the United States by the National Criminal Justice Commission (NCJC), at the end of the twentieth century, women who sought help from battered women shelters were often turned away for lack of space, while the amount of prison space for women convicted of crimes was increasing dramatically.[37]

So if any case can be made with official statistics or research findings, it not that women, even "liberated" women, are becoming more like men in terms of violent offending. If the so-called liberation of women did make women more like men in terms of violence, it was in terms of violent victimization rather than violent offending. Perhaps that explains why, in the face of a public outcry about a new female offender, Dwayne Smith was prompted to ask in the title of a 1987 article, "Is There a 'New Female Victim'?"[38] While his analysis of NCVS victimization data for the years 1973 to 1982 showed that women during that period did increasingly become victims of property crimes, though not necessarily violent crimes, it does not preclude the conclusion that women are more likely to be victims rather than perpetrators of violence. In either case, public policy makers and the media continue to define the problem as one of growing numbers of female offenders.

Women and the Criminal Justice System

Early evening on February 3, 1998, in Huntsville, Texas, a lethal dose of sodium thiopental was injected into the veins of Karla Faye Tucker. Minutes later she was dead, the first woman executed in Texas in more than 100 years. In fact, she was only the second woman executed under government authority in the United States in more than a quarter century, during which time more than 300 men were executed, the plurality of them in Texas.[39] Before becoming a born-again Christian in prison, by her own admission the 38-year-old woman had participated in the vicious 1983 slaying of a man and a woman, bludgeoning them repeatedly with a pickax while, in her own words, feeling sexual pleasure each time the ax plunged into her victims.

Early morning on February 4, even before the sun came up on the day after the execution, all the national news programs—*Today* on NBC, *Good Morning America* on ABC, *This Morning* on CBS, and, of course, CNN—were telling the story of Karla Faye Tucker and her untimely death. One after another the newscasters had the opportunity to interview together the former husband and the brother of the woman whom Tucker had murdered. Both had been present at her execution, but they disagreed vehemently about what they had witnessed. To some extent, their different moods reflected the different feelings of the people of the nation. The husband rejoiced in having been witness to the vengeance taken for the death of his wife. The brother despaired in the pain he said he felt at the death of a woman whom he had come to know as someone who had overcome a violent past and had found religion and faith.

That same morning, newspapers all over the United States told of the execution, and those with sites on the World Wide Web made their stories immediately available to millions of people all across the country. A search of selected Web sites on the morning of February 4, 1998, turned up the following.

- A headline on the first page of the *Washington Post* read, "Texas Executes Karla Faye Tucker." Based on an Associate Press report by Sue Anne Pressley, the theme of the article was specified in its first sentence: "Hunstville, Tex., Feb. 3—Karla Faye Tucker, the Pickax Killer turned born-again Christian, died of a lethal injection tonight, closing a long fight for her life as a crowd outside the Texas death house prayed for her soul."

- The *Los Angeles Times* had an article written by staff reporter Jesse Katz called, "Texas Executes Born-Again Woman After Appeal Fails." The focus of that article likewise was the contrast between the bloodthirsty ax murderer of 1983 with the saintly death row inmate of 1998, but also noted, "The virtual moratorium on female executions in Texas was lifted Tuesday evening."

- "Tucker is put to death in Texas" was the headline on the front page of the *Philadelphia Inquirer*. The story by John Moritz of the *Fort Worth Star Telegram* told again of Karla Faye Tucker, the Christian woman who had been venerated by Pope John Paul II and by televangelist Pat Robertson but also of the life she led as a "drug-crazed teenage prostitute" and about the details of the murder.

- The article in the *New York Post* by Gersh Kuntzman told a similar story, but shifted the emphasis a little by opening with the headline, "Karla's Last Words: 'I Love You All.'"

- The *Chicago Tribune* took a slightly different view of the story, emphasizing that a woman had been executed and presenting details of the impact the execution was having on a variety of people, including the former husband of the female victim, the religious witnesses who prayed for her soul, and the civil rights activists who demonstrated against all executions. In an article called "Karla Tucker Put to Death in Texas," Cornelia Grumman wrote, "Outside more than 1,000 onlookers and protesters on all sides of the capital-punishment issue sang gospel songs, yelled football game chants, said prayers and played a video of Tucker."

With few exceptions, while the story of the execution of Karla Faye Tucker was included in every newspaper, it was not the lead story in most papers around the country. Naturally, in Texas it was.

The *Houston Chronicle* not only had an article about the execution as its "Top Story," it had related articles and editorials about "revamping" capital punishment in Texas, the "media marathon" in response to the case, the meaning of justice in a "pickax murderer's execution," the governor's prayers, and so on. In addition, the newspaper's Web site listed and provided access to related articles that had been published about the case going back several weeks. Still, the main article, "Tucker dies after apologizing," did what the other newspapers did, wondered aloud about the meaning and value of the execution of "Karla Faye Tucker, the 38-year-old pickax murderer who charmed television audiences worldwide with her coquettish smile and talk of Jesus."

On the morning of February 4, 1998, a Web site dedicated to the Dallas/Fort Worth area led to an interactive voting Web page called "Voting Booth: DFW News." Visitors to this site were asked to vote, responding to the question: "Should women get to skip the death penalty?" Agreement with a response already supplied by a previous voter could be registered, or another could be added. As of that morning, 701 people had voted. Of those, 374 (53 percent) recorded their agreement with the comment of one voter who said, "No. No. NO." The next largest group of voters, 152 (22 percent) agreed with the voter who wrote, "For hundreds of years women have demanded equal rights. As a female, I believe I should have the same treatment as any male who commits an equaly (sic) horrendous crime. For crying out loud, she killed him with a PICK AX!" Another 23 voters called for "life in prison, instead," while 22 agreed with the comment "Killer! Being a woman shouldn't get her off and neither should 'finding God.'" Twenty-one agreed with, "As a woman I believe in 'Equal' rights, she did the crime so she should do the time, even if it means the death penalty." The remaining responses were mixed, and no one got more than a few votes. Overall, in this very unscientific sample, a vast majority of voters agreed that the criminal justice system should treat a woman the same way it would treat a man.

On February 4, 1998, the *Seattle Times* carried an Associated Press report on the Karla Faye Tucker story, but gave it less attention than it had received almost anywhere else. The people of Seattle had their own story of a woman who had been caught up in the criminal justice system for a crime that was legally an act of violence against another person. The *Seattle Times* had three articles—two stories and a timeline—about Mary Kay LeTourneau. According to the timeline, in the summer of 1996, "LeTourneau becomes sexually involved with the victim, then a sixth-grader, whom she also taught when he was in second grade. The boy later tells police he and LeTourneau had sex about six times in 1996, mostly at her home or in her car." Then, in May 1997, "LeTourneau gives birth to a girl fathered by the boy." In August 1997 she pleaded guilty in King County Superior Court to "two counts of second-degree child rape," and in November she was sentenced to seven and a half years in prison, suspended after six months in jail followed by completion of a treatment program. The story was back in the news in February 1998 because, after having been released from jail just a month earlier, at the beginning of the month "LeTourneau is arrested for violating the conditions of her probation when she is found with the boy in a parked car near her home at about 2:40 A.M."

The main story in the *Seattle Times* on February 4, 1998, "LeTourneau on suicide watch," by Carol M. Ostrom and Arthur Santana, told of the event that resulted in her return to custody, the criminal justice implications of her rearrest, and mostly about her state of mind and need for treatment. In a way, the related article by Jack Broom and Carol M. Ostrom was more interesting. In "LeTourneau's gender drew attention to the case," the reporters noted, "Hundreds of sex offenders are sentenced each year in King County Superior Court, but few draw a fraction of the media attention Mary Kay LeTourneau has received. Part of the crush of publicity stems from the fact that as a teacher, she was in a position of trust. But a greater factor is the most obvious one: She's a woman." The reporters went on to raise the question of the significance of her gender when they wrote, "Much media attention and cocktail-party conversation has centered on whether her case has been handled differently because of her gender." When they asked a criminal-defense lawyer and a therapist with a sex-offender treatment practice, they were told that the legal system does not distinguish men from women. To the extent that the public is less concerned with sex offending by women, the experts told the reporters, it is the product of the media, for having fueled "a popular fantasy about the beautiful teacher," and neighbors, for having welcomed home LeTourneau while reviling male sex offenders, even those who have demonstrated successful participation in a treatment program.

Whatever the claims of one defense lawyer and one therapist, and whatever the views of an unscientific sample of Web crawlers, there is strong evidence that in the areas of crime and criminal justice, gender matters. Perhaps over time we can move beyond rhetoric and politics and appropriately and adequately turn our attention from the problem of offending by women to the problems of women who are victims of violence.

Conclusion

A myth is a story invented by people to explain their present in terms of a sacred past, a story "once widely believed to be true, and which served to explain, in terms of the intentions and actions of supernatural beings, why the world is what is and why things happen as they do."[40] The myth of the liberated woman tells the story of women who are freed from the constraints of patriarchy and male domination to act more like men, most notably by engaging in the various forms of violent offending long held to be the distinctive domain of men. The myth explains what would happen if women left their traditional role and function in their homes and families and ventured out into the wider world of unrestrained opportunity. In doing so, it effectively justifies and commends the world as it was prior to their liberation.

Unfortunately for women, the myth does not include the part of the story about the extent to which women living in a world dominated by men have been victims of violence in their own homes. Ultimately, despite the fact that the notion that liberated women would be more violent could never be established with empirical evidence, the myth serves the interests of those who are more concerned with preserving the world as it has been and with discrediting any movement to help women achieve social equality. It also diverts attention from the growing evidence that the real problem of women and violence was and remains that women are more likely to be victims of violence, particularly in their own homes and families.

After we completed our study of women incarcerated for homicide, Barry Spunt and I joined with Debbie Baskin and Ira Sommers to study women who had engaged in either robbery or assault. By their inclusion, all of the women in our sample had done something violent, and many had participated in the drug trade. One of the women interviewed explained how, despite the fact that she was a drug dealer, as a woman she remained especially vulnerable to violent victimization.[41]

According to her account, there was a time when she was a very successful drug dealer, earning perhaps $1,300 to $1,400 every day. Eventually she began free-basing, though not, by her own standard, excessively. She would work all day selling heroin, stop at a crack spot on the way home to buy about $50 worth, and head home where she would smoke what she bought and then go to bed. She suspected that people were watching her and knew that she was carrying large amounts of cash from Manhattan, where she worked, to the Bronx, where she lived, so she hid her money in the lining of her coat.

One night she was walking past a building on her way to the crack spot when three men stopped her. They were wearing hats and their faces were covered. They asked her for a light. She said she did not have one. Then one of the men said yes, she did, and he pulled a gun on her. She started to fight, and the man hit her in the mouth with the handle of the gun. Some of her teeth were broken, and blood poured from her mouth. She became frightened. They made her take off her clothes and began to go through her garments looking for her money. They could not find any and threatened to take her clothes. She begged them not to, and they ran away. She got dressed and left, with her money still hidden in her coat.

Endnotes

1. Libit, H. and Hudson, J. (1997). "Howard teacher collapses, dies after effort to break up brawl." *The Sun* (Baltimore) May 15:1A, 15A.

2. The percent increase in County population is based on figures from *The Sourcebook of County Demographics*, Tenth Edition, published in 1997 by CAC Marketing Systems.

3. Friedan, B. (1963). *The Feminine Mystique.* New York: Dell, p. 364.

4. Friedan, B.:69.

5. Brownstein, H. .H.., Spunt, B. J., Crimmins, S. M., and Langley, S. C. (1995). "Women Who Kill in Drug Market Situations." *Justice Quarterly* 12:473–98. Curran D. J. and C. M. Renzetti (1994). *Theories of Crime.* Boston: Allyn and Bacon. Jurik, N. C. and Winn, R. (1990). "Gender and Homicide: A Comparison of Men and Women Who Kill." *Violence and Victims* 5:227–42.

6. Curran and Renzetti 1994.

7. Simon R. J. (1975). *Women and Crime.* Lexington, MA: Lexington.

8. Simon 1975:40.

9. Adler, F. (1975). *Sisters in Crime: The Rise of the New Female Criminal.* New York: McGraw-Hill, p. 15.

10. Adler 1975:251.

11. Baskin, D. R. and Sommers, I. B. (1998). *Casualties of Community Disorder — Women's Careers in Violent Crime.* Boulder, CO: Westview.

12. See, for example, Curran and Renzetti 1994; Daly, K. and Chesney-Lind, M. (1988). "Feminism and Criminology." *Justice Quarterly* 5:497–538. Maher, L. and Curtis, R. (1995). "In Search of the Female Urban 'Gansta': Change, Culture, and Crack Cocaine." Pp. 147–66 in B. R. Price and N. J. Sokoloff (eds.), *The Criminal Justice System and Women — Offenders, Victims, and Workers.* New York: McGraw Hill. Miller, E. M. (1986). *Street Women.*

Philadelphia: Temple University. Miller, J. (1998). "Up It Up: Gender and the Accomplishment of Street Robbery." *Criminology* 36:37–66. Smart, C. (1978). "The New Female Criminal: Myth and Reality." *British Journal of Criminology* 19:50–59.

13. Miller, J. 1998:62.

14. Simon, R. J. and Landis, J. (1991). *The Crimes Women Commit, The Punishments They Receive.* Lexington, MA: Lexington, p. 122.

15. *Newsweek* 1975:35.

16. Federal Bureau of Investigation. (1997). *Crime in the United States, 1996.* Washington, DC: U.S. Government Printing Office.

17. Maguire, K. and Pastore, A. L., (eds.). (1997). *Sourcebook of Criminal Justice Statistics 1996.* U.S. Department of Justice, Bureau of Justice Statistics. Washington, DC: U.S. Government Printing Office.

18. Campbell, A. (1993). *Men, Women, and Aggression — From Rage in Marriage to Violence in the Streets How Gender Affects the Way We Act.* New York: BasicBooks, p.1.

19. FEMDREIM # 014.

20. FEMDREIM # 440.

21. Brownstein et al. 1995. Inciardi, J. A. Lockwood, D. and Pottieger, A. E. (1993). *Women and Crack Cocaine.* New York: MacMillan. McCoy, H. V., Inciardi, J. A., Metsch, L. R., Pottieger, A. E., and Saum, C. A. (1995). "Women, Crack, and Crime: Gender Comparisons of Criminal Activity among Crack Cocaine Users." *Contemporary Drug Problems* 22:435–51.

22. Johnson, B. D., Hamid, A., and Sanabria, H. (1992). "Emerging Models of Crack Distribution." In T. Mieczkowski (ed.), *Drugs, Crime, and Social Policy: Research, Issues, and Concerns.* Boston: Allyn and Bacon, p. 60.

23. Brownstein et al. 1995.

24. Maher, L. and Daly, K. (1996). "Women in the Street-Level Drug Economy: Continuity or Change?" *Criminology* 34:465–91. Mieczkowski, T. (1994). "Experiences of Women Who Sell Crack: Descriptive Data from the Detroit Crack Ethnography Project." *Journal of Drug Issues* 24:227–48.

25. Maher and Daly 1996:483.

26. Craven, D. (1996). *Female Victims of Violent Crime.* NCJ-16602. Washington, DC: Bureau of Justice Statistics, p. 1.

27. Craven, D. (1997). *Sex Differences in Violent Victimization, 1994.* NCJ-164508. Washington, DC: Bureau of Justice Statistics.

28. Rand, M. R. with K. Strom. (1997). *Violence-Related Injuries Treated in Hospital Emergency Departments.* NCJ-156921. Washington, DC: Bureau of Justice Statistics.

29. Rand amd Strom 1997:5.

30. Wilt, S. A., Illman, S. M. and BrodyField, M. (1997). *Female Homicide Victims in New York City 1990–1994.* New York: NYC Department of Health.

31. Spunt, B. J., Brownstein, H. H., Crimmins, S. M. and Langley, S. (1994). *Female Drug Relationships in Murder.* A Final Report submitted to the National Institute on Drug Abuse. New York: National Development and Research Institutes.

32. DeKeseredy, W. S. and Hinch, R. (1991). *Woman Abuse — Sociological Perspectives.* Toronto, Canada: Thompson Educational Publishing. Donziger, S. R., (ed.). (1996). *The Real War on Crime — The Report of the National Criminal Justice Commission.* New York: HarperPerennial. Dobash, R. E. and Dobash, R. (1979). *Violence against Wives — A Case against the Patriarchy.* New York: The Free Press. Gelles. R. J. (1997). *Intimate Violence in Families.* Third Edition. Thousand Oaks, CA: Sage. Millett, K. (1971). *Sexual Politics.* New York: Equinox.

33. Dobash and Dobash 1979: ix.

34. Donziger 1996. Fagan, J. (1996). *The Criminalization of Domestic Violence: Promises and Limits.* Research Report. Washington, DC: National Institute of Justice. Gelles 1997.

35. Fagan, 1996. Gelles 1997; 147

36. Fagan 1996.

37. Donziger 1996:146–58. See also Bureau of Justice Statistics. (1997). *Correctional Populations in the United States, 1995*. Executive Summary. NCJ-163917. Washington, DC: U.S. Department of Justice.

38. Smith, M. D. (1987). "Changes in the Victimization of Women: Is There a 'New Female Victim'?" *Journal of Research in Crime and Delinquency* 24:291–301.

39. Snell, T. L. (1997). *Capital Punishment, 1996.* Bulletin. December. Washington, DC: Bureau of Justice Statistics.

40. Abrams, M. H. (1957). *A Glossary of Literary Terms*. New York: Holt, Rinehart and Winston, p. 52.

41. FEMDREIM2 # ROS.

7

The Age of the Superpredators: A Fable

On October 17, 1997, not long after the start of a new school year, Maria Alvarez of the *New York Post* wrote a story about the spread of youthful violence, describing how it had permeated the lives of the students and teachers at one New York City high school. "Fear & Violence Rule at City Horror High" told how two teachers at Martin Luther King, Jr., High School had been attacked by students, one having been kicked down a flight of stairs, and how two students had been chased by others wielding boxcutters. It told how one girl had been sexually assaulted as part of a gang initiation. It quoted parents who were angry, students who were fearful, and school officials who said an investigation was underway. It reported that parents, students, and teachers believed that violence ruled the school.

The story of widespread violence in an urban high school was old news and did not generate much interest on the national level. Rather, the school violence story of the year was what the *New York Post* on May 22, 1998, called "school massacres" at rural and suburban schools. One spring day near the end of the school year, the *Oregonian* and most every other newspaper and television news program in the nation told the story of a 15-year-old boy who killed two classmates and wounded more than 20 others when he opened fire in a school cafeteria in Springfield, Oregon, on May 21, 1998. With its telling of that story, the New York *Daily News* listed other notable shootings that had taken place at U.S. schools during the year. In October 1997, a 16-year-old boy in Pearl, Mississippi opened fire on school grounds and shot nine fellow students, killing two. On December 1, a 14-year-old boy fired at a prayer circle in the hallway of his high school in Paducah, Kentucky, killing three students and wounding five. On December 15, a 14-year-old boy in Stamps, Arkansas, fired at classmates and wounded two. On March 24, 1998, a teacher and four young girls were killed when two boys, ages 9 and 11, stood in the woods and fired gunshots at their school. On April 24, an Edinboro, Pennsylvania, teacher was shot to death by a 14-year-old student at a school dance. In Pomona, California, on April 28, a 14-year-old boy was charged with shooting to death two teenage boys playing basketball at an elementary school. On May 19 in Fayetteville, Tennessee, an 18-year-old boy started shooting in a school parking lot and killed a classmate.

In all, the *Daily News* identified nine accounts of "school massacres" during the 1997–1998 academic year. That year there were reported to have been 44,351 public and private secondary schools[1] and 91,661 public and private elementary schools[2] in the United States, for a total of 136,012 schools. Assuming that schools are in session an average of 180 days per year, school was in session for the day at various places throughout the nation a total of 24,482,160 times. The nine school massacres represent 0.00003% of the approximately $24\frac{1}{2}$ million times when a school was in session for the day somewhere in America. Certainly we could argue that the nine events mentioned by the *Daily News* underestimate the true number of school massacres, or that nonlethal forms of violence are commonplace in urban, inner-city schools. And we could argue with certainty that every act of violence is itself a personal tragedy. Nonetheless, no matter what we say, we can be confident that, given the number of days individual schools in America are in session, most days in most places it is safe for a child to go to school.

Despite the small numbers and percentages, as we face the dawn of the third millennium, such stories of youthful violence are used by the news media to present us with an ominous warning of violent times ahead. As early as five years before the end of the twentieth century, on December 4, 1995, *Newsweek* introduced an article about violence by young people with a foreboding question that was followed with a troubling answer. The question came in the title, "The Lull Before the Storm?"; the answer came in the subtitle, "Crime really is down, but teenagers are more violent than ever— and some cops and experts believe 1995 may turn out to be the good old days." One expert quoted was James Alan Fox of Northeastern University, who predicted "'The Coming of Super-Predators'—teenage boys who routinely carry guns, who 'have absolutely no respect for human life' and who 'kill and maim on impulse, without any intelligible motive.'"

Early the next year, *Newsweek* followed the story of the coming of the superpredators with an article on January 22, 1996, announcing that they had arrived. The article told the story of a 5-year-old boy in Chicago who died when two other boys, ages 10 and 11, dropped him from the roof of a 14-story building because he had refused to steal candy for them. This time the question of the subheading was, "Should we cage the new breed of vicious kids?"

This chapter is about of the relationship between age and violence, particularly the argument that a class of youthful "superpredators" will lead an assault of violent crime on the United States during the early years of the twenty-first century. Both official statistics and ongoing research have supported the conclusion that younger people are more involved in violence than are older people, and that the level of participation of younger people in violence has been increasing in recent years. Those conclusions are not being disputed. What is being questioned is whether we should believe those whose claims warn of the coming of the superpredators, a new breed of vile and callously violent youngsters who stalk other people as animals stalk their prey.

Changing Patterns of Youthful Violence

Based on her experience as a physician and public health official, Deborah Prothrow-Stith concluded, "A certain attraction to violence is probably a normal adolescent trait, from a developmental viewpoint. The insecurity adolescents feel—their need to take risks; their abundant energy; their sense of invincibility—propel them toward behavior adults might label foolhardy."[3] So it is not surprising that young people are now and historically have been disproportionately involved as both violent offenders and as victims of violence.

In the late spring of 1994, the federal Office of Juvenile Justice and Delinquency Prevention (OJJDP) produced two fact sheets about trends in the involvement of young people in violence. In *Juvenile Violent Crime Arrest Rates 1972–1992*, Howard Snyder reported that after a period of relative stability in "the overall juvenile violent crime rate" for a period of nearly 20 years, something happened in the later years of the 1980s that brought "more and more juveniles into the justice system charged with a violent offense."[4] For the period 1988 to 1992, the report indicated that "the juvenile Violent Crime Index arrest rate increased by 38%," reaching 198 arrests per 100,000 juveniles in 1992. That is, violent crime by juveniles was on the rise.

To make his case, Snyder used statistics from the Federal Bureau of Investigation's (FBI) Uniform Crime Reports (UCR) program, the official crime statistics of the U.S. government. Rates were calculated as the number of arrests of juveniles (defined as persons under the age of 18) for every 100,000 juveniles in the nation for each of four offenses included in the UCR violent crime index (murder, forcible rape, robbery, and aggravated assault). The most obvious increases were in arrests for murder and aggravated assault, with the rate of juvenile arrests for robbery actually having declined from the middle years of the 1970s to the beginning of the 1990s.

Snyder did note in the report that the UCR rate was based on the number of arrests made, not on the number of juveniles arrested. Theoretically, then, a small number of juveniles could have accounted for all the arrests. We have no way of knowing that from these statistics. He did not mention any of the other reasons that the UCR statistics might not be an adequate measure of violent offending, by juveniles or anyone else. For example, one thing that always struck me when I was responsible for the UCR program in New York State was that the number of arrests police departments reported to us (a total count of all arrests submitted monthly) never matched the number of arrests reported by the same departments for the fingerprint identification program (individual arrests reported at the time the arrest is made).

The second OJJDP report was not so certain in its findings. In *Juvenile Victimization: 1987–1992*, Joseph Moone reported that from 1987 to 1992 the rate of violent victimization of persons between the ages of 12 and 17 increased by almost 23 percent.[5] But the report was filled with so many qualifications and comparisons that it was difficult to determine exactly what Moone was trying to say. Apparently, violence against people between the ages of 12 and 17 did increase more than did violence against people over age 35, but the increase was about the same as that for people between age 18 and 24.

The OJJDP report on the violent victimization of juveniles was based on statistics from the Bureau of Justice Statistics' (BJS) National Crime Victimization Survey (NCVS). Beyond noting that the survey counts incidents of victimization rather than actual victims, the report included some discussion of the nature of the survey and the problems related to using these statistics as a measure of victimization. For example, interviews are only conducted with a national sample of persons ages 12 and older. Included in the NCVS are data on what are called personal crimes, and the OJJDP report selected from among these assault, robbery, and rape as indicative of violent victimization. Victims of homicide, naturally, cannot be interviewed.

Toward the end of 1994, OJJDP issued another fact sheet that provided highlights of its conclusions about trends in juvenile violent offending and victimization. This report summarized the findings of the two earlier reports, demonstrating with graphs and statistics that, increasingly, juveniles had become both violent offenders and victims of violence.[6] The report also used the Supplementary Homicide Reports (SHR) data from the UCR to show that the changing pattern of violent victimization of juveniles varied by sex and race, with the increase being greatest for young black males. It also included a few statistics showing increasing rates of suicide among teenagers and increasing reports of maltreatment of children.

In August 1995, OJJDP issued *Juvenile Offenders and Victims: A National Report*, a 188-page glossy report designed to provide "the most current and reliable information available in the fall of 1994 on juvenile offending and victimization and the juvenile justice system."[7] This report was updated with shorter volumes in 1996 and 1997.[8] All three reports included large numbers of graphs and statistics from a variety of government sources showing trends in the violent offending and violent victimization of young people. Along with UCR and NCVS statistics were statistics from the National Center for Education Statistics, the National Center on Child Abuse and Neglect, and the Bureau of the Census. The 1997 report also included statistics from a number of available research reports. Though all three were obviously intended as reference documents or sources of information to be consulted as needed, it could be concluded from the material provided in each that violence by and against young people was continuing its rise, though not necessarily to the extent that was earlier thought. The 1997 edition was accompanied by a "Dear Colleague" letter from Shay Bilchik, the administrator of OJJDP. In it he wrote, "While these new arrest figures tend to diminish the likelihood of the predicted onslaught of youth violence in the first decade of the twenty-first century, there is ample evidence presented in this report that the level of violence involving our nation's youth, both as victims and perpetrators, remains unacceptably high."

What probably gave the administrator pause was his obvious knowledge of a report OJJDP was ready to release one month after the release of the 1997 update. In a "From the Administrator" box on the cover of *The Youngest Delinquents: Offenders Under Age 15,* Bilchik wrote:

> While confirming the recent disproportionate increase in the number of young offenders, [this] Bulletin reports that juvenile offenders as a group have not become markedly younger in the past decade. An additional encouraging finding is that the number of violent index crime arrests, which declined 3% between 1994 and 1995 for all juveniles, dropped 6% among youths ages 13 and 14.[9]

So, given what they could tell from official statistics as a measure of violence, the federal government could not be so sure that a class of violent young superpredators was on the way.

In our study of boys and girls detained in youth facilities in New York State for one of a variety of violent offenses, my colleagues and I did interview a few youngsters who seemed to have engaged in senseless violence.[10] One boy told the interviewer that he had killed a man in what might be considered a minor altercation. He and the man had an argument, a fight broke out, and he stabbed the man. The interviewer asked what the argument was about. The boy replied that the man had come down to his apartment to tell him that he was making too much noise. The man was angry because he could not sleep and, according to the boy, came down "swinging." He tried to hit the boy in the face. A few other people broke up the fight, and the man returned to his upstairs apartment. But the boy was not satisfied. He knew where the man lived, so he went upstairs to find him. When he got there the man continued to come at him. The boy thought the man was provoking a fight, so he started fighting. The boy took a screwdriver he happened to have in his pocket and swung it at the man, stabbing him in the chest.

Another boy who was interviewed for the same study more obviously committed violence for the sake of violence.[11] He had been detained in the youth facility for robbery, a robbery he had committed with his cousin. They took a train to an area they knew they could find people to rob. They saw two men playing a video game. They simply walked up to them and robbed them. Then they left the area. Asked why, the boy said, "No reason. I just wanted to rob them. I just wanted to rob somebody."

The senselessness of such aimless violence was clear in what still another boy told the interviewer.[12] He had robbed a drug dealer in a place he described as a "junkie park." Asked why he did it, he told the interviewer, "I did it, I did it cause—I didn't really need money. I just wanted—I don't know, man! I was lookin' to start trouble." Asked what led up to the robbery, he said, "I wanted to buy a moped. I asked my step-pops and he said he ain't buying me no moped because I never got a license. That was one of the reasons. I don't know why, man! It was like after my mom died I didn't really care if I did a crime or not, or got to jail."

What each of these boys did was hurtful to another person. It could easily be argued that the behavior described in each example shows insufficient respect for human life. Similarly, it could be argued that the boys each showed a lack of remorse for the wrong done. Arguably, if what they did reflects what they regularly do in their lives, then each one of these boys could be called a violent predator. But there is no way to know whether these incidents reflect who these boys are or how they normally relate to other people. And even if individually these boys and other boys and girls who do such things can be characterized by their violence, that does not necessarily mean they represent a new breed of particularly savage, ferocious, and murderous kids who should be called superpredators.

Theories of Youthful Violence

Throughout the twentieth century, social scientists have been attracted to the notion that crime and violence are too often the domain of the young. Since Frederic Thrasher studied gangs of youngsters in Chicago in the earliest years of the twentieth century,[13] numerous studies have looked at gangs and tried to understand the nature and extent of crime and violence in terms of the peer relationships of young people.[14] Most recently, as part of an OJJDP study, Terence Thornberry and James Burch concluded, "These results clearly indicate that gang members account for the lion's share of delinquent acts, especially the more serious delinquent acts."[15]

The search for an explanation of the relationship between age and crime and violence has also led to studies of the importance of family bonds.[16] Cathy Spatz Widom, for example, studied 1,575 youngsters from childhood through young adulthood and hypothesized a "cycle of violence," suggesting that a childhood history of physical abuse or neglect would predispose a person to violence in later years.[17] More recently in a *Research Preview* for the National Institute of Justice (NIJ), Widom wrote that a "key finding was that neglected children's rates of arrest for violence were almost as high as physically abused children's. Neglect was defined by the court as excessive failure by caregivers to provide food, clothing, shelter, and medical attention."[18]

Others have sought an answer in the relationship between crime, violence and the nature of community relations, particularly the extent to which the people and institutions of a community offer a safe and secure environment.[19] In a recent review of official crime statistics for NIJ, Alfred Blumstein showed how drugs contributed to increasing violence by young people during the late 1980s and early 1990s.[20] In particular, he noted the link between increasing juvenile violence and the illicit drug industry, highlighting "the community disorganization effect of the illicit drug industry and its operations in the larger community."[21]

Though observed changes in the level and nature of violence by young people has made the search for an explanation for juvenile violence particularly pronounced today, it is not without precedence and history. Over the years, criminologists have argued that class and cultural distinctions or dislocations strain the ability of young people to adhere to social norms.[22] Others have suggested that the criminal or violent behavior of young people results from their not having been taught to act appropriately or their inability to learn to act in an appropriate manner.[23] Still others have argued that young people engage in crime and violence because they are not bound to their society or community in ways that are likely to promote acceptable behavior.[24] Some have even argued that attention should be shifted away from the action itself and instead placed on the labels that others attach to it and hence to the young actors.[25]

From their recent study of what they call *serious* street crime by young people, James Inciardi and his associates suggested that while the research done to date provides some useful findings about youth and crime, it cannot explain violence by young people since the advent of crack cocaine. They opened their book with the words, "In the mid-1980s, six decades' worth of scientific research on delinquency proved dismayingly useless in explaining the latest youth crisis: crack-related crime."[26] They agreed with the claims that young people were offending more and that their offending had become more violent. Their argument was with the research that had been done, which they suggested was too out of touch with the streets to contribute to an adequate understanding of the changes. The problem, then, was how to make sense of what was happening and how to respond to it.

The explanation that emerged in the early 1990s—that something new was happening and new ways of responding would be necessary—was not necessarily based on new research, but rather on interpretations of official statistics. True or not, the case for an increase in the level of violent crime by young people was easily made with available statistics. The claim that the nature of violence by young people had changed was more difficult to support. That claim had to be made ideologically, and for that purpose a new breed of youthful offender was constructed, the superpredator.

The Notion of the Superpredator

When *Newsweek* announced the coming in 1995 and the arrival in 1996 of youthful superpredators, it was not alone in doing so. Following the release of a report by the federal OJJDP on juvenile offenders and victims,[27] an Associated Press article was released out of Washington, D.C. As it appeared in the *Sun* of Baltimore, the article was called "U.S. children: Armed and dangerous." It cited the government report and notified the public that the "juvenile arrest rate for violent crimes may well double in the next 15 years."[28] It went on to quote James Alan Fox of Northeastern University—who only months later would provide *Newsweek* with a definition of the superpredator[29]—as saying, "This generation is the young and the ruthless. This generation has more deadly weapons in their hands, more dangerous drugs in their bodies and a much more casual attitude about violence."[30]

On January 30, 1996, Howard Bluth wrote an editorial for the Baltimore *Sun*. He told the story of Isaac Coley, a 10-year-old boy who was arrested on the streets of Baltimore "for selling three rocks of crack cocaine." Bluth took the position that to save Isaac and the people he will inevitably victimize, Isaac must be saved from the poverty of his home and community. Nonetheless, for his commentary he turned to contemporary experts on the subject to try to understand what was propelling Isaac toward a life of crime. He found John DiIulio, Jr., whom he identified as a criminologist at Princeton University, who told him, "There's a tornado coming. We can't stop it; we must prepare for it." That tornado, he was told, would come in the form of Isaac and other kids like him, "a new breed of juvenile offender, described by . . . DiIulio as lacking significant adults in their lives, and having little capacity for remorse."

Bluth did not call on the expertise of Fox of Northeastern, but rather DiIulio of Princeton. It was a good choice. Though Fox is well known for his belief in the imminent arrival of large numbers of extremely violent youth, DiIulio is widely credited with creating and promoting the notion of the youthful superpredator.

Around that time in 1994 when warm weather was finally reaching the northern half of the American continent, John J. DiIulio, Jr., issued a storm warning. He was a professor of politics and public affairs at Princeton University and a nonresident senior fellow at the conservative Brookings Institution in Washington, D.C. In an essay called "America's Ticking Crime Bomb and How to Defuse It,"[31] he foretold of an impending crisis of crime and, as he had done metaphorically with his tornado warning to Bluth, offered a proposal for how we should prepare to disarm it.

DiIulio's 1994 essay in *Wisconsin Interest* provided a listing of "Ten Things to Know About Crime in America Today,"[32] followed by an admonition in the form of an answer to the question, "Waiting for the Bomb to Explode?" After discussing each of the ten things, he summarized them as follows:

> In sum, crime is concentrated in inner cities. Crime is getting worse among juveniles. Substance abuse, including liquor abuse, drives much of the crime problem. There is a real danger that crime will spread from the inner cities later in this decade. To combat adult and juvenile crime, we need to target-harden inner-city neighborhoods in every way possible. We also need more cops, more prisons, and less 1960s-style nonsense about the "root causes" of crime. The only truly radical solutions are ones that would remove at-risk juveniles from at-risk settings.[33]

He concluded with a call for government to address the "disappointment and desperation of decent, struggling, fearful, inner-city citizens," or soon it will be too late and we will all be sharing their pain.

Youthful violence was not the obvious focus of DiIulio's essay. The explicit theme was what he called "the ticking time bomb." Crime is growing and spreading and soon will be out of control, a danger to us all. DiIulio suggested that while the problem may be intractable and a lasting solution may be out of reach, there is a simple and immediate response that should be pursued.

> Unless and until massive target-hardening and effective local economic development measures are taken to restore order and economic opportunity to the inner cities, something must be done to remove at-risk children and youth from these debilitating, disorderly, criminalistic, and life-threatening environments—from their parents, their neighbors, their schools, and their neighborhoods.[34]

The real key to defusing the bomb is implicit in this proposal. We are being asked to distinguish the "decent, struggling, fearful, inner-city citizens," especially the young ones, from the "chronic violent offenders under 18 years of age" who prey on those good citizens. While he did not call them superpredators at the time, DiIulio had identified a distinctive breed of violent, predatory youth.

After DiIulio first introduced the term *superpredator* in a "small-circulation magazine in 1995," the conceptualization almost immediately became a media darling.[35] With William Bennett, a fellow at the Heritage Foundation, and John Walters, executive director of the Council on Crime in America, in 1996 he institutionalized the theoretical construct, portraying it as an objective reality. In *Body Count*, the idea of a "new generation of street criminals" who were the "youngest, biggest, and baddest generation any society has ever known" took form.

> Based on all that we have witnessed, researched, and heard from people who are close to the action, here is what we believe: America is now home to thickening ranks of juvenile "superpredators"—radically impulsive, brutally remorseless youngsters, including ever more preteenage boys, who murder, assault, rape, rob, burglarize, deal deadly drugs, join gun toting gangs, and create serious communal disorders. They do not fear the stigma of arrest, the pains of imprisonment, or the pangs of conscience. They perceive hardly any relationship between doing right (or wrong) now and being rewarded (or punished) for it later. To these mean-street youngsters, the words "right" and "wrong" have no fixed moral meaning.[36]

While they did acknowledge that "it is impossible to know exactly how much worse, on average, today's youth criminals are than those of previous eras," it took them fewer than five pages with a few statistics to conclude, "here come the superpredators."[37]

Defining and Identifying the Problem

Others before DiIulio and his colleagues had considered the idea that a new class of violent young criminals was on the way. In a 1991 book written for teenagers, Elaine Landau asked, "Is a new breed of young perpetrator emerging—individuals who don't feel sorry or guilty, at least initially, and who can shrug off their victim's suffering?"[38] But Landau was a news reporter and youth librarian, and the references in her book were all to news articles, none to any scholarly work. DiIulio, Bennett, and Walters are all respected scholars, and two had served as high-ranking government officials. Their work was more credible to a broader public audience and would have a greater impact on public policy.

On November 19, 1995, an Associated Press article appeared in the *Boston Sunday Globe* under the headline "Major crimes show 3-year decline—Juvenile arrests climb 7% in US as violence drops in big cities, FBI says."[39] Scholars were cited as having linked the decline to the aging of the baby boom population, politicians to the increase in time served by offenders in prison. Whatever the explanation, that was the good news. The bad news was that "arrests of youths under age 18 for violent crimes surged by

7 percent." That statistic was identified as a problem and explained by James Alan Fox of Northeastern University. "This is the calm before the crime storm. An impending crime wave of teen violence is facing us as the adolescent population begins to rise in America."

On May 6, 1996, after the FBI released statistics showing a decline in serious crime throughout the United States for the fourth straight year, an Associated Press article published in the *Washington Post* reported, "Experts hailed the data but unanimously warned that the large national trends mask an alarming rise in teenage violence."[40] Quotes from a number of "experts" followed. Republican U.S. Representative Bill McCollum from Florida, chairman of the House crime subcommittee, was reported as saying, "We shouldn't be lulled into a false sense of security." Professor Fox of Northeastern University was quoted as saying, "[T]his calm before the crime storm won't last much longer."

In fact, expert opinion never really was unanimous. On July 28, 1996, a headline in the *Philadelphia Inquirer* read, "A divide on what's fueling youth crime. Teens raised for violence or just well-armed?"[41] After noting that there are crime experts who have warned of the coming of superpredators, the article then pointed out that other scholars do not believe that such "mutants" exist. Alfred Blumstein of Carnegie Mellon, Daniel Webster of Johns Hopkins, and David Kennedy of Harvard, for example, were cited as experts who believed that the real difference between kids in the 1990s and kids from decades before was the availability of guns. The article duly noted that the National Rifle Association (NRA) naturally disagreed with this position and directed the reader to the work of DiIulio on superpredators. But the weakness of that position was identified by Howard Snyder of the National Center for Juvenile Justice (NCJJ) when he said, "I don't know of anybody doing work showing that kids are getting consistently more violent. Everybody believes that just because it sounds good."

Not everybody. An article by Franklin Zimring, a prominent professor of law at the University of California at Berkeley, appeared in the August 1996 issue of *Overcrowded Times*, a bimonthly newsletter supported by the Edna McConnell Clark Foundation. Zimring summarized the warnings about the coming of juvenile superpredators and called the issue "hogwash."[42] His argument was with both the "colorful language and the sense of alarm" used by DiIulio and others to demonstrate the seriousness of the problem. For example, Zimring claimed (referring to statistics used by DiIulio to calculate the coming of 270,000 additional superpredators by the year 2010) that the 6 percent of boys statistically responsible for half of all police contacts involving boys under age 18, the so-called "chronic delinquents [who have] five or more police contacts for any cause," the boys who DiIulio and others had argued were candidates to become superpredators, were not violent offenders but actually were kids repeatedly doing things like shoplifting and playing hooky.[43] Zimring concluded that the "faulty arithmetic and conceptual sloppiness that produced the projections" about superpredators were the consequence of a political need of the time "for a youth crime wave set in the future so that government can shadow box against it by getting tough on juvenile crime in advance."[44]

It is not all that clear that the government was in the mood at that time to shadow box. In the fall of 1996, OJJDP held its national conference in Baltimore. From December 12 to 14, speakers at panel and plenary sessions and workshops shared what they knew about juvenile offending and juvenile justice. The program did include a track called "Changing Nature of Juvenile Offenders," but there was no mention of superpredators. The focus was on questions rather than answers, on programs rather than polemics.

During the meeting in Baltimore, an interesting news story broke. On the front page of the weekend edition of *USA Today* dated December 13–15, 1996, a small headline read, "Study eases fear of teen crime wave." The article opened, "Criminologists and other law enforcement officials now believe a predicted wave of juvenile violence will not occur." Even Fox was quoted as saying, "I never meant there would be a bloodbath. Some of it was part of getting people's attention." Jack Levin, a colleague and collaborator of Fox's at Northeastern, was quoted as saying, "I was wrong." The article, the conclusion, and the comments were in response to statistics released by the FBI showing that arrests of juveniles for violent crimes, especially those juveniles ages 10 to 14, had declined in 1995. A second article called "Juvenile crime 'wave' may be just a ripple" appeared in the same paper with a picture of a smiling U.S. Attorney General Janet Reno. A similar story called "Violent Crime Drops Among Young Teens" appeared that weekend on December 13 on the front page of the *Washington Post*.

It was no wonder the OJJDP conference program did not mention superpredators. "Juvenile Arrests 1995," the federal report with the FBI statistics, had been prepared and released by OJJDP itself through the National Center for Juvenile Justice (NCJJ), a research organization in Pittsburgh that analyzes official juvenile crime and justice data for the federal government. Prepublication copies were distributed at the conference. The report used official government data to prepare and present 10 pages of statistics, graphs, and text saying, ultimately, that the number of arrests of juveniles for violent crimes declined.[45] On the front page was a note from the OJJDP administrator, Shay Bilchik, in which he wrote, "Juvenile arrests for violent crime declined in 1995 for the first time in nearly a decade. Most encouraging is that this decline was greatest among younger juveniles." The line separating the experts had been firmly drawn, and OJJDP, a federal agency, had not supported the claim that superpredators were on their way.

Much earlier, there were signs that OJJDP would take this position. In May 1994, just before federal crime statistics had convinced observers that violent crime in the United States was really on the decline, the agency released a fact sheet prepared by Howard Snyder that asked the question,

"Are Juveniles Driving the Violent Crime Trends?" Using FBI UCR statistics, Snyder concluded, "In summary, juveniles are not driving the violent crime trends; however, their responsibility for the growth in violent crime in the U.S. has increased."[46]

In March 1996, OJJDP released a major report called *Combating Violence and Delinquency: The National Juvenile Justice Action Plan.* The plan was the work of the Coordinating Council on Juvenile Justice and Delinquency Prevention, which is chaired by Attorney General Janet Reno and has nine federal members, most of whom are secretaries of executive agencies, and nine practitioner members. The council was established by an act of Congress and is responsible for the coordination of federal programs concerning juveniles.

The OJJDP report issued "An Urgent Call to Action" with the words, "In the 1990's, pervasive problems with juvenile violence threaten the safety and security of communities across the country, and projections for the future are cause for nationwide alarm."[47] Quick then to note that "[p]rojections and trends are not destiny," the report followed with 105 pages of great detail about patterns and trends of violence by young people and a broad array of recommendations for policy and program development. Recommendations were generally guided by a "broad vision for reforming the juvenile justice system and strengthening communities to reduce both the number of juvenile victims and the number of juvenile offenders."[48] Specific recommendations were arranged by objectives and included improving risk classification and needs assessment procedures for youth brought into the system, creating graduated sanctions, expanding legal mechanisms for transferring juveniles to adult criminal justice authority, reducing firearms availability, making schools safer, boosting family and community support, and so on.

So while OJJDP statistical reports clearly were not supporting the notion that the United States was about to be overrun by a new breed of youthful superpredators, the action report did not dismiss the possibility that they might be on their way. And the recommendations of the report were vague and broad enough that the federal, state, and local governments could interpret them however they wished. Consequently, policy makers chose to define the problem and design and implement programs and policies in ways that would allow them to appear to have made progress toward a solution.

Youth, Violent Crime, and Public Policy

Writing about U.S. adolescents in the 1990s, Mike Males called them a "scapegoat generation." He suggested that perhaps adults are "so mad at them" because "they act just like us."[49] That may be true, but for policy

makers, the motivation to classify our youth as a particularly violent generation is more complicated than that.

Public policy and programs are developed in the context of recurrent
political cycles (for example, the procession of civic elections, the prepara-
tion of administrative budgets, the development of annual governing agenda or messages) and the immediacy of crisis management.[50] For this reason,
they are inevitably designed and implemented so that outcomes are easy to
measure and output is easy to interpret as successful.[51] Unfortunately, policies and programs that would engage families and communities to help kids
find their way out of the cycle of violence are slow to show progress, and
their success is difficult to measure. For example, how would you show that
violence was reduced by a program of late-night basketball tournaments
that kept kids occupied and off the streets when they might otherwise
engage in violence? The apparent success of policies and programs that
emphasize getting tough with youthful offenders is easier to measure,
whether the measures are adequate or the success is real. For example, a
strict law enforcement effort against juvenile offenders might not reduce
violence, but at least it would create statistics that showed increases in the
number of arrests, convictions, sentences to prison, and so on. Maybe a program to transfer juveniles brought to the attention of the criminal justice system from juvenile to adult authority would not reduce violence, but at least
policy makers could cite statistics on the number of transfers to the tougher
adult system.

It was no surprise, then, that the policies and programs developed and
implemented to deal with youthful crime and violence in the last years of
the twentieth century tended to be based on the assumption that youthful,
violent superpredators were on their way. This was true for state and local
governments as well as for the federal government.

The year prior to the publication of its action plan in 1996, OJJDP had
released a 255-page document as a guide for communities seeking to deal
with the problem of juvenile violence.[52] In it, the federal agency identified
the problem as increasing youth violence committed largely by a small proportion of all offenders, most of whom started at an early age. The solution,
it suggested, needed to be comprehensive, focusing "prevention and juvenile justice resources on the serious, violent, and chronic juvenile offender."[53] So while OJJDP had not necessarily endorsed the notion that a new
breed of depraved youth were coming to wreak violence on us, and while
the plan set forth by the agency may have been comprehensive, in the end
the federal government had pointed its finger at the superpredators.

Juvenile and criminal justice are primarily functions of state and local
government, but the federal government does provide leadership and support. In terms of leadership, there have been public pronouncements and
proposals pointing to superpredators as a source of our problems. During
the presidential election in 1996, Alexander Cockburn suggested that the

candidates had declared a "war on kids."[54] Republican candidate Bob Dole told potential voters, "Unless something is done soon, some of today's newborns will become tomorrow's superpredators, merciless criminals capable of committing the most vicious of acts for the most trivial of reasons."[55] Dole was not elected president. No matter. Democratic candidate and winner Bill Clinton opened his second term with a proposal for legislation that would "provide grants to states that stiffen penalties for juveniles who commit violent crimes or serious drug offenses."[56] At the same time, Republicans in Congress proposed a bill that, among other things, would permit younger offenders to be prosecuted as adults under the federal system, would offer grants to states to encourage them to treat as adults juveniles who committed violent crimes, and would create task forces to apprehend "armed violent youth."[57]

During this period, the federal government did provide some support for programs designed to deal with underlying problems of violence. For example, through the SafeFutures project, OJJDP provided $1.4 million over five years to each of six communities.[58] Those funds were for a "coordinated approach to prevention, intervention, and treatment" that was "designed to serve a community's juveniles and encompasses both the human service and the juvenile justice systems, including health, mental health, child welfare, education, police, probation, courts, and corrections."[59] There was also OJJDP support for local curfew programs[60] and programs dealing with school truancy.[61] But for the most part, federal resources for dealing with the problem of youth violence favored enforcement programs that got tough with the hypothesized core of violent juvenile offenders, the superpredators. There were evaluations of juvenile "boot camps," designed "to provide constructive intervention and early support to a population of juvenile offenders who were at high risk of chronic delinquency."[62] There were assessments of state efforts to transfer "serious juvenile offenders" from juvenile justice systems to the authority of the adult criminal justice systems.[63] In 1998, a federal bill was proposed that, according to a February 6 editorial in the *Washington Post*, "brings a kind of punitive zeal to the subject of juvenile justice" and effectively federalizes juvenile crimes by giving federal prosecutors the power to "get involved in juvenile cases" that otherwise would be the province of individual states.

In the end, the federalization of juvenile justice might not make much difference for the juveniles who come into contact with the justice system. The interest and activity on the state level was not much different from that of the federal government. For example, in response to reports of increasing violence among youth, the New York State Division for Youth in 1993 published a report on youthful violent offenders under its custody and concluded, "The type of youngster for whom care must be provided, at least with respect to the nature of her/his admitting offense, is radically different than was the case just a few years ago."[64] The difference observed was fundamentally in terms of "admitting offense," which reflects not only what the youngster did but more important how what he or she did was defined by the juvenile or criminal justice community. Nonetheless, in 1995 the state arrested 71,210 kids under the age of 16, an increase of more than 14 percent since 1990.[65] And favoring control over guidance, the state increasingly developed policies and programs to transfer juveniles to the authority of the adult criminal justice system. As reported in an article on page 1 of the *New York Times* on December 10, 1995, "Gov. George E. Pataki proposed new legislation today that would impose significantly tougher rules for prosecuting and sentencing juvenile offenders, in effect prodding the state's prosecutors and courts to treat more teen-agers like adult criminals." In the words of the governor, "We have to continue our aggressive approach to crime by going after youths who are violent predators." Pataki declared the juvenile justice system an "abysmal failure" and called for a system that would punish rather than rehabilitate.

In 1994, a study of juvenile offenders and violent crime by the Illinois Criminal Justice Information Authority concluded that "violent crime arrestees are generally adults."[66] Nonetheless, since January 1995 "the state's attorney has been empowered to petition for a presumptive transfer [of juveniles to adult criminal courts] for most [serious] felonies and some other limited circumstances," meaning the youngster rather than the court is faced with "the burden of rebutting the presumption [that a transfer is warranted]."[67] In North Carolina, a review by the state Criminal Justice Analysis Center of arrest statistics for children below age 16 found that a total of 16 juveniles were arrested for murder in 1995 compared to 5 in 1985, and 241 were arrested for robbery in 1995 compared to 66 in 1985.[68] Without noting how small the numbers were that they were reporting, the authors of the state report concluded that their finding "not only shows that the number of crimes committed by juveniles appear to be increasing, it also shows that the nature of juvenile crime has changed in ways that are frightening to the public."[69] The report concluded with vague recommendations emphasizing the need to "take steps to control whether juvenile crime continues to become more serious, more violent, and more frightening to the public."[70]

Findings of a 1996 crime survey in Minnesota found that from 1992 to 1995 the level of violent crime in the state had remained about the same, from 1993 to 1996 the number of people in the state who were fearful of being the victim of a violent crime had declined, and most violent assailants in the state were adults.[71] Nonetheless, under legislation enacted in Minnesota in 1994, in cases of "serious crimes against the person," youth in the state are presumptively transferred to adult court with "the burden of proof on the juvenile to show that he or she should be processed in juvenile court."[72]

During this period, local governments likewise treated youth violence as a serious problem. To deal with that problem, they too introduced programs grounded in a belief that there is a new breed of violent kids known as superpredators. According to a 1997 poll of cities by the U.S. Conference of Mayors, both nighttime and daytime curfews have become a popular way for cities to try to reduce crime by keeping young people off the streets.[73] As reported by the Associated Press, "276 of 347 responding cities has a nighttime curfew [and] sixty-six had a daytime curfew."[74] This might reduce crime by youngsters, but it ignores the findings of the various state reports and statistics showing that adults commit most of the violent crime.

Early in 1998, I began to hear from different people in the Baltimore City Police Department that the department was planning to announce a new program to deal with youthful crime and violence. On January 23, an article appeared on the front page of the *Sun* declaring, "Police plan clampdown on Baltimore youth gangs." According to the article, the police defined the problem as juvenile crime having "spiraled out of control [due to] children who terrorize neighborhoods with drug dealing and shootings." Baltimore police officials, who often look to other cities for programs that work, found a program in Boston that incorporates "law enforcement and street counseling" and has been "credited with that city's plummeting juvenile crime rates." But in terms of things like the level of violent crime and the nature of street gangs, Baltimore is not Boston, so it is not surprising that police officials in Baltimore were quoted as saying that their program would target the few known violent street gangs in the city, telling their members that "we won't tolerate the violence anymore" and that if they did not cooperate "the full wrath of law enforcement" would come down on them.

As president of the American Society of Criminology in 1993, Delbert Elliott chose as the theme for its annual conference "Violence and Its Victims." In his presidential address to the membership of the society, he spoke of his own research and his involvement with the National Youth Survey, "a projected longitudinal study of a national probability sample of 1,725 youths age 11–17 in 1976" who were interviewed nine times, most recently (then) in 1993.[75] After defending the value of self-reported data, he presented his analysis and concluded, "The possibility that 25% of all males at age 17 are involved in some form of serious violent offending is alarming—even more so if these youths now have access to, and are carrying, guns."[76] In sounding this alarm, however, he did not announce the coming of the superpredators. Rather, he announced that "[t]he need for theoretically and empirically grounded policy and prevention strategies is urgent."[77] Too bad his audience was largely made up of academic criminologists. It was the federal, state, and local policy makers who needed to hear his message.

Conclusion

A fable is a fiction, a narration designed to support a favored truth. It tells a story that illustrates a moral thesis "in which animals talk and act like human beings."[78] In the fable of the superpredators, our young people become animals who prey on the weakness of others. They represent evil against good. John DiIulio, Jr., and his associates described them as "radically impulsive" and "brutally remorseless."[79] James Alan Fox said they have no respect for human life and kill without reason.[80] The moral of the story is that unless we stop them, good people will be victimized by their evil.

On January 11, 1998, Vincent Schiraldi, the director of the Justice Policy Institute in Washington, D.C., wrote an editorial that was published in the *Washington Post*. In "The Latest Trend in Juvenile Crime: Exaggeration by the News Media," he thrashed legislators, policy analysts, and especially the news media for having misstated and misrepresented trends in juvenile crime in order to "return us to a [juvenile justice] system that more closely resembles 19th-century jurisprudence." He cited official statistics and reports showing, for example, that "fewer than one-half of 1 percent of America's juveniles were arrested for a violent crime in 1995" and that the number of arrests of juveniles for violent crimes had declined by 23 percent from 1973 to 1995. Against these numbers, he contrasted poll results showing that U.S. citizens believe that "juveniles commit 43 percent of all violent crime" and that legislative proposals have been introduced to get tougher with juvenile offenders. His main targets, however, were "the many media outlets" and "Princeton professor John J. DiIulio," whom he said have suggested that there is a "'rising tide of superpredators.'"

DiIulio, the original author of the fable of the superpredators, is no fool. Effectively acknowledging the significance of the conflicting evidence for the story he tells, he had already modified his rendition and was quick to set the record straight. In response to Schiraldi's editorial, he wrote a letter published in the *Washington Post* on January 31, 1998, in which he said:

> I have written a number of articles in major newspapers and journals, and have testified in Congress, to correct the misperception that a large fraction of juvenile offenders are "superpredators." Also, I have been on record for more than two years now in opposition to efforts to incarcerate violent juveniles in adult facilities.

Despite the contradictory evidence and the new version of the story being told by its main storyteller, others who tell the fable of the superpredators have found ways to preserve its original motif. In September 1997, almost a year after the OJJDP meeting in Baltimore, James Alan Fox was the featured speaker at the annual conference of the federal Bureau of Justice Statistics and the Justice Research and Statistics Association held in Miami

Beach. He called his presentation "The Young and the Ruthless" and argued that "as bad as things are, things are going to get worse."[81] To support his conclusion, he offered his own interpretation of official government statistics on crime and justice, the same statistics used by those who argue that there is no coming wave of youthful superpredators.

Late in 1997, a professional basketball player earning millions of dollars was fired by his team and suspended for a year, by the National Basketball Association after first strangling his coach and later returning to assault him further. It was announced that after the year he would be allowed to return to league play, and several teams immediately expressed interest. Irwin Stelzer, the director of regulatory policy studies at the American Enterprise Institute, used this story to make a point about role models in an editorial that appeared in the *New York Post* on December 17, 1997. In his commentary, Stelzer wrote, "Unfortunately, the role models the [professional basketball] league is providing are more likely to signal the emerging superpredators that violence pays—and pays big—than that the path to riches is paved with discipline, teamwork and obedience to authority."[82] Thus, despite the doubts that had been raised about its validity as a meaningful social construct, the question of whether youthful superpredators are on their way was no longer an issue. Their claim that they exist had been taken for granted as real.

Endnotes

1. Moody, W. (1998) *Patterson's American Education.* 1998 Edition. Volume XCIV. Mount Prospect, IL: Educational Directories, p. vii.

2. Moody, W. (1998) *Patterson's Elementary.* 1998 Edition. Volume X. Mount Prospect, IL: Educational Directories, p. vii.

3. Prothrow-Stith, D. (1991). *Deadly Consequences.* New York: HarperCollins, p. 23.

4. Snyder, H (1994). *Juvenile Violent Crime Arrest Rates 1972–1992.* Fact Sheet # 14. May. Washington, DC: Office of Juvenile Justice and Delinquency Prevention.

5. Moone, J. (1994). *Juvenile Victimization: 1987–1992.* Fact Sheet # 17. June. Washington, DC: Office of Juvenile Justice and Delinquency Prevention.

6. Allen-Hagen, B., Sickmund, M. and Snyder, H. (1994). *Juveniles and Violence: Juvenile Offending and Juvenile Victimization.* Fact Sheet # 19. November. Washington, DC: Office of Juvenile Justice and Delinquency Prevention.

7. Snyder, H. N. and Sickmund, M. (1995). *Juvenile Offenders and Victims: A National Report.* August. Washington, DC: Office of Juvenile Justice and Delinquency Prevention.

8. Snyder, H. N., Sickmund, M., and Poe-Yamagata, E. (1996). *Juvenile Offenders and Victims: 1996 Update on Violence—Statistics Summary.* February. Washington, DC: Office of Juvenile Justice and Delinquency Prevention. Snyder, H. N., Sickmund, M. and Poe-Yamagata, E. (1997). *Juvenile Offenders and Victims: 1997 Update on Violence—Statistics Summary.* February. Washington, DC: Office of Juvenile Justice and Delinquency Prevention.

9. Butts, J. A. and Snyder, H. N. (1997). *The Youngest Delinquents: Offenders under Age 15.* Juvenile Justice Bulletin. September. Washington, DC: Office of Juvenile Justice and Delinquency Prevention.

10. LAVIDA # 214.

11. LAVIDA # 298.

12. LAVIDA # 219.

13. Thrasher, F. M. (1927). *The Gang*. Chicago: University of Chicago Press.

14. See, Block, C. R. and Block, R. (1993). "Street Gang Crime in Chicago," *National Institute of Justice Journal*. August. Washington, DC: U.S. Department of Justice. Fagan, J. (1989). "The Social Organization of Drug Use and Drug Dealing among Urban Gangs." *Criminology* 27:633–69. Klein, M. W. (1971). *Street Gangs and Street Workers*. Englewood Cliffs, NJ: Prentice-Hall. Klein, M. W., Maxson, C. L. and Cunningham, L. C. (1991). "'Crack,' Street Gangs, and Violence." *Criminology* 29:701–17. Miller, W. B. (1958). "Lower Class Culture as a Generating Milieu of Gang Delinquency." *The Journal of Social Issues* 14:5–19. Thornberry, T. P. and Burch, J. H. (1997). "Gang Members and Delinquent Behavior." Juvenile Justice Bulletin. June. Washington, DC: Office of Juvenile Justice and Delinquency Prevention. Whyte, W. F. (1943). *Street Corner Society*. Chicago: University of Chicago Press. Yablonsky, L. (1962). *The Violent Gang*. New York: MacMillan.

15. Thornberry and Burch 1997:3.

16. See Dembo, R. et al. (1994). "The Relationships among Family Problems, Friends' Troubled Behavior, and High Risk Youths' Alcohol/Other Drug Use and Delinquent Behavior: A Longitudinal Study." *The International Journal of the Addictions* 29:1419–42. Denton, R. E. and Kampfe, C. M. (1994). "The Relationship between Family Variables and Adolescent Substance Abuse: A Literature Review." *Adolescence* 29:475–95. Fagan, J. and Wexler, S. (1987). "Family Origins of Violent Delinquents." *Criminology* 25:643–69. Glueck, S. and Glueck, E. (1950). *Unraveling Juvenile Delinquency*. New York: Commonwealth Fund. Goetting, A. (1994). "The Parenting-Crime Connection." *The Journal of Primary Prevention* 14:169-86. McCord, J. (1991). "Family Relationships, Juvenile Delinquency, and Adult Criminality." *Criminology* 29:397–417. Nye, F. I. (1958). *Family Relationships and Delinquent Behavior*. New York: John Wiley. Widom, C. S. (1992). "The Cycle of Violence." National Institute of Justice Research in Brief. Washington, DC: U. S. Department of Justice. Wright, K. N. and Wright, K. E. (1994). *Family Life, Delinquency, and Crime: A Policymaker's Guide*. Washington, DC: Office of Juvenile Justice and Delinquency Prevention.

17. Widom 1992:1.

18. Widom, C. S. (1996). "The Cycle of Violence Revisited." National Institute of Justice Research Preview. Washington, DC: U.S. Department of Justice, p. 1.

19. See Shaw, C. R. and McKay, H. D. (1942). *Juvenile Delinquency and Urban Areas*. Chicago: University of Chicago Press; Park, R. E., Burgess, E. W., and McKenzie, R. D. (1967). *The City*. Chicago: University of Chicago Press.

20. Blumstein, A. (1995). "Violence by Young People: Why the Deadly Nexus." *National Institute of Justice Journal*. August. Washington, DC: U.S. Department of Justice, pp. 2-9.

21. Blumstein 1995:6.

22. Agnew, R. (1992). "Foundation for a General Strain Theory of Crime and Delinquency." *Criminology* 30:47-87. Cloward, R. A. and Ohlin, L. E. (1960). *Delinquency and Opportunity*. New York: The Free Press. Cohen, A. K. (1955). *Delinquent Boys*. New York: The Free Press. Merton, R. K. (1938). "Social Structure and Anomie." *American Sociological Review* 3:672–82. Miller 1958; Sykes, G. M. and Matza, D. (1957). "Techniques of Neutralization." *American Sociological Review* 12:664–70.

23. Akers, R. L. (1977). *Deviant Behavior: A Social Learning Approach*. Belmont, CA: Wadsworth. Sellin T. (1938). *Culture Conflict and Crime*. New York: Social Science Research Council. Sutherland, E. H. (1924). *Principles of Criminology*. Philadelphia: J. P. Lippincott.

24. Hirschi, T. (1969). *Causes of Delinquency*. Berkeley: University of California Press.

25. Becker, H. S. (1963). *Outsiders — Studies in the Sociology of Deviance*. New York: The Free Press.

26. Inciardi, J. A., Horowitz, R. and Pottieger, A. E. (1993). *Street Kids, Street Drugs, Street Crime: An Examination of Drug Use and Serious Delinquency in Miami*. Belmont, CA: Wadsworth, p. 1.

27. Snyder, H. and Sickmund, M. (1995). *Juvenile Offenders and Victims: A National Report.* August. Washington, DC: Office of Juvenile Justice and Delinquency Prevention.

28. Associated Press. (1995). "U. S. children: Armed and dangerous." *The Sun* (Baltimore) September 8:3A.

29. Morganthau, T. (1995). "The Lull before the Storm?" *Newsweek* December 5:40–42.

30. Associated Press 1995:3A.

31. DiIulio, J. J., Jr. (1994). "America's Ticking Crime Bomb and How to Defuse It." *Wisconsin Interesl* Spring/Summer:1-8.

32. DiIulio 1994:1.

33. DiIulio 1994:7.

34. DiIulio 1994:7.

35. Bennett, W. J., DiIulio, J. J., Jr. and Walters, J. P. (1996). *Body Count—Moral Poverty. . . and How to Win America's War against Crime and Drugs.* New York: Simon and Schuster, p. 35. See also DiIulio, J. J., Jr. (1995). "Crime in America—It's Going to Get Worse." *Reader's Digest* August:55–60.

36. Bennett, DiIulio and Walters 1996:27.

37. Bennett, DiIulio and Walters 1996:29,33.

38. Landau, E. (1991). *Teenage Violence.* Englewood Cliffs, NJ: Julian Messner, p. 17.

39. Associated Press. (1995) "Major crimes show 3-year decline." *The Boston Sunday Globe* November 19:12.

40. Associated Press. (1996). "Reported Serious Crime Drops for 4th Straight Year." *The Washington Post* May 6:A9.

41. Montgomery, L. (1996). "A divide on what's fueling youth crime. Teens raised for violence or just well-armed?" *The Philadelphia Inquirer* July 28.

42. Zimring, F. E. (1996). "Desperadoes in Diapers?" *Overcrowded Times* 7:3.

43. Zimring 1996:3.

44. Zimring 1996:2.

45. Snyder, H. (1996). *Juvenile Arrests 1995.* Juvenile Justice Bulletin. December. Washington, DC: Office of Juvenile Justice and Delinquency Prevention.

46. Snyder, H. (1994b). *Are Juveniles Driving the Violent Crime Trends?* Fact Sheet # 16. May. Washington, DC: Office of Juvenile Justice and Delinquency Prevention.

47. Coordinating Council on Juvenile Justice and Delinquency Prevention. (1996). *Combating Violence and Delinquency: The National Juvenile Justice Action Plan—Report.* March. Washington, DC: Office of Juvenile Justice and Delinquency Prevention, p. 1.

48. Coordinating Council on Juvenile Justice and Delinquency Prevention 1996:105.

49. Males, M. (1996). *The Scapegoat Generation—America's War on Adolescents.* Monroe, ME: Common Courage, p. 35.

50. Brownstein, H. H. (1998). "The Drugs–Violence Connection: Constructing Policy from Research Findings." In Jensen, E. L. and Gerber, J. (eds.), *The New War on Drugs—Symbolic Politics and Criminal Justice Policy.* Cincinnati: Anderson. Brownstein, H. H. (1996). *The Rise and Fall of a Violent Crime Wave.* Guilderland, NY: Harrow and Hestron, p. 88; Brownstein, H. H. (1995). "The Social Construction of Crime Problems: Insiders and the Use of Official Statistics." *Journal of Crime and Justice* 18:17–30. Brownstein, H. H. and Goldstein, P. J. (1990). "Research and the Development of Public Policy: The Case of Drugs and Violent Crime." *Journal of Applied Sociology* 7:77–92.

51. Brownstein 1996.

52. Howell, J. C. (ed.). (1995). *Guide of Implementing the Comprehensive Strategy for Serious, Violent, and Chronic Juvenile Offenders.* June. Washington, DC: Office of Juvenile Justice and Delinquency Prevention.

53. Howell 1995:6.

54. Cockburn, A. (1996). "The War on Kids." *The Nation* June 3, v. 262:7-8.

55. Associated Press. (1996). "Dole urges crackdown on youth violence." *The Sun* (Baltimore) July 7:10A.

56. Hosler, K. (1997). "Tough bill on youth crime." *The Sun* (Baltimore) May 9:1A.

57. Suro, R. (1997). "White House, Hill GOP Offer Get Tough Measures on Juvenile Crime." *The Washington Post* May 8:A4.

58. Kracke, K. and Special Emphasis Division Staff. (1996). *SafeFutures: Partnerships to Reduce Youth Violence and Delinquency*. Fact Sheet # 38. June. Washington, DC: Office of Juvenile Justice and Delinquency Prevention, p. 1.

59. Kracke 1996:1.

60. LeBoeuf, D. (1996). *Curfew: An Answer to Juvenile Delinquency and Victimization?* Juvenile Justice Bulletin. April. Washington, DC: Office of Juvenile Justice and Delinquency Prevention.

61. Garry, E. M. (1996). *Truancy: First Step to a Lifetime of Problems*. Juvenile Justice Bulletin. October. Washington, DC: Office of Juvenile Justice and Delinquency Prevention.

62. Peters, M., Thomas, D., Zamberlan, C. and Caliber Associates. (1997). *Boot Camps for Juvenile Offenders*. September. Washington, DC: Office of Juvenile Justice and Delinquency Prevention, p. 12.

63. Parent, D., Dunworth, T., McDonald, D. and Rhodes, W. (1997). *Transferring Serious Juvenile Offenders to Adult Courts*. Research in Action. January. Washington, DC: National Institute of Justice. Scalia, J. (1997). *Juvenile Delinquents in the Federal Criminal Justice System*. Special Report. January. Washington, DC: Bureau of Justice Statistics.

64. Baccaglini, W. F. et al. (1993). *Violent Offenders. Research Focus on Youth*. Rensselaer, NY: NYS Division for Youth, p. 6.

65. Ely, R. E. et al. (1996). *1995 Crime and Justice Annual Report*. Albany, NY: NYS Division of Criminal Justice Services, p. 107.

66. Bensinger, P. B. et al. (1994). *On Good Authority—Juvenile Offenders and Violent Crime*. Chicago: Illinois Criminal Justice Information Authority, p. 2.

67. Przybylski, R. et al. (1997). *Trends and Issues 1997*. Chicago, IL: Illinois Criminal Justice Information Authority, p. 157.

68. Rosch, J. and Ajygin, S. (1997). *SystemStats—Understanding Juvenile Crime Trends and What Can and Cannot Be Done about Them*. Raleigh: North Carolina Criminal Justice Analysis Center, p. 1.

69. Rosch and Ajygin 1997:1.

70. Rosch and Ajygin 1997:4.

71. Lewis, R., Erickson, L. Storkamp, D. and Weber, C. (1996). *1996 Crime Survey—Changing Perceptions*. St. Paul: The Criminal Justice Center at Minnesota Planning, pp. 8, 10, 11.

72. Sondheimer, H. et al. (eds.). (1995). "Is Waiver to Adult Court the Best Response to Juvenile Crime?" *Juvenile Justice Update* 1:13.

73. Associated Press. (1997). "Poll of U. S. Cities Finds Increase in Curfews." *The Washington Post* December 1:A4.

74. Associated Press 1997: A4.

75. Elliott, D. S. (1994). "Serious Violent Offenders: Onset, Developmental Course, and Termination—The American Society of Criminology 1993 Presidential Address." *Criminology* 32:3.

76. Elliott 1994:19.

77. Elliott 1994:19.

78. Abrams, M. H. (1957). *A Glossary of Literary Terms*. New York: Holt, Rinehart and Winston, p. 2.

79. DiIulio et al. 1996:27.

80. Morganthau 1994:41.

81. Justice Research and Statistics Association. (1997). "BJS/JRSA Conference Features Fox on 'The Young and the Ruthless.'" *The (JRSA) Forum* 15:12.

82. Stelzer, I. M. (1997). "Teaching the Wrong Lessons." *New York Post* December 17:29.

8

The Parable of Poor and Minority Violent Offenders

On a personal level, the ways we choose to distinguish ourselves from others can serve as a basis for fear, hatred, and even violence. Such was the case for a troubled young man who spoke to an interviewer during our study of men incarcerated in New York State for homicide.[1] He was a white man who caused the death of a girl he did not know simply because her ancestors had come from Asia.

During the 1970s, the young man had served in the Peace Corps in Thailand. After coming home to New York City, he regularly returned to Thailand to have sexual relations with prostitutes. As an adult, he only had sex with Asian prostitutes. He became obsessed with this practice, telling the interviewer that he lived to go to Thailand.

Though he saw nothing wrong with what he was doing, his friends and other people who knew him tried to get him to stop going to Thailand. They told him to stop having sex with prostitutes. They told him they thought he was "hung up" on Asian women. At that point, he felt a conspiracy against him had been hatched. He told the interviewer that "a dwarf living in his neighborhood" was always watching him. He was a teacher, and he believed his students were suspicious of him. For seven years, he believed, they conspired to change him, to make him stop going to Thailand to have sex with Asian prostitutes.

One day he received notice from the school where he worked that he was being fired. Teaching was his life, and now it was being taken from him. It occurred to him that without his teaching salary he could no longer travel to Thailand. This seemed to him to be the culmination of the conspiracy against him. So, he decided, his only option was to have himself thrown in jail.

That night he went to Chinatown for dinner, a meal of duck with three bottles of Chinese beer. Then he walked to the subway station and downstairs to the uptown platform. His plan was to find an Asian girl and push her in front of a moving train. The first girl he looked at looked back at him. This startled him, and he backed away. He walked down the platform and saw another girl. This was the one. He remembers feeling jealous and angry. If he could not go to Asia, she could not come here. This would tell everyone who had meddled in his life what their intrusion had done. The girl was wearing a sweater and carrying a shopping bag. As the train approached, he walked toward her. Arms raised, he ran towards her and pushed her just as the train approached. One more second, he thought, and she would have bounced off the side of the train.

This story shows how a person can become *a victim of violence* because of nothing other than his or her race. In the United States, however, the stories we tell about violence just as often end with someone being *characterized as a violent offender* because of his or her race or class. To the extent that we routinely treat distinctions of race and class as meaningful or consequential, the likelihood that an otherwise virtuous person will be perceived as a violent offender is increased.

This chapter discusses the relationship between race, class, and violence. From stories about the experiences of poor and minority people in America—their dominant place as the victims of violence as well as the targets of our official response to it—the moral becomes clear. It is as Eldridge Cleaver wrote from his cell in Folsom prison in California at a time in the United States when the simple desire of *Negroes* for civil rights was giving way to the rage of *black men and women* for power in a land that for hundreds of years they had called home. He wrote, "The price of hating other human beings is loving oneself less."[2] Official criminal justice and public health statistics and research findings are used to demonstrate the extent to which minorities and the poor have been not only the most frequent officially designated perpetrators of violence, but also its principal victims. In that sense, it undermines the often-told parable of the young, minority male as a violent offender.

Race, Class, and Violence

In the United States, race and class matter. They matter not only in the degree to which individuals are likely to be violent offenders or are liable to be its victims, but also in terms of how we view violence and the people who behave in violent ways. In fact, race and class even matter in terms of whether we are likely to believe that a person could have been the perpetrator or even the victim of violence.

On December 14, 1987, a story called "Bias Cases Fuel Anger of Blacks" appeared in the *New York Times*. It told of three recent events that took place just north of New York City, each of which mobilized local black citizens to rally in angry protest. Perhaps the most notable of the events, and the one given the most attention in the article, was the assault on a young black girl by a group of white men.

> Poughkeepsie, N.Y., Dec. 13. Tawana Brawley, a popular 15-year-old high school student was found Nov. 28 curled in a fetal position inside a plastic bag behind an apartment house in Wappinger's Falls, six miles south of here.
>
> Miss Brawley, who is black, had been beaten. "Nigger" and "KKK" had been written in charcoal or marker on her torso, feces had been smeared across her body and her hair had been chopped off, the police said. She later told her family and law enforcement authorities she had been abducted and sexually assaulted by six white men—one of whom wore a police badge.[3]

Immediately after the story was published, public outrage over the assault was widespread. It was particularly intense in the black community. Religious leaders, including the Rev. Louis Farrakhan and the Rev. Al Sharpton, and legal advisors, including Alton H. Maddox, Jr., and C. Vernon Mason, came to her side. She began speaking only to her aunt, mother, and advisors, and there were demands for a special prosecutor. According to the newspaper account, the Rev. Farrakhan warned, "You will not do to another black girl in America what you did to Tawana Brawley and get away with it."

The case became too big for the local prosecutor, and the governor of New York, Mario Cuomo, became involved. By the end of the next month, the *New York Times* reported that the Governor had appointed a special prosecutor.[4] It was Robert Abrams, the state's Attorney General. Abrams announced that the case would be "'the highest priority investigation in my office." Tawana Brawley's advisors announced that they were not satisfied, and Alton Maddox said that the girl "would not cooperate with the inquiry."

The lines between whites and blacks became more pronounced as the girl's story began to unravel under the investigation of the attorney general's office. On March 24, 1988, the *New York Times* reported, "In a puzzling new twist in the Tawana Brawley mystery, school books the teen-ager was believed to have been carrying on the day she disappeared in November turned up last week in her former high school in Wappinger's Falls, N.Y., according to people familiar with the investigation."[5] The *Times* report noted that, under counsel of her advisors, the girl had not been participating with the investigation, and this was one of a number of confusing pieces of information that were "haunting investigators."

In addition to the state investigation of the assault, the federal government had initiated an investigation of whether Tawana Brawley's civil rights had been violated in the attack. Hidden in a small article, the *New York Times* announced on April 29, 1988, "The Federal Bureau of Investigation, unable to corroborate any violation of Tawana Brawley's civil rights, said yesterday that it had reassigned three of the four agents on the case to other investigations."[6] While continuing to counsel Miss Brawley not to talk to investigators, her advisors reportedly "denounced" the action by the FBI.

As time went by, new information continued to raise questions about the story she had told, and Tawana Brawley continued to refuse to talk to investigators. On May 5, 1988, a story in the New York Times reported that investigators had evidence that the girl was seen at a party in a nearby town during the time that she was supposed to have been missing. On June 4, 1988, the Times reported that the attorney general had urged the girl's legal advisors to testify before the grand jury established especially for this case. Not only did they refuse, but they announced plans to hold a hearing to "describe racism in the criminal justice system" and repeat-edly accused an assistant district attorney in the county where the assault took place of having participated in the assault.[7] On June 15, 1988, the Times reported that Governor Cuomo had written a letter of rebuke to the Brawley family and their advisors for not participating with the grand jury investigation.

After seven months without cooperation from the victim, the grand jury investigation was coming to a close. On September 27, 1988, in advance of the grand jury report, the New York Times reported, "Evidence Points to Deceit by Brawley." Among other things, the grand jury concluded that Tawana Brawley "concocted, alone or with an accomplice, the degrading condition in which she was found—by smearing herself with dog feces, writing racial slurs on her body, tearing and scorching her clothes, crawling into a garbage bag and pretending to be in a traumatized state."[8] Under the subheading "National Symbol of Racism," the Times reporters wrote, "Thus it appears that a case that became a national symbol of racism, that mired the state's highest officials in political quicksand, that stymied law-enforce-ment authorities for nearly 10 months and inflamed racial passions in New York, originated as little more than the fantasy of a troubled teen-ager, and became grist for the racial and political agendas of her advisors." That is, according to the extensive evidence provided in the news account, Tawana Brawley was not the victim of a racist attack, but rather the perpetrator of a pernicious hoax. Of course, her advisors and their now large following dis-agreed with the findings.

On September 29, 1988, the Times reported "Brawley Rejects Evidence Cited To Grand Jury."[9] In a media event held in Newark, New Jersey, Al Sharpton and Alton Maddox denounced the article from the Times, with Sharpton calling it "'a bunch of reckless speculations that was beneath a porno magazine to print.'" On October 7, 1988, the grand jury report was released, and the Times published another article on the findings.

With the investigation closed, people were ready to form opinions about what had happened. Those who wanted to conclude that Tawana

Brawley had made up the story and that there was no racial assault in Wappinger's Falls in November 1987 could point to the grand jury findings. For them, this was just another story of an irresponsible black girl lying to avoid facing the consequences of her actions. Those who wanted to believe that there was such an assault, and that a racist criminal justice system was conspiring to hide the fact, could argue that Tawana Brawley never had the opportunity to tell her side of the story to investigators. For them, this was just a modern-day version of white slave masters sexually assaulting a black woman they believed they owned. Observers were free to reach conclusions about whether or not a young girl had been the victim of racial violence on the basis of their own views of the nature and extent of racism in U.S. society and particularly in the criminal justice system.

According to the *New York Times Index* for the year 1988, during that year the newspaper published at least one article about the case on each of 111 days. But by the end of 1988, the Tawana Brawley story was old news. It did not surface again until December 1997 when the lawsuit filed against Brawley's advisors by Steven Pagones, the local assistant district attorney accused of being one of the white men to assault the young girl, reached the courts.

On December 3, 1997, the *New York Times* reported that 800 people turned out in the Bedford Stuyvesant section of Brooklyn, New York, to hear Tawana Brawley speak. Speaking in defense of her advisors, who were the subject of Pagones's defamation lawsuit, she did not disappoint them. According to the *Times*, "A confident and defiant Tawana Brawley told a roaring audience of supporters last night the same thing she did [ten years earlier]: that she had told the truth."[10] She told them of her new life since the event and the investigation that followed it, claiming that on occasion she had been followed by the Central Intelligence Agency (CIA) and once was "stopped at gunpoint" by law enforcement officials.

The next day, the *Times* headlined its Metro section with an article about the opening of the court case and included a side article, "Grand Jury Found Nothing to Back Claim." The *Times* reminded readers that after seven months and 180 witnesses, not including Tawana Brawley, the grand jury found no evidence to support her claims and concluded that she had "concocted her account of being kidnapped and raped by white men."[11] Still, the *New York Post* that same day announced findings from a survey of 1,200 adults living in the New York City area with the headline, "Poll: Majority of Blacks Believe Her Story."

In the face of so much evidence, it is difficult to understand how anyone, black or white, could still believe that Tawana Brawley was telling the truth about her assault. In the face of U.S. history, it is easy to understand how someone, a black person especially, could believe that perhaps she was. Easier still is it for a white person to believe that a black man accused of violence probably did it, while a black person might see the same situation as that of a black man being falsely incriminated by a racist system of justice. Even class and celebrity could not protect O. J. Simpson from such judgment.

On October 3, 1995, the *Los Angeles Times* published an extra edition with a headline larger even than its own name. The headline read, "Simpson Not Guilty." O. J. Simpson, a successful and beloved American football hero and a passable if not talented entertainer, had been arrested and charged in the brutal killing of his wife and an acquaintance on June 12, 1994. Despite a strong circumstantial case against him, Simpson never admitted guilt, and a jury found him not guilty. The next day in its regular edition, the *Los Angeles Times* ran another front-page story about the acquittal, accompanied by several pages of related reports. One front-page story announced the results of a *Times* poll under the heading, "Half of Americans Disagree With Verdict." That national poll taken immediately after the verdict could not distinguish respondents by race, but did show that "[t]hose who make $50,000 a year or more—ironically, O. J. Simpson's former earnings range—were far harsher on the jury and also more likely to believe Simpson was guilty of first-degree murder than those making less than $30,000 a year."[12] That is, class mattered in how respondents judged the guilt or innocence of O. J. Simpson.

The following Sunday, the *Los Angeles Times* published on its front page the results of another poll. That poll was conducted with 760 adults living in Los Angeles County. Pollsters found that "[c]ountywide, 65% of whites disagreed with the guilty verdict, including 51% who said they disagreed strongly."[13] Similarly, they found that among blacks, however, "77% agreed with the verdict, including 68% who agreed strongly and only 12% who disagreed." The reporter concluded that the poll "illustrated the deep racial divide on the Simpson matter." That is, race mattered in how respondents judged the guilt or innocence of O. J. Simpson.

During the week that the *Los Angeles Times* was devoting the headline of its front page to the acquittal of O. J. Simpson, a report was released in Washington, D.C., that was relevant to the public response to the verdict. The *Los Angeles Times* began this story in a small box at the center of its first page on Thursday, October 5, 1995, a day when the headlines were reserved for comments by jurors and Simpson about the trial and the verdict. The small headline read, "Sentencing Study Sees Race Disparity." The article opened, "Washington—Nearly one in three African American men in their 20s is in jail, prison, on probation or parole—a sharp increase over the approximately 25% of five years ago, a study concluded."[14] The report issued by the Sentencing Project went on to cause quite a reaction in its own right, but at that moment the emphasis was on one of its pronouncements. As stated in the *Times* article, "The report, written before a jury's acquittal Tuesday of O. J. Simpson, said: 'Regardless of where one stands on his guilt or innocence, what is clear is that a wealthy and famous African American was able to assemble a very formidable defense. This is contrasted with the typical scene in almost every courthouse in cities across America, where young African Americans and Hispanic males are daily processed through the justice system with very limited resources devoted to their cases'."[15]

Minorities as Violent Offenders

Despite being hidden in the shadow of the O. J. Simpson verdict, the findings of the Sentencing Project study could not be ignored. The Sentencing Project is a nonprofit organization dedicated to reforming sentencing policies and practices in the United States. It focuses on promoting alternatives to incarceration, especially for indigent offenders. In a 1990 study funded largely by the Edna McConnell Clark Foundation and the Public Welfare Foundation, Marc Mauer and the research staff of the Sentencing Project found that, on any given day in the United States, *1 of every 4* black men between the ages of 20 and 29 was under arrest, on probation or parole, in jail or prison, or somehow under the control of the criminal justice system.[16] This compares to 1 of every 16 white men and 1 of every 10 Hispanic men in the same age group. For women, the numbers were much smaller, but the proportions were comparable. One of every 37 black women, 1 of every 56 Hispanic women, and 1 of every 100 white women were under the control of the criminal justice system on any given day. The follow-up report (the one issued at the time of the O.J. Simpson verdict) found that only five years after the initial report was published, *one in every three* black males between the ages of 20 and 29 was under the control of the criminal justice system.[17]

Most people processed as violent criminal offenders in the United States are white males. Of more than 600,000 people arrested for a violent crime in 1995, 85 percent were male and 54 percent were white.[18] Still, Americans have been and remain quick to think of people of color as violent and to think of violent offenders as black.[19] Perhaps these stereotypes are sustained by the statistical knowledge that while whites account for the greater number, proportional to their representation in the total population blacks account for more than their share of those arrested for violent offenses. In 1995, African Americans accounted for almost 44 percent of all people arrested for a violent crime, but less than 14 percent of all people in the total United States population.[20] In addition, almost 49 percent of all inmates in state prisons and almost 37 percent of all inmates in federal prisons in 1995 in the United States were black, not including those who were both black and Hispanic.[21]

Because a category of people are officially overrepresented as violent offenders does not necessarily mean that they are responsible for more violent offending. Those people included in criminal justice statistics represent only those who were caught in the web of the criminal justice system. Further, official crime statistics and self-report data (even given that each has its own limitations) are not always consistent in terms of this question. Findings from some studies involving interviews with survey respondents, for example, show that observed differences in the violent offending patterns of white and African American males are not significant.[22] In a review of the research on race and crime in the United States, Samuel Walker and his associates concluded that they had limited confidence in conclusions about the "racial makeup of the offender population." They wrote, "Although African Americans obviously are arrested at a disproportionately high rate, particularly for murder and robbery, it is not clear that this discrepancy reflects differential offending rather than selective enforcement of the law."[23] That is, to understand the disproportionately high rate of violent offending attributed by the criminal justice system to African Americans, we need to understand how the criminal justice system treats people in relation to their race and class.

The Favors of the Criminal Justice System

One Saturday afternoon in the springtime of 1970, I was visiting my students in the Bushwick section of Brooklyn, New York, where I was a fourth grade teacher. I was standing on Putnam Avenue outside a student's home talking to his mother. Suddenly, a fast-moving car turned the corner, bounced from side to side off parked cars, and just missed hitting children playing on the street. The car stopped and was immediately surrounded by an irate crowd of 50 or more people. At that point, I realized that besides the driver of the car, I was the only white person on the block. A black woman who saw the incident went into her house and called the police. People were screaming and waving their arms. There was much anger, and any minute violence could have erupted. Fortunately, it did not. By my watch the police did not arrive for almost 30 tense minutes, at which time two officers told the crowd to disperse, took statements, and sent the driver away.

Not long after, I was driving home from a day of teaching along my usual route, a street in Bedford Stuyvesant lined with once elegant brownstone homes. In my rearview mirror I noticed a car coming up very fast behind me. I pulled to the left to let the other driver pass, but he chose instead to follow me, and his car swiped the side of mine. I stopped as he sped by. He then hit a parked car as he turned right onto the next street and disappeared. I saw a man come from a house near the corner to look at the damage to the car he had parked just outside. I drove over to where he was standing and got out of my car to talk to him. There was no reason to suspect immediate danger to anyone. We were both victims of another driver who had already driven away. We agreed that we should call the police to report the accidents. The other man, who was black, asked me to go into his house to make the call. Hearing the voice of a white man coming from an accident scene in Bedford Stuyvesant, the police were waiting for us by the time we got back outside to our cars.

Nearly three decades later, my experience with law enforcement on the streets of Brooklyn was reflected in my observations in courtrooms of Baltimore. During the first few days of January 1998, days that felt more like spring than winter, I spent my mornings in various courtrooms in the city of Baltimore. A young man I knew, really just a boy, had been arrested and charged with possession of a handgun. Both of his parents had died before he was 18, the victims of drugs and AIDS he told me, and his remaining relatives seemed either unable or unwilling to care for him. So I went to court to appear on his behalf, a middle-aged white man speaking for a young black boy.

Worlds collide in criminal courtrooms. Nicely dressed and mostly white stewards of the law, including the judge and assorted lawyers, go about their business with precision and confidence in a domain that is clearly theirs to command. Law enforcement officers, ready to tell the tales of offending that the court will adjudicate, sit together in the first rows of benches, sharing stories from the field and waiting to he heard. Behind them sit the defendants. A few, most of them white and neatly dressed, wait quietly with a private attorney at their side. The others are mostly young black men sitting alone, a few with a mother or grandmother who looks too weary, confused, or frightened to be of much help. Other defendants, again mostly young black men, all with shackles restraining their gait and metal cuffs holding their hands at their backs, are brought from detention for their cases to be heard.

Invariably, there are too many cases to manage, and a surprising number are summarily dismissed, usually because no one is inclined or really cares to go forward. When the prosecution does proceed, having an attorney, someone who can speak to the court in its own language, makes a difference. So the number of young black men and boys who stand before the judge alone is remarkable. They listen while the judge asks a few questions they probably do not understand and mumble when told that they have waived their right to an attorney. Then they are asked to decide by themselves how and when judgment should be passed. Fortunately for them, nowadays more often than not their charge involves possession of drugs, and their conviction results in a term of probation. They walk out of the courtroom with what they think is a victory, no one having explained to them in a way they can understand the significance of having been convicted of a crime.

Having someone at your side does make a difference. When I met with the public defender who was initially assigned to help my young friend, he told me the case was hopeless and the boy would almost certainly go to prison. Over the next few days, I spoke on his behalf to each public defend-er assigned to the case, and I wrote a letter to the court suggesting that this was a boy in need of help rather than incarceration. I do not know every-thing that happened behind the scenes, but I do know that the court did not proceed with its case against the boy. He was released, given one more chance to stay out of trouble.

On an individual level, there must be countless cases of boys and girls, men and women, who are devoured by a criminal justice system that is too overloaded and too overworked to be blind to race and class. Perhaps of greater concern, however, is the extent to which these biases are taken for granted as inevitable in a criminal justice system with a workload too large to manage effectively, efficiently, and fairly all at the same time.

There is no question that people who are poor or members of certain minority groups are overrepresented among those whom we have arrested, prosecuted, convicted, sentenced, and incarcerated during the last decades of the twentieth century in the United States.[24] The question is whether this disparity is the result of differences in patterns of offending or discrimina-tion in the criminal justice system. Some studies have suggested that the level of disparity is small or that it is not necessarily the result of discrimi-nation.[25] Others have suggested that the disparity is real and is, in fact, a function of systemic bias based on race, socioeconomic status, or both.[26] Whatever it is, it is not something that policy makers are eager to address.

According to the President's Crime Commission in the late 1960s—not to mention Articles IV, V, VI, VIII, and especially XIV of the U.S. Constitution—a principal objective of any comprehensive plan to reduce crime is "to eliminate injustices so that the system of criminal justice can win the respect and cooperation of all citizens."[27] But, as the commission report went on to say, "Injustice will not yield to simple solutions."[28] For policy makers, for whom the best problems are the ones that are easily solved and the best solutions are those that appear to be making progress toward an established goal, this is unfortunate. As claims makers trying to show that bringing justice to the criminal justice system is a manageable problem, it is better to argue that the system is already just than to recognize that it is not and have to find ways to make it so.

In the years when I was an employee of New York State government, a member of our research staff at the Division of Criminal Justice Services (DCJS) was working on an analysis of disparity in the processing of first misdemeanor and then felony criminal cases in the state courts. The state legislature had issued a mandate and allocated funds for the study. The plan was to produce a series of reports. The researcher had come to the agency from a major university where he taught statistics. His methodology was highly sophisticated and very well regarded, not only by other research staff in the agency, but also by prominent social scientists who, over the years, would have the opportunity to review his work for publication in professional journals, presentation at conferences, or as part of the agency's external review process.

A draft of the first report was ready in 1989. It analyzed "the combined effects of processing decisions that occurred between arrest and final disposition by modeling whether blacks and Hispanics were sentenced to jail or prison more often than whites," showed that, in fact, minorities "were incarcerated more than whites," and identified the counties in the state in which the disparity was greatest.[29] By the time the draft was being circulated internally in March 1989, the findings were not in question. Nonetheless, agency officials were reluctant to release the report. There was concern that if results were presented at that time, the legislature would not continue funding for the project. There was also concern about identifying counties by their disparity level. So, the research director never formally showed the draft to the agency head.

Months passed. Suddenly, in December 1989, bureaucratic procrastination was replaced by political urgency. Outside interest in the report was somehow aroused, and the agency head, who was also an aide to Governor Mario Cuomo, had asked for a briefing from the researcher. By that time, I was designated as acting research director and attended the meeting. It was decided that while we could not yet release a written report, we could plan a conference on the theme to be held in March 1990. Over the next few months, the researcher and I met with the agency head about plans for the conference and the substance of the report. Should we delay the conference until after the state budget was approved? Could we identify better economic indicators to distinguish between racial and economic effects?

Early in 1990, the researcher and I attended planning meetings with representatives of the two universities that agreed to cosponsor the conference with us. We decided that the researcher would present the findings and conclusions of the work and would be followed at the podium by a number of prominent criminologists. Their job would be to respond to his conclusions (having earlier reviewed a written draft) and to put the work in a broader criminal justice context.

We also met with the governor's aides about the findings that would be presented at the conference and in the report. After about a month of delays, in March 1990, we met with them downtown on "The Second Floor," as the governor's suite of offices was called. The researcher briefly presented his findings and conclusions, they asked a few questions, and then told the researcher that, once it was released, the press would label him "the guy who wrote the racist report." He was undeterred. We asked if we could send the draft to the district attorney in each county to get his or her feedback. Not a good idea, we were told; someone in the media would surely get a copy and we would lose control over the interpretation of the findings. Also, we were told that the district attorneys were not as interested in their constituents as they were in their political battles. Whatever material we provided with names of counties on it would be used in those battles. Then, they looked over the rankings of counties, considering which district attorneys would be hurt by the findings and whether they cared about those district attorneys. Next, we talked about the plans for the conference. They liked the format, but told us to wait before we sent anyone a draft of the report.

The conference was scheduled for May 29, 1990, in New York City at John Jay College, one of our cosponsors. On May 18, I received a call from the governor's aide. A group of students at John Jay had taken over a few offices on campus and disrupted a government function there after a Latino professor had been denied tenure. The call was to tell me that a decision had been made to postpone the conference. It would be held no later than September, but it would not be in New York City. We would move it to Albany, where there was likely to be less media attention. It would be held at the State University of New York at Albany, our other cosponsor. The other speakers had to be notified. Plans had to be canceled. The researcher saw this as part of the continuing effort to delay the release of a report that had been ready for release more than a year earlier.

The conference was held in Albany on July 26, 1990. A few of the original speakers were able to make the new dates; others had been replaced. About 70 or 80 people attended, mostly state agency employees; no one from the news media attended. The findings and conclusions from the report, that there was racial disparity in criminal case processing in New York State, were out, though with little fanfare. The media did not report on the event or the findings.

A year later, July 1991, the researcher finally got permission from the governor's aide to proceed with the release of the written report. However, the decision was made to first send a draft to the governor, Mario Cuomo, for his approval, with a recommendation that to avoid bringing too much attention to the findings the report be issued without a press release. A month later, a cover letter was prepared and signed by the state director of criminal justice, and permission to print 500 copies was granted. Another month later, the report was still not out, delayed this time by a debate over the press release issue. Finally, on September 24, 1991, the report was in the mail. There was no press release. Nonetheless, someone did notify the press, and, on September 30, a story appeared in the Albany *Times Union*. Despite two years of delay and countless bureaucratic decisions, the headline on the front page of the *Times Union* read, "Reports find minorities face tougher justice." That was about the extent of the response.

In November 1995, several years after the initial report was released and several months after I had left New York, the report on *felony* processing[30] was released. It was mailed with a cover letter from the state director of criminal justice in which he downplayed the findings of disparity. He called the report "a sophisticated research report" and wrote, "The research found that whites and minorities were processed in similar ways at most, albeit not all, decision points." On the first page of the executive summary of the report, however, the researcher wrote, "After controlling for differences in prior criminal histories, seriousness of arrest charges, type of arrest charges, gender, county, and youthful offender eligibility, the analyses demonstrate that minorities were held in jail at indictment and sentenced to incarceration more often than comparably situated whites."[31] These are not minor decision points.

Though, like the first, the second report was released without a press notice, five months later, a headline in the April 10, 1996, *New York Times* read, "A Hushed Study Shows Disparity in Sentencing." The article by Clifford J. Levy began, "A little-noticed study released last fall by the Pataki administration concluded that black and Hispanic people sentenced for minor felonies or misdemeanors in New York were treated more harshly than whites in similar circumstances." The news report continued, "Some experts have hailed the study as ground-breaking, but Gov. George E. Pataki's own aides have now disavowed it."

The Poor and Minorities as Victims of Violence

In their classic study of ethnic groups living together in New York City during the middle of the twentieth century, Nathan Glazer and Daniel Patrick Moynihan concluded, "The interplay between rational economic interests and the other interests or attitudes that stem out of group history makes for an incredibly complex political and social situation."[32] The interplay they observed proved to be a source of ethnic identity, but it also lays a foundation for ethnic conflict. Students of ethnic relations have long known that in open societies such as ours, the competition between and among similarly situated ethnic groups for the scarce resources available to them may result in violence.[33] Thus we get the story of the robberies of the Korean storekeepers in Baltimore.

The headline of an editorial on January 30, 1997, of the Baltimore *Sun* asked the question, "Are Korean Americans crime targets?" The point of the editorial was that even with 35 robberies every day in the city, the number of robberies of Korean American shopkeepers was striking, if not alarming. Four recent examples of such robberies were mentioned, including one during which a man was "shot twice in the back in front of his wife after he had complied with a demand for money." The editorial argued, "The unknown African-American suspects seem to be more concerned with inflicting fear, pain and death among the Korean-American community than in the money they steal." An explanation for this violence was then offered in terms of interethnic rivalry: "Hold-ups have occurred in largely African-American neighborhoods where there is resentment toward Korean merchants. Some jealously see them as interlopers."

The details and at least one of the groups involved in this violence may be new, but the story is not. It is not different from the stories Kenneth Clark heard about Jews and blacks in Harlem during the middle of the twentieth century.[34] It is the story of people stuck at the lower end of the social order struggling to control the small part of the economy that is even in their sights. And inevitably they lose. Those who gain control end up as oppressors, much in the way described in David Caplovitz's *The Poor Pay More*,[35] a book that demonstrated scientifically to the satisfaction of liberal scholars what poor black people living in housing projects across the United States already knew. From research conducted through the Bureau of Applied Social Research at Columbia University, he showed how and why our economic system routinely forces lower-income people to pay more for goods and services than do people of greater means. And those who lose control become angry and jealous, turning to violence against those who have wrested from them the small rewards that they hoped would be theirs.

In the end, the poor and minorities who do not move up through the social order, away from the scratching and fighting for the scarcest portion of society's scarce resources, end up the victims of violence. They become victims both of the violence of poverty and of the violence of the people who remain angry and frustrated with them at the lower end of the economic scale.

What we know about violent victimization largely comes from official statistics. For homicide victims we turn to the Supplementary Homicide Reports (SHR) of the Uniform Crime Reports (UCR) program. For victims of other violent crimes, we turn to the criminal justice statistics of the National Crime Victimization Survey (NCVS) and the public health statistics of the hospital Emergency Department (ED) Summary.

For 1996, the SHR reported 8,239 homicide victims in the United States.[36] White people, who accounted for more than 80 percent of all people in the United States,[37] were the victims of only 50 percent of all homicides. Black people, who accounted for fewer than 14 percent of all people in the United States, were the victims of almost 47 percent of all homicides. It was not surprising when the national Centers for Disease (CDC) Control examined mortality statistics for the years 1978 to 1987 and found that "annual homicide rates for young black males were four to five times higher than for young black females, five to eight times higher than for young white males, and 16 to 22 times higher than for young white females."[38] Nor is it surprising when SHR statistics regularly show that most white victims are killed by white offenders (84 percent in 1996) and most black victims are killed by black offenders (92 percent in 1996).

In terms of other forms of violent victimization, an analysis of NCVS data by the federal Bureau of Justice Statistics (BJS) in 1997 showed that, during the middle years of the 1990s, rates of both violent and nonviolent victimization declined and that this observed "downward trend in criminal victimization can be seen across demographic groups such as sex, race, and income."[39] The same analysis, however, showed that, in 1996, black people were three times as likely as white people to be victims of robbery, and twice as likely as white people to be victims of aggravated assault. Similarly, that analysis showed that "Hispanics were twice as likely as non-Hispanics to fall victim to robbery and personal theft."[40] An earlier analysis of NCVS data focusing specifically on the victimization of young black males found in 1992 that "black males age 12 to 24 experienced violent crime at a rate significantly higher than the rates for other age or racial groups."[41] And an analysis by BJS of hospital emergency room data from 1994 found that "Blacks, who constitute about 13% of the Nation's population, represented 24% of those treated for violence-related injuries."[42]

Conclusion

For poor and minority people who live their lives with limited access to the resources and rewards of society, the danger and risk of violent victimization is obvious. As Deborah Prothrow-Stith observed from her years of clinical experience, "An epidemic of violence in the poorest of our poor neighborhoods is decimating a generation of young men of color. The shattering impact of living in an environment saturated with violence and fear is reshaping the lives of poor children."[43] More than two decades earlier, the members of the National Commission on the Causes and Prevention of Violence suggested that the same forces that result in the violent victimization of poor, minority youngsters may lead to their violent victimization of others. The commission reported:

> To be a young, poor male; to be undereducated and without means of escape from an oppressive urban environment; to want what society claims is available (but mostly to others); to see around oneself illegitimate and often violent methods being used to achieve material success; and to observe others pursuing these means with impunity—all this is to be burdened with an enormous set of influences that pull many toward crime and delinquency.[44]

Prothrow-Stith made this conclusion plain when she wrote, "We know this, too—that growing up in violence places young people and their communities at terrible jeopardy. For the fact is, those who are the witnesses and victims of violence often become its perpetrators."[45]

For those of us who are more likely to be the beneficiaries of the resources and rewards of our society and not the direct targets of its violence, the impact of that violence is nonetheless real. Taxpayers must pay the economic cost, including, but not limited to, the expense of a vast criminal justice system to process and then house those who are charged with the commission of violence. Citizens must pay the moral cost of being recog-

nized throughout the world as a nation that allows violence to disproportionately affect the lives of those most vulnerable among them. Writing for
the Commission on Criminal Justice, Steven Donziger noted:

> [W]hether the cause is higher crime or discrimination or both, this country is
> on the verge of a social catastrophe because of the sheer number of African-
> Americans behind bars—numbers that continue to rise with breathtaking
> speed and frightening implications. The reason: our criminal justice policies
> are preventing many African-Americans from claiming their stake in the
> American dream, thereby contributing to the destruction of our national ideal
> of racial harmony. [46]

Why, then, do we tell the stories we tell about poor and minority people and violence, particularly the parable about the poor, young, African
American male as a violent offender? A parable tells a story from which a
moral may be drawn, "a short narrative, presented so as to bring out the
analogy, or parallel, between its elements and a lesson that the speaker is
trying to bring home to [the reader]."[47] The moral most often drawn from
this particular parable is that we are correct to concentrate our criminal justice resources on the surveillance and control of poor, young, African
American males.

Such a view of society identifies a problem that is relatively easy to
address, especially compared to a view that would see the problem as having to redistribute society's resources to make them equally available to
all people. Unfortunately, it ignores another moral lesson from our history,
one inscribed in stone on a monument prominently placed in one of our
earliest cities. Walk west along Benjamin Franklin Parkway in Philadelphia,
with City Hall at your back and the steps of the Art Museum ahead. As
you pass the Free Library on your right and the Franklin Institute on your
left, you are greeted by towering stone monuments rising above the trees
on either side of the elegant and expansive boulevard. At the top of the
monument on your left is a pillar dedicated to those who fought in the
Civil War for the union of our nation. On it are words that reflect the
thinking of Franklin not long before he died in 1790, a former slaveholder
who became "sensitive to the anomaly of slavery in a society proclaiming
human rights."[48] Immortalized in stone are words spoken by Abraham
Lincoln in his annual message to Congress in December, 1862: "In giving
freedom to the slave, we assure freedom to the free."

Identifying one group of people as the cause of violence, particularly
one from a relatively powerless segment of society, permits us to concentrate our resources on those people. By arresting, prosecuting, convicting,
and sentencing to prison more young, black men, we can say we are doing
something to reduce violence. Identifying the problem as one of bias in our
social institutions, particularly the institutions of our criminal justice system, is not a simple problem to solve. To reduce bias is to shift the balance

of our overall social reward structure. Public officials who make policy, especially those who, at one time or another, must face a public election, favor simple, manageable problems. Recall what happened in New York when a government researcher simply established that bias did exist in the state's criminal justice system.

The problems of real people are often difficult to solve, not a good thing for officials trying to show they are effectively taking action to help the public. After Dan Rostenkowski was released from prison in 1998, an article in *Newsweek* suggested that the former congressman who had been incarcerated for defrauding the government was the last of a dying breed, a representative who legislated by arm-twisting and deal making. "By and large, modern-day congressmen are more interested in ideological posturing than in legislating."[49] That is only partially true. On the state and local level, and probably on the national level as well, posturing has become more important, but deal making remains a central component of the process of making policy and law.

Endnotes

1. DREIM # 118.

2. Cleaver, E. (1968). *Soul on Ice*. New York: Dell, p. 17.

3. Iverem, E. (1987). "Bias Cases Fuel Anger of Blacks." *The New York Times* December 14:B1.

4. Barron, J. (1988). "Abrams Office to Investigate Attack on Black Teen-Ager." *The New York Times* January 27:B3.

5. Blumenthal, R. (1988). "Brawley's Texts Founds At School." *The New York Times* March 24:B1.

6. Blumenthal, R. (1988). "F.B.I. Pulls Back in Brawley Case." *The New York Times* April 29:B3.

7. Blumenthal, R. (1988). "Abrams Urges Brawley Lawyers To Testify on What They Know." *The New York Times* June 4:31.

8. McFadden, R. D. et al. (1988). "Evidence Points to Deceit by Brawley." *The New York Times* September 27:A1.

9. Shipp, E. R. (1988) "Brawley Rejects Evidence Cited To Grand Jury." *The New York Times* September 29:B4.

10. Yardley, J. (1997). "Brawley Comes to Rally and Repeats Charge of an Attack." *The New York Times* December 3:B1.

11. Barron, J. (1997). "Grand Jury Found Nothing to Back Claim." *The New York Times* December 4:B12.

12. Decker, C. and Stolberg, S. (1995). "Half of Americans Disagree With Verdict." *Los Angeles Times* October 4:A11.

13. Decker, C. (1995). "Most in County Disagree With Simpson Verdicts." *Los Angeles Times* October 8:A36.

14. Ostrow, R. J. (1995). "Sentencing Study Sees Race Disparity." *Los Angeles Times* October 5:A1.

15. Ostrow 1995:A17.

16. Mauer, M. (1990). *Young Black Men and the Criminal Justice System: A Growing National Problem*. Washington, DC: The Sentencing Project.

17. Mauer, M. and Huling, T. (1995). *Young Black Americans and the Criminal Justice System: Five Years Later*. Washington, DC: The Sentencing Project.

18. Maguire, K. and Pastore, A.L. (eds.). 1997. *Sourcebook of Criminal Justice Statistics, 1996*. U.S. Department of Justice, Bureau of Justice Statistics. Washington, DC: U.S. Government Printing Office, pp. 380, 382.

19. Curtis, L. (1974). *Criminal Violence—National Patterns and Behavior*. Lexington, MA. Lexington. Donziger, S.R. (ed.). (1996). *The Real War on Crime—The Report of the National Criminal Justice Commission*. New York: HarperCollins. Mann, C. R. (1993). *Unequal Justice*. Bloomington: Indiana University Press. President's Commission on Law Enforcement and Administration of Justice. (1968). *The Challenge of Crime in a Free Society—The Complete Official Report*. New York: Avon.

20. Horner, E. R. (1997). *Almanac of the 50 States—Basic Data Profiles with Comparative Tables*. Palo Alto, CA: Information Publications. Maguire and Pastore 1997.

21. Bureau of Justice Statistics. (1997). *Correctional Populations in the United States, 1995*. Executive Summary. Washington, DC: Bureau of Justice Statistics.

22. Walker, S., Spohn, C. and DeLone, M. (1996). *The Color of Justice—Race, Ethnicity, and Crime in America*. Belmont, CA: Wadsworth.

23. Walker, Spohn, and DeLone 1996:56.

24. See, for example, Black, D. J. and Reiss, A. J., Jr. (1970). "Police Control of Juveniles." *American Sociological Review* 35:63–78. Blumstein, A. (1982). "On the Racial Disproportionality of United States' Prison Populations." *Journal of Criminal Law and Criminology* 73:1259–81. Blumstein, A. and Graddy, E. (1983). "Prevalence and Recidivism in Index Arrests: A Feedback Model." *Law and Society Review* 16:279–80. Christianson, S. (1981). "Our Black Prisoners." *Crime and Delinquency* 27:364–75. Mauer 1990; McDonald, D. C. and Carlson, K. E. (1993) *Sentencing in the Federal Courts: Does Race Matter? The Transition to Sentencing Guidelines, 1986–90*. Washington, D.C. Bureau of Justice Statistics. Tonry, M. (1995). *Malign Neglect: Race, Crime, and Punishment in America*. New York: Oxford University Press.

25. See, for example, Kleck, G. (1985). "Life Support for Ailing Hypotheses: Modes of Summarizing he Evidence for Racial Discrimination in Sentencing." *Law and Human Behavior* 9:271–85. Petersilia, J. (1983). *Racial Disparities in the Criminal Justice System*. Santa Monica, CA: Rand. Wilbanks, W. (1987). *The Myth of the Racist Criminal Justice System*. Belmont, CA: Wadsworth.

26. See, for example, Crutchfield, R. D. and Bridges, G. S. (1985). *Racial and Ethnic Disparities in Imprisonment: Final Report*. Seattle: University of Washington Press. Lizotte, A. J. (1978). "Extra-Legal Factors in Chicago's Criminal Courts: Testing the Conflict Model of Criminal Justice." *Social Problems* 25:564–80. Nelson, J. F. (1994). "A Dollar or a Day: Sentencing Misdemeanants in New York State." *Journal of Research in Crime and Delinquency* 31:183–201. Nelson, J. F. (1992). "Hidden Disparities in Case Processing: New York State, 1985–86." *Journal of Criminal Justice* 20:181–200. Reiman, J. (1998). *The Rich Get Richer and the Poor Get Prison*. Boston: Allyn and Bacon. Sampson, R. (1986). "Effects of Socioeconomic Context on Official Reaction to Juvenile Delinquency." *American Sociological Review* 51:876–85. Thornberry, T. P. (1973). "Race, Socioeconomic Status, and Sentencing in the Juvenile Justice System." *Journal of Criminal Law and Criminology* 64:90–98.

27. President's Commission 1968:44.

28. President's Commission 1968:45.

29. Nelson, J. F. (1991a). *The Incarceration of Minority Defendants: An Identification of Disparity in New York State, 1985–1986*. Albany, NY: NYS Division of Criminal Justice Services, p. i. See also Nelson, J.F. (1991b). *Racial and Ethnic Disparities in Processing Persons Arrested for Misdemeanor Crimes: New York State, 1985–1986*. Albany, NY: NYS Division of Criminal Justice Services.

30. Nelson, J. F. (1995). *Disparities in Processing Felony Arrests in New York State, 1990–1992*. Albany, NY: NYS Division of Criminal Justice Services.

31. Nelson 1995:i.

32. Glazer, N. and D. P. Moynihan. (1963). *Beyond the Melting Pot—The Negroes, Puerto Ricans, Jews, Italians, and Irish of New York City*. Cambridge: The MIT Press, p. 17.

33. Glazer, N. and D. P. Moynihan. (1975). *Ethnicity—Theory and Experience*. Cambridge: Harvard University Press. Shibutani, T. and K. M. Kwan. (1965). *Ethnic Stratification—A Comparative Approach*. London: MacMillan, pp. 372ff.

34. Clark, K. (1965). *Dark Ghetto—Dilemmas of Social Power*. New York: Harper & Row.

35. Caplovitz, D. (1963). *The Poor Pay More—Consumer Practices of Low Income Families*. New York: The Free Press.

36. Federal Bureau of Investigation. (1997). *Crime in the United States, 1996*. Washington, DC: U.S. Government Printing Office.

37. Horner 1997.

38. Centers for Disease Control. (1990). "Homicide among Young Black Males—United States, 1978–1987." *Morbidity and Mortality Weekly Report* 39:870.

39. Ringel, C. (1997). *Criminal Victimization 1996—Changes 1995–96 with Trends 1993–96*. National Crime Victimization Survey. Washington, DC: Bureau of Justice Statistics, p. 9.

40. Ringel 1997:4.

41. Bastian, L. D. and Taylor, B. M. (1994). *Young Black Male Victims*. National Crime Victimization Survey. Washington, DC: Bureau of Justice Statistics, p. 1.

42. Rand, M. R. and Strom, K. (1997). *Violence-Related Injuries Treated in Hospital Emergency Rooms*. Special Report. Washington, DC: Bureau of Justice Statistics, p. 3.

43. Prothrow-Stith, D. (with M. Weissman). (1991). *Deadly Consequences*. New York: HarperCollins, p. 64.

44. National Commission on the Causes and Prevention of Violence. (1969). *Final Report: To Establish Justice, to Insure Domestic Tranquility*. Washington, DC: U.S. Government Printing Office, p. 35.

45. Prothrow-Stith 1991, p. 64.

46. Donziger 1996, p. 99.

47. Abrams, M. H. (1957). *A Glossary of Literary Terms*. New York: Holt, Rinehart and Winston, p. 3.

48. Crane, V. W. (1954). *Benjamin Franklin and a Rising People*. Boston: Little, Brown, p. 203.

49. Klaidman, D. and Thomas, E. (1998). "Rosty's Difficult Winter." *Newsweek* January 12:36.

9

The Tale of the Worker Gone Mad

With personal demands so great and social expectations so high, the Christmas season is a stressful time for everyone. For some of us, it is a time of joy; for others, it is a time of frustration and even depression or anger. Working people who routinely deal with the public, such as retail store employees and postal workers, face the potential strain of longer hours and increased customer contact, but they also may enjoy the benefit of earning bigger paychecks. We really do not know how those people feel about their added workload, whether they see it as a burden or an opportunity. Still, it is not hard to imagine that they are under particular pressure. So, we are rarely surprised when the Christmas season arrives and a postal worker loses control and becomes violent.

In 1997, the Christmas tale of the postal worker gone mad unfolded in Denver. On Christmas Day, most big city newspapers took the story written by Martha Bellisle for the Associated Press, or a comparable story from other wire services, and published an account of the event somewhere inside their first section. The opening lines introducing the story were repeated across America.

- "A fired postal employee held seven people hostage at a regional mail center before surrendering to police yesterday, ending a $9\frac{1}{2}$-hour Christmas Eve standoff." (*Philadelphia Inquirer*)
- "A dismissed postal worker surrendered to the police today after releasing unharmed seven people whom he had held hostage at a regional mail center and ending a $9\frac{1}{2}$-hour Christmas Eve standoff." (*New York Times*)
- "A fired postal employee who held seven people hostage at a regional mail center surrendered to police Wednesday, ending a $9\frac{1}{2}$-hour Christmas Eve standoff." (*Chicago Tribune*)

- "A fired postal employee who held seven people hostage at a regional mail center surrendered on Christmas Eve after a $9\frac{1}{2}$-hour standoff with police." (*Washington Post*)

The story was similarly introduced in the *Los Angeles Times* and the *Baltimore Sun*. Then, after recounting the details of the event, all the newspaper stories concluded with a similar proposition. As written in the *Philadelphia Inquirer*, "In the last decade, shootings by postal employees have become all too common." A few papers, including the *Washington Post* and the *Chicago Tribune*, added a second conclusion. They printed a response from the Postal Service indicating that workplace violence is not limited to postal service workers.

Naturally, in Denver, the story received the most attention. The *Denver Post* had a cover story by its own staff writer, Jim Hughes, and four attendant articles on various aspects of the story. There was one about the hostages, another about the suspect, a third about the security at the facility, and a fourth about the psychology of such violence in the workplace. Each was written by a different staff writer.

The main story provided great detail about the event, the suspect, the hostages, the local postal facility, and the response of local police and the Postal Service. The story, as told simply and directly by Jim Hughes, was summed up in a quote from Sgt. Dennis Cribari of the Denver Police Department. "No one is injured. They've been through a terrible ordeal [the hostages], but that will heal. Physically, they were not harmed. What a nice Christmas present."

The side stories in the *Denver Post* on December 25, 1997, each were more thematic. In a story under the heading "Safe release 'the best' present," Steve Lipsher wrote about some of the people who were the hostages, giving them human faces and highlighting their dedication to their jobs. The hostage taker was made human in a story by Carlos Illescas called "Standoff 'wasn't like' suspect." After speaking to friends and relatives of the man, the reporter learned that despite "several run-ins with supervisors," he was known to the people around him as "a doting father figure, an avid fisherman and a man who dreamed of selling aquariums made of wine bottles." The story by Cate Terwilliger that emphasized the psychological aspect of workplace violence, "Seizing of workers 'rageful,' experts say," added to the picture of the man as a human being by explaining how a seemingly decent person could be forced to do such a horrible thing. Drawing on what she learned from speaking to a variety of "experts," she wrote that the "Christmas Eve hostage-taking was an 'incredibly angry and rageful' act that may have been triggered by a dangerous mix of holiday depression, financial woes and a chronic sense of being victimized and unappreciated, experts said Wednesday."

The villain of the story was finally identified in a *Denver Post* story by Cindy Brovsky called "Security called lax at facility." She opened the story with the words, "Employees at Denver's regional mail center said job stress combined with unreasonable management expectations have caused numerous morale problems in the past few months." Then, she went on to quote a representative of the local postal workers who pointed the finger at the Postal Service. "'This was a nightmare waiting to occur in Denver,' said Paul Mendrick, president of the Denver Local American Postal Workers Union. 'This is happening at post offices across the country, and this time it was our turn.'" Brovsky included a few words from Postal Service representatives and a few other postal workers who did not see things quite the same way, but then returned to the union steward, who again focused on management, specifically the ability of management to maintain a secure workplace. She quoted Wendy Thoreaux as saying, "Their security system has been a sham since it was installed."

None of the Denver news stories said anything about the overall number of cases of violence by postal workers, or anything about the extent to which violence is more or less common among postal workers as compared to other workers. Neither did the stories in most of the other newspapers. The *Chicago Tribune* and the *Washington Post* cited Roy Betts, the Postal Service spokesperson, as saying that, nationwide, there are about 20 people killed in the workplace each week, and with 800,000 employees the post offices around the country are likely to have their share. The *Washington Post* concluded its story with another statistic attributed to Mr. Betts: "[T]he number of assaults by one employee on another had declined from 488 in 1995 to 436 in fiscal 1997." If that number is accurate, then we can estimate that no more than 0.05% of all 800,000 postal employees in 1997 participated in an act of interpersonal violence against a fellow employee.

The story of the postal worker losing control and becoming violent is one that has become almost as familiar as a recurring childhood nightmare. In the United States during the last years of the twentieth century, a new phrase describing when a worker becomes violent entered the lexicon: "going postal." That being the case, perhaps we should avoid all contact with the Postal Service. But how extensive really is the problem of violence by postal workers—or any workers—who have lost control? And how does the risk of violence by disgruntled or otherwise fractious workers compare to the risk resulting from other forms of violence that emanate from the world of work and business? For example, how does it compare to the risk from corporate offending? This chapter looks at the stories we tell and claims we make about violence related to the workplace and includes a discussion of that violence in the context of official crime, health, and occupational statistics and relevant research.

The Relationship among Work, Daily Life, and Violence

When the story of a man becoming violent in his workplace involves people and places we know, we are better able to see that it is more than just a story of workplace violence. Because a man or woman becomes violent at the place where he or she works does not always mean that his or her violent actions were related to that workplace.

Throughout the evening of March 6, 1998, the network, local, and cable television news stations told the story of a man identified as a "lottery worker" who had killed his boss and several coworkers. That night, an Associated Press version of the story by Strat Douthat found its way onto the World Wide Web home pages of newspapers across the country. A story on Washingtonpost.com called "Gunman Kills 4, Self in Connecticut" began, "A state lottery accountant who returned from stress-related disability only last week gunned down three supervisors, then chased down the lottery chief in the parking lot and killed him, too."

March 6 was a Friday, and the story of the state lottery employee Matthew E. Beck continued to receive media attention throughout the weekend. On March 7, in the *Washington Post* was a front-page story by Blaine Harden called "Worker Kills Four at Conn. Lottery." Harden wrote, "The shooting in this bedroom suburb five miles south of Hartford fit a grisly American pattern of lethal violence in the workplace, a pattern that in recent years has claimed about 120 lives a year, according to Joseph Kinney, executive director of the nonprofit National Safe Workplace Institute in Charlotte, N.C." The account continued with more information about workplace violence, including estimates of its costs, tips for workplace security, and a listing of six of the "several recent workplace shootings in the United States."

That same day, the story appeared in the Baltimore *Sun* under the headline, "Conn. man fatally shoots supervisors, then himself." The account, from wire reports, summarized what was known to have happened, with a mention of the "stress-related problems" that the worker had been experiencing. The cover of the *New York Post* that day declared in large, bold letters, "Gunman's chilling words as he executes his bosses—BYE, BYE!" The next two pages were given to three different stories, along with photographs of the gunman, his victims, and the scene. The headline across most of the two inside pages read, "CONNECTICUT LOTTERY BLOOD-BATH." That story, by Angela Mosconi in Connecticut and Tracy Conner in New York, provided the details of how "[a]n accountant carrying a grudge and a semi-automatic pistol gunned down the chief of the Connecticut state lottery and three other supervisors yesterday—and then blew his brains out." A related story by Angela Mosconi was about the people who were killed. Another related story by Angela Mosconi was called "Massacre capped slayer's long slide into depression" and told about the mental health problems of the young man who had shot his coworkers.

The focus of all these accounts of the shooting were on workplace violence. They largely told the story of a man who had lost control and turned work-related stress into violence against other workers. A few mentioned the man's history of mental illness, but even those typically emphasized that his mental health problems were related to the stress of his job. In that local readers would be more likely to be familiar with the people and situations involved, I was interested in how this story was presented in the community where it had happened.

On the afternoon of March 9, just days after the violent assault, I entered the World Wide Web and worked my way through the CNN channel to the home page of the *Hartford Courant*. I clicked on the word *lottery* and was transfered to a page with the heading, "SPECIAL REPORT: Lottery Shooting." Below that were two subheadings. "Latest Stories" listed four articles: one about the physical damage of the violence, another about security measures being considered, a third about the ways that surviving workers were dealing with their fears, and the fourth about the surviving husband of one of the victims.

The second subheading of the special report, "Recent Stories," listed 21 articles that had been published in the newspaper since the violent event had occurred. A few of these were specifically about the shooting, such as "Worker Kills 4 at Lottery Headquarters" and "Horrified Workers Witness Killing." Most of these, however, were about people. There were articles about the people who died, such as "New Britain Mourns Loss of Former Mayor" and "A 'Most Solid Family Man' Loses His Life." There were articles about the ways in which the community was grieving, and articles about the letter of apology written by the parents of the young man who had committed the violence. And there were articles about the mental health of the young man and about the things that people who knew him knew about his problems, problems not limited to his workplace experience.

In "When A Job Is All That Matters," written by Liz Halloran and Andrew Julien for the *Courant* on March 8, 1998, the reporters quoted Dr. Leslie M. Lothstein, "director of psychology at the Institute of Living/Hartford Hospital," as saying, "Stressful environments don't create murderers. This is a person who has suffered very much in his life, and he really wanted to kill himself. But he wanted to take down everyone with him." The doctor did not know Beck, but people who did had seen evidence that her assessment was correct. On March 7, "Friends Saw Anger Growing in Beck," an article by Andrew Julien, Lyn Bixby, and Colin Poitras, noted that about a year earlier Beck had suffered an "emotional breakdown" and had been "hospitalized twice." According to a man identified as a "close friend" of Beck, the problem was related to a "combination of personal problems and difficulties at work." On March 8, the *Courant* published "Lottery gunman's parents: 'We love you Matt—but why?'" According to that article, which did mention the salary dispute that was the focus of Beck's grievance with his employer, the young man's father told reporters that "his youngest son's adult life had been marked by a battle against depression and several suicide attempts." His father further told them that the young man "had been under a doctor's care and on prescribed medications for his depression since January, 1997."

Certainly, Matthew Beck did face stress in relation to his job. There was the grievance about his salary, and there was the frustration over limited opportunities for advancement. But those are not unusual. What made the case of Matthew Beck different was his inability to cope with that stress. The anger or rage that grew into violence could have evolved in the context of any stressful situation. In this case, as Halloran and Julien pointed out in "When A Job Is All That Matters," for Matthew Beck "the workplace became the ultimate stage for the expression of his rage." So, despite the way the story was told by the media around the country, locally it was the story of a young man unable to cope with the conditions of his life and how the people of his community suffered as a result.

What may present itself to a distant public as the story of a worker gone mad over working conditions or disputes with fellow workers may be better understood as the story of a man or woman with a troubled life. Such was the case of Matthew Beck in Connecticut. His was the story of a young man unable to cope with life in general. His was a story of mental health. When, then, can we say that an act of violence is actually related to the workplace?

Defining Workplace Violence

In Chapter 1, violence was defined generally as social activity that threatens, attempts, or uses physical force for the purpose of gaining dominance (broadly defined) over others. It was also acknowledged that this is a narrow definition of violence, limited only to violence in the social arena. It was suggested, however, that even from this narrow view, it is apparent that what we call violence is dependent on who we are, where we are placed in society, and how violence is defined and measured for us as members of the public.

In terms of the workplace, there are several different social activities that could be viewed as forms of violence. Workplace violence could be the product of what workers do, as in the case of workers who physically assault coworkers or consumers. Or workplace violence could be what happens to workers at their workplace, such as accidents that are the result of intentional negligence by management. Or workplace violence could be viewed in terms of the impact on workers, consumers, or the public generally as a result of corporate decisions and actions, such as death or disease related to the intentional dumping of toxic waste.

Books and reports with the words *workplace violence* in their titles are typically about violence by workers. Effectively, then, they contribute to the social construction of the meaning of violence related to the workplace. In *Workplace Violence—A Continuum from Threat to Death*, Millie Southerland and her associates open by reminding readers that, in 1984, when he was surgeon general of the United States, C. Everett Koop declared violence in the workplace to be a significant public health problem.[1] Then, based on a content analysis of news accounts, they define workplace violence as any violent incident that occurs at a site that can be classified as a workplace and involves the relationship of a worker to that setting.[2] *Workplace Violence: Before, During, and After* by Sandra Heskett is more immediately practical, being about the need to deal with and how to deal with workers who "use threatening or intimidating actions" to get their way, workers whom she suggests are acting abnormally.[3] With support from the federal Bureau of Justice Assistance, in the middle of the 1990s the International Association of Chiefs of Police published a bulletin called *Combating Workplace Violence— Guidelines for Employers and Law Enforcement*. In it, the association suggests that worker violence is a serious problem that needs programs to effectively deal with it; it then goes on to suggest such programs.[4]

The social meaning of workplace violence is also influenced by the data available to study its scope and nature. Because they are more readily available, data about workplace homicides are often used in studies of workplace violence. Having based their analysis of workplace violence on newspaper articles, Southerland and her associates argued that their selection of this secondary data source was appropriate since the sources of data traditionally used to study workplace violence (including "death certificates from each states' vital statistics reporting unit, workers compensation claims, OSHA [Occupational Safety and Health Administration] fatality files, and organization surveys") have resulted in a focus of this research on only those incidents that result in death.[5]

The Bureau of Labor Statistics (BLS) conducts an annual Census of Fatal Occupational Injuries that is used to compile an account of the number of workplace homicides in the United States. For that compilation, data are collected "in cooperation with Federal, State, and local administrative sources including death certificates, workers' compensation reports and claims, medical examiner reports, police reports, and reports to various regulatory agencies."[6] In 1995, there were 1,024 workplace homicides reported through this program, with 80 percent involving wage and salary workers, 76 percent involving males, more than half involving people between the ages of 25 and 44, 65 percent involving whites, and 74 percent involving shootings.[7]

Of the 1,024 reported workplace homicides in 1995, 71 percent involved a robbery or other crime, and only 11 percent involved a relationship between work associates.[8] That is, arguably no more than 113 people were killed when one of their fellow workers lost control and became violent. Each of these 113 deaths is a personal tragedy, but in a nation with more than 130 million working people known to the BLS, all together they are not a widespread social problem.

As should be clear by this time, however, claims makers of social problems are not apt to allow statistical findings or conclusions to interfere with their claims making. From an analysis of a variety of statistics and research reports about murder in the workplace, Michael Kelleher[9] concluded that, from 1980 to 1989, homicide accounted for only 12 percent of all fatalities in the workplace, and the annual rate of workplace homicide was about half the annual rate of workplace fatalities due to automobile accidents.[10] Those findings did not prevent him from declaring that "[v]iolence in the workplace is now at epidemic levels,"[11] from devoting the rest of his book to identifying the behavioral characteristics of violent workers, or from suggesting ways to prevent lethal violence by these workers.

This is not to say that people being killed by coworkers in the workplace is not a problem. But a much greater number of people are estimated annually to be victims of nonlethal violence in their workplaces. Using National Crime Victimization Survey (NCVS) statistics, the Bureau of Justice Statistics (BJS) in 1994 concluded that annually nearly 1 million individuals became victims of violent crime while working.[12] More recently, using the same survey data, a BJS report showed that annually between 1992 and 1996, compared to 1,000 workplace homicides, there were reportedly about 1.5 million simple assaults and 396,000 aggravated assaults.[13] Still, all cases of violent victimization in the workplace, lethal and nonlethal, represent only about 15 percent of all violent victimizations reported to BJS.[14]

The task of properly measuring and defining the problem of workplace violence is further complicated in that the number of people who report they are victims of intentional workplace violence pales in comparison to the number of ostensibly unintentional deaths and injuries involving people simply doing their jobs in the workplace. Each year, the National Safety Council (NSC) uses data from the BLS, the National Center for Health Statistics (NCHS), and state vital statistics and industrial commission reports to estimate the extent and costs of unintentional injuries and deaths of U.S. workers while doing their jobs. In 1996, reportedly more than 126 million workers in all industries suffered unintentional injuries while at work, including 4,800 who died and 3.9 million who suffered a disabling injury.[15] Proportional to the size of the workforce, these numbers have declined dramatically over the course of the twentieth century. According to the NSC report, "Between 1912 and 1996, unintentional work deaths per 100,000 population were reduced 90%, from 21 to 2."[16] This is good news. Nonetheless, 4,800 deaths is considerably more than 1,024 deaths, and 126 million injuries is far greater than 1 or 2 million violent victimizations, not all of which necessarily result in injury. If these unintentional deaths and injuries are, in fact, avoidable, then perhaps we need to think differently about workplace violence.

Corporate Violence

Thus far, we have considered definitions of workplace violence in terms of the death or injury of people in work settings due to violent actions by individuals against other individuals. Another way to look at workplace death or injury that has a greater impact than violence at the hands of workers gone mad is what Ronald Kramer called "corporate violence," which he defined as "corporate behavior which produces an unreasonable risk of physical harm to employees, the general public, and consumers, which is the result of deliberate decision-making by persons who occupy positions as corporation managers or executives, which is organizationally based, and which is intended to benefit the corporation itself."[17] Similarly, in his anthology on the subject, sociologist Stuart Hills defined corporate violence as "actual harm and risk of harm inflicted on consumers, workers, and the general public as a result of decisions by corporate executives or managers, from corporate negligence, the quest for profits at any cost, and willful violations of health, safety, and environmental laws."[18]

While there is not a single or comprehensive source of data that estimates the extent of death or injury from corporate violence, accounts such as those described in the Hills anthology show that the risk and actual occurrence of death or injury from corporate violence is perhaps greater than that of all other sources of workplace violence. One well-known example is the case of the Ford Pinto, a story originally told by Mark Dowie in *Mother Jones* in 1977 and reprinted in Hills's book. Dowie reviewed and reported on secret Ford Motor Company documents that showed that for seven years Ford corporate executives sold an estimated 11 million cars that they knew could burst into flames upon impact in even a slow rear-end collision, thereby saving no more than $11 dollars per car in manufacturing costs.[19] Dowie argued that studies by independent consultants and the Highway Traffic Research Institute had shown that the lives of 40 percent of the 3,000 people who died annually in 400,000 automobile fires could have been saved had automobile manufacturers complied with proposed industry regulations.[20]

Naturally, automobile manufacturers were not quick to agree with the Dowie's claims. Both he and they can be seen as claims makers, as can others who describe cases of what they consider corporate violence and those corporate managers and executives who argue that they are wrong. Given that the potential number of victims of corporate violence is so great, and given the enormous amounts of money involved,[21] claims from both sides about corporate violence are not uncommon.

On December 28, 1986, in an editorial column in the *Washington Post*, Taft Broome, then director of the Large Space Structure Institute at Howard University and chair of the ethics committee of the American Association of Engineering Societies, looked at the responsibility of engineers for corporate violence.

Until now, engineers would have been judged wicked or demented if they were discovered blatantly ignoring the philosopher Cicero's 2,000-year-old imperative: In whatever you build, "the safety of the public shall be the highest law." Today, however, the Ford Pinto, Three-Mile Island, Bhopal, the Challenger, Chernobyl and other technological horror stories tell of a cancer growing on our values. These engineering disasters are the results of willful actions. Yet these actions are generally not seen by engineers as being morally wrong. They are judged to be ordinary. What's more, some engineers now espouse a morality that explicitly rejects the notion that they have as their prime responsibility the maintenance of public safety.

Even if he is correct, an engineer pointing his finger at engineers, engineers alone are not to blame. Still, to the extent that he is correct, events such as those he mentions account for potentially enormous amounts of violent death and injury. Of course, claims are made on both side of the argument.

Consider the nuclear energy industry. On August 31, 1989, an article in the *Washington Post* called "Reactor Cracks Detected" reported from news service reports that "[a] television camera lowered into Three Mile Island's damaged Unit 2 reactor confirmed small cracks in a steel liner." Recalling what happened in 1979, local citizens became alarmed. In 1979, the worst accident in the history of the U.S. nuclear power industry occurred at Three Mile Island (TMI) in Pennsylvania. Just months before the crack was discovered, around the tenth anniversary of the original TMI accident, an article by Cass Peterson of the *Washington Post* appeared on March 28, 1989, recalling that accident. According to that news account, "A malfunctioning pump, a stuck valve and a series of operator errors had combined to drain water from the core of the reactor, exposing its intensely hot and highly radioactive fuel rods. In industry vernacular, the reactor had suffered a 'LOCA'—a loss-of-cooling accident—so perilous that it is the 'worst-case scenario' in the safety manuals." Reportedly, at that time, industry officials tried to calm people living in the area by telling them that "[t]he containment features of the reactor worked, holding in what utility officials estimate was 18 billion curies of radioactivity—more than 100 times the amount believed to have been released in the 1986 nuclear accident at the Chernobyl reactor in the Soviet Union." Thirty-one people died in Chernobyl, and no one died in Pennsylvania. So, industry officials claimed there was nothing to fear. Still, people living in the area were concerned about the long-term health effects. The industry assured them it was safe. When a year later Gordon MacLeod, the Pennsylvania health secretary, "found an abnormal number of thyroid problems in newborns in three counties surrounding TMI," he was "abruptly replaced." Then, in 1981, the state epidemiology director concluded that "the accident would cause 'no significant physical health effects.'" Still, residents worried. Over time, they experienced unexplained symptoms, including "a 'metallic taste' in their mouths immediately after the accident" and, of greater concern, "skin rashes, nausea and respiratory problems." Apparently, they need not have worried. According to the news account, "Medical experts dismissed the complaints as symptoms of stress." Nonetheless, 200,000 people fled their homes, 2,000 people filed physical injury lawsuits, and $1 billion were spent cleaning up the mess. According to the article, the reactor could not be used again and has since become a tourist attraction.

Of course, it could be argued that even if thousands of people had died, the TMI incident was not a case of corporate violence, in that any death or injury from the accident was not necessarily the result of malicious or indifferent corporate decision making. Unfortunately, that conclusion is not so easily reached. On December 21, 1987, in the *Washington Post* was an article by Cass Peterson called "NRC Bows to Industry, Panel Says." The article began, "The Nuclear Regulatory Commission [NRC] has an 'unhealthy empathy' for the industry it regulates and is compromising public health and safety in its zeal to promote nuclear power, a House subcommittee [the House Interior and Insular Affairs oversight subcommittee] report charged yesterday." Effectively, though without explicitly saying so, the House panel was claiming that accidents such as the one at TMI were, in fact, examples of corporate violence. Naturally, not everyone agreed. According to the article, "Three Democratic members signed the report; two Republican members signed a brief dissent calling it 'overly critical and in some instances vicious.'" In addition, Lando W. Zech, Jr., then chair of the NRC, was quoted as saying that, despite not having yet read the report, he was of the opinion that the NRC had been "a tough regulator," as evidenced by the closing of 10 nuclear power plants in the United States for safety reasons. Those supporting the claim being made by the report argued, that despite the closings, "commission members and top agency officials have repeatedly bowed to industry pressure on such critical issues as drug abuse and fire prevention in nuclear power plants."

In another article by the same reporter just a few months earlier, on April 2, 1987, the *Washington Post* published an article called "NRC's June Report Praised Reactor's Staff." The subtitle was "Agency now cites 'total disregard' for duties as reason for immediate shutdown." Apparently, after the NRC inspected the Peach Bottom nuclear power plant in Delta Pennsylvania, in June 1986, the commission wrote that the plant was "operated by well-qualified individuals with a positive attitude toward their positions and for nuclear safety." Then, after it was learned that reactor operators were literally asleep on the job, the NRC closed the plant accusing those "well-qualified individuals with a positive attitude" of "sleeping on the job in 'total disregard' for their duties" and "a lack of appreciation for what those duties entail."

The nuclear industry is not the only industry about which questions of corporate violence can be raised. Remember the Ford Pinto. The Ford Motor Company, however, is not the only automobile manufacturer that has been accused of corporate violence. On October 23, 1988, an article appeared on the first page of the *Washington Post* as part of a series on courts and justice. Written by Elsa Walsh and Benjamin Weiser, it was called "Court Secrecy Masks Safety Issues." It claimed that General Motors had deliberately developed a strategy to hide its liability for the death and injury from auto crashes involving a poorly placed fuel tank.

> Over the last five years, in defending itself against scores of lawsuits filed by victims of fiery car crashes, General Motors Corp. has used court secrecy procedures throughout the nation to keep closely held and controversial documents about auto safety from becoming public. GM's legal approach, which is becoming a favored way of preventing the disclosure of sensitive information in civil lawsuits, has helped avoid a public debate about whether the company placed financial considerations ahead of safety concerns in designing the fuel tanks used in most GM cars until the early 1980s. Fuel leaks are a key factor in starting fires, which can cause deaths in otherwise survivable accidents. The documents that have been kept from public view show that company officials were told in 1970 that the gas tank was vulnerable to puncture during some high-speed crashes. In 1971, the company decided not to move the tank to a more protected location after top engineers concluded that the traditional design was adequate, and that the design change was too expensive and would reduce trunk space. GM's estimates for the cost of the change ranged from $8.59 a car to $11.59.

The reporters noted that while General Motors officials would not respond to requests for interviews during litigation, they did suggest that the memoranda were being read out of context and that the placement of the gas tank was as safe as it could be "given that cars cannot be made totally safe and still be affordable."

Conclusion

A tale is "a narrative of real or imaginary events," a story that emphasizes happenings over character.[22] When the site of a killing or other violence is a workplace, more attention is given by public observers to the setting and happenings than is given to the people involved and their character or life experiences. As told by the national media, this was clearly the case in the story of Matthew Beck of Connecticut when he was charged with shooting at coworkers in March 1998. Similarly, stories about individuals who commit violence in the workplace are somehow more interesting than stories about corporations whose executives and managers take actions and make decisions that result in real or potential injury or death among their workers, consumers, or both.

If available measures clearly show that death and injury due to corporate violence far exceed death and injury due to the actions of individual workers at their workplace, why do claims makers emphasize violence by individuals rather than violence by corporations? If closer examination of stories about individual workers who become violent at their workplaces demonstrates that the violent actions of such workers often is related to psychological or social issues unrelated to their work experience, why do claims makers stress the context of work when telling these stories rather than the context of mental health or family life?

The mass media in the United States serves not only as a social institution to inform the public, but also as a business institution, the primary function of which is to earn the greatest possible profit for its shareholders.[23] The communications received by local community people either in print or over airwaves are not simply the product of things local people want to share with their neighbors and friends but also are the product of corporate activity and decision making. Consider the following examples, taken from the Web sites of selected communications corporations, of the extent of corporate control over local media.

- The Hearst Corporation considers itself "one of the nation's largest diversified communications companies, with interests in magazine, newspaper, book and business publishing; television and radio stations; newspaper comics and feature syndication; cable television networks; television production and syndication; and news media activities." The 12 daily and 7 weekly newspapers published by the Hearst Corporation include the *Houston Chronicle*, the *San Francisco Examiner*, the Albany (NY) *Times Union*, and the *Seattle Post-Intelligencer*.

- Gannett Company identifies itself as "a large diversified news and information company in the USA" with approximately 39,000 employees, 280 million shares of common stock held by 14,000 shareholders, and operating revenue in 1997 of $4.7 million. The company publishes 84 daily newspapers, including *USA Today* ("the largest-selling daily newspaper, with a circulation of approximately 2 million") as well as owning and operating "21 television stations covering 16.6 percent of the USA" and participating in several other business ventures.

- The Times Mirror Company "publishes five metropolitan and two suburban daily newspapers" including the *Los Angeles Times*, the Baltimore *Sun*, and the *Hartford Courant*. The company also considers itself "the nation's leading publisher of leisure-oriented, special-interest magazines, reaching nearly 40 million readers each month." On its Web page, the company explained its plan in 1995 to improve its financial performance as follows: "To achieve its financial goals, the company exited a number of businesses where it did not have a competitive advantage; streamlined operations and improved efficiencies; and took a number of steps to reinvigorate its remaining businesses, all while sustaining editorial, product and service excellence."

There is nothing wrong with being a corporation. The problem is that while the mission of a corporation acting as a business may be to serve its customers or to fulfill a public need, the sine qua non of such a corporation is to maximize its profits. Therefore, in making decisions, and hence making claims, about what is workplace violence—for example, whether acts of individuals that result in death or injury should be given more attention than acts of corporations that have similar outcomes—the media are not neutral observers and reporters. Neither are business consultants.

The job of a consultant is to provide information and advice to organizations and agencies. To make organizations and agencies interested in the information or advice they have to offer, they engage in activities, such as writing books, to advertise or sell themselves or their program. Consider, for example, the consultant described earlier who wrote a book offering ideas about how to prevent lethal violence by workers, this after showing in his book that lethal violence by workers accounts for only a small proportion of all workplace fatalities and is a much smaller problem than deaths of workers due to automobile accidents.[24]

Consider also a book by Marianne Minor, a social worker and management consultant. Her book is a self-study guide with exercises, activities, assessments, and cases designed to be used individually or at workshops and seminars to train people to deal with workplace violence.[25] She defines workplace violence broadly as "any situation that may: increase in intensity and threaten the safety of an employee, have an impact on any employee's physical and/or psychological well-being, [or] cause damage to company property." Yet, she limits her examples to actions involving individuals, particularly workers, such as "threats," "work-related conflict," "personal conflict," "taking hostages," or "attack by an outsider."[26] She also cites statistics (such as "[h]omicide in the workplace is the fastest growing form of murder; the rate has doubled in the past 10 years") and makes statements (such as "[m]ost U.S. companies have no plan to deal with the crises of violence in the workplace"), though she does not support them with citations or place in them in context.[27] No matter. They nicely lead the reader to the program she has to offer, and the book concludes with checklists, worksheets, guidelines, and case studies to help businesses get started before they call in a consultant to help them solve this problem.

Endnotes

1. Southerland, M. D., Collins, P. A., and Scarborough, K. E. (1997). *Workplace Violence—A Continuum from Threat to Death*. Cincinnati: Anderson, p. 1.

2. Southerland, Collins and Scarborough 1997:21.

3. Heskett, S. L. (1996). *Workplace Violence: Before, During, and After*. Boston: Butterworth-Heinemann, pp. 12–14.

4. Timm, H. W. and Chandler, C. J. (n.d.) *Combating Workplace Violence—Guidelines for*

Employers and Law Enforcement. Alexandria, VA: International Association of Chiefs of Police, p. 1.

   5. Southerland et al. 1997:20.

   6. Maguire, K. and Pastore, A.L. (eds.). (1997). *Sourcebook of Criminal Justice Statistics 1996*. U.S. Department of Justice, Bureau of Justice Statistics. Washington, DC: U.S. Government Printing Office, p. 342.

   7. Maguire and Pastore 1997:342.

   8. Maguire and Pastore 1997:342.

   9. According to the note at the back of his book, Kelleher is a consultant who "specializes in strategic management, human resource management, staff education, and in threat assessment and management crisis resolution for organizations in the public and private sectors."

   10. Kelleher, M. D. (1996). *New Arenas for Violence—Homicide in the American Workplace*. Westport, CT: Praeger, p. 19.

   11. Kelleher 1996:20.

   12. Bachman, R. (1994). *Violence and Theft in the Workplace*. Crime Data Brief. Washington, DC: Bureau of Justice Statistics, p. 1.

   13. Warchol, G. (1998). *Workplace Violence, 1992–96*. Bureau of Justice Statistics Special Report. Washington, DC: Bureau of Justice Statistics, p. 2.

   14. Bachman 1994:1.

   15. National Safety Council. (1997). *Accident Facts 1997 Edition*. Itasca, IL: National Safety Council, p. 48.

   16. National Safety Council 1997: 48.

   17. Kramer, R. C. (1983). "A Prolegomena to the Study of Corporate Violence." *Humanity and Society* 7:166.

   18. Hills, S.L. (ed.) (1987) *Corporate Violence—Injury and Death for Profit*. Totowa, NJ: Rowan and Littlefield, p. vii.

   19. Dowie, M. (1987). "Pinto Madness." Pp. 13–29 in S. L. Hills (ed.), *Corporate Violence—Injury and Death for Profit*. Totowa, NJ: Rowan and Littlefield, pp. 15, 21.

   20. Dowie 1987:23–24.

   21. See Derber, C. (1996). *The Wilding of America—How Greed and Violence Are Eroding Our Nation's Character*. New York: St. Martin's. Hills 1987. Reiman, J. (1998). *The Rich Get Richer and the Poor Get Prison—Ideology, Class, and Criminal Justice*. Boston: Allyn and Bacon.

   22. *The American Heritage Dictionary of the English Language*. Third Edition. Electronic version. 1992. Houghton Mifflin.

   23. Brownstein, H. H. (1991). "The Media and the Construction of Random Drug Violence." *Social Justice* 18:85–103. Koch, T. (1990). *The News as Myth—Fact and Context in Journalism*. New York: Greenwood. Lee, A.M. (1973). *The Daily Newspaper in America—The Evolution of a Social Instrument*. New York: Octagon Press; Lee, A. M. (1988). *Sociology for People—Toward a Caring Profession*. Syracuse, NY: Syracuse University Press. Mayer, M. (1987). *Making News*. Garden City, NY: Doubleday.

   24. Kelleher 1996.

   25. Minor, M. (1995). *Preventing Workplace Violence—Positive Management Strategies*. Menlo Park, CA: Crisp Publications.

   26. Minor 1995:3, 4.

   27. Minor 1995:5.

10

The Social Reality of
Violence and Violent Crime

One morning late into the winter of 1998, just weeks before the cherry blossoms reached their full bloom in our nation's capital, I went to the National Museum of American Art to see an exhibition of photographs by Ansel Adams. Adams is best known for his pictures of natural settings, especially our national parks, and especially Yellowstone. His images in black and white reveal the beauty of a place in ways you would never have imagined possible, even a place you had seen for yourself.

I drifted quietly from room to room looking at pictures from places like Yellowstone in California, Monument Valley in Utah, and Santa Fe in New Mexico. Then, in the midst of these magnificent and majestic scenes from nature, I saw a picture of a rose placed purposefully on a piece of plywood. The marker on the wall said it was called "Rose and Driftwood, California, 1942." Adams knew this picture of a rose from his mother's garden would puzzle people accustomed to his scenic landscapes, so he included it in his book, *Examples: The Making of 40 Photographs*. In that book, he describes how he had conceived of and then fashioned 40 different photographs. The image of the rose on a piece of wood is a "contrived subject," while most of his other photographs are pictures of "found objects."[1] Found objects, he suggests, are there to be found and are then "subject to analytic consideration," while contrived subjects are purposefully and consciously arranged to make a statement before their image is taken.[2] In this sense, the beauty of the photograph of a found object is in the likeness of the object as reflected through the eyes of the photographer.

Reading about the rose that Ansel Adams found in his mother's garden, it occurred to me that, like the beauty of Adams's pictures of nature, the violence of a social act essentially is a social and cultural reflection of a found object. We observe people acting and then see the act as violent when our eyes reflect on it as an act of brutality or coercive domination. That is, we define a social act as violent when we recognize and understand it as an attempt by one or more people to force their dominance over others. The question is who holds the lenses to the action so that its reflection appears to us as violent. From what we have seen in each of the preceding chapters, it should be clear that the people holding the lenses are the people social scientists refer to as claims makers.

Whereas action by itself is just movement, social action is meaningful. Action becomes social when it involves people sharing a common experience.[3] To be able to know how to act in relation to one another, the people involved give meaning to the ways they act toward each other. That meaning is grounded in a social and cultural context, so the meaning attached to an action can be derived from how people define themselves and how they define their relationship with the others. For example, people who consider themselves friends will act differently toward one another than will people who consider themselves business associates. Or it can be derived from how people define the objective or purpose of their action. For example, athletes trying to win a game might use force during the game in ways that they might not in other social situations. Without such a context or framework through which to interpret them, it cannot be known for certain what particular acts or actions mean, or what the person doing them means to do. If a person runs into another person and knocks that person down, does that necessarily mean he or she is trying to hurt the other person? Maybe not, for example, if they are playing hockey or football.

Claims makers—from individuals acting as moral entrepreneurs to participants in organized social movements or groups—compete to provide the context or framework through which we interpret and understand social actions. They try to convince us that we should attach particular meanings to particular actions. To do so, they must make simple what is inherently complex, to explain what is intrinsically enigmatic. Stories are often used to simplify and make meaningful what is otherwise confusing and abstruse. The stories we tell about violence have been and continue to be used in this way. Throughout this book, we have seen how the ongoing competition among claims makers has shaped our knowledge and understanding of the nature and extent of violence in our society.

The Measure of Violence and Violent Crime

In the winter of 1991, when the annual number of officially recorded violent crimes in the United States was still climbing and just before anyone had noticed that it was about to begin falling, Christopher Jencks asked a simple question. In the title to an article in *The American Prospect*, he asked, "Is Violent Crime Increasing?"[4] In the article, Jencks did not argue that at that time the violent crime rate, or even violent crime itself, was not higher than it had been "at many times in the past." However, after considering the impact of the mass media, government statistics, law enforcement estimates, social and cultural conditions, demographic trends, and shifts in public policy and values, he concluded, "Few subjects inspire as much nonsense as violent crime."[5]

The point Jencks was making was that whatever violent crime is or is not, and however much of it there is or is not, as a social concept it serves political purposes very well. Violence may be difficult to define and measure, but it nonetheless has great symbolic value. Whatever it is and however much of it there is, people know they would rather avoid being its victim. So, as Jencks noted, politicians from both major political parties in the United States welcome the opportunity to run a campaign "in which they fault their opponent for being 'soft' on crime."[6] Similarly, policy makers and practitioners are encouraged to develop policies, programs, and practices that can show constituents an immediate and apparent, if not real, impact on violence. Unfortunately, without a clear and precise definition of what we mean by violence and a reliable and valid measure of how much of it there is, any claims made about violence inevitably are misleading.

Chapter 1 discussed the various ways in which violence has been officially defined and measured. It was noted that, in the United States, concepts used to define violence and statistics used to estimate its extent are typically derived from the worlds of public health or criminal justice, with criminal justice definitions and statistics predominating. That said, it has become common practice for any serious scholar writing about violence in the late twentieth century to remind his or her readers that violence, as well as the more narrow concept of violent crime, is neither easily nor precisely measured. For example, writing for the Committee on Law and Justice of the Panel on Understanding and Control of Violent Behavior of the National Research Council, Albert Reiss and Jeffrey Roth wrote, "There is no single way to define, classify, and measure the domain of violent events, because each counting system involves some evaluation of people's observations and reports of what they perceive as violent events."[7] Similarly, writing specifically about crime statistics, Victor Kappeler and his associates wrote, "Crime statistics must be treated with great caution and not an inconsiderable amount of skepticism."[8]

In the end, we do not have any precise or simple measure of violence in our society. We do not even have agreement on how to define violence, or when and how to identify particular acts or actions as violent. An article in the *Sun* on August 4, 1998, was called "Reported rapes in Balto. increase." In the article, Jamie Stiehm reported that, according to the Baltimore police, given its rate of occurrence over the first six months of the year, the total number of rapes reported to them would be greater in 1998 than it had been in the previous year. As a police spokesperson told the reporter, however, an increase in reported rapes does not necessarily mean more rapes occured. The increase may actually reflect a change in how rape was being defined by people in Baltimore. The article quoted Lt. Frederick Taber, head of the department's unit responsible for investigating sex offenses and child abuse, as saying, "Before, females thought they couldn't be raped by their husband or ex-boyfriend." With a growing awareness in the city that marital or acquaintance rape is still rape, in 1998, 53 percent of the people in Baltimore who reported being raped knew the person they said had raped them, compared to only 45 percent in 1997.

The problem of knowing how much violence there is in society is further complicated in relation to the problem of what we mean by violence. We do not agree about when to recognize a behavior or activity we do define as violent as a social problem, demanding a greater share of our public resources. For example, during the school year from September 1997 to June 1998, the national news media reported on at least nine different instances in which a student arrived at school with a gun and opened fire on classmates and teachers, often killing and wounding several of them. After one such shooting in Oregon, on May 22, 1998, the New York *Daily News* listed eight previous incidents under the heading "Young and Dangerous—Kids slaughtering kids to settle scores at small-town schools has become an all-too-common phenomenon recently." That same day, the *New York Post* ran an editorial among its reports of the Oregon incident called "Idyllic small towns face the same woes as our inner cities." The next day, the Baltimore *Sun* had a cover story called, "School violence's 'contagion effect.'"

With a grant from the Annie E. Casey Foundation, known for its concern for children, the Justice Policy Institute of the Center on Juvenile and Criminal Justice produced a report to place the events in a meaningful context. Acknowledging that children do face some threats to their safety in society or in schools, the authors of the report examined available research and statistics and concluded, for example, that "children face a one in a million chance of being killed at school," that "school shooting deaths have declined slightly since 1992," and that "the number of children killed by gun violence in schools is about half the number of Americans killed annually by lightning strikes."[9] Nonetheless, in 1998, it was easy to convince frightened parents and outraged taxpayers to support the suspension and expulsion from school of youngsters involved in offenses that otherwise would be considered minor, to reduce or even eliminate afterschool programs, and even to pay for more police officers in schools and for the processing of more youngsters in the adult criminal justice system.[10]

In that we cannot measure or even know for certain what we mean by violence, we are able to disagree about how much violence there is and about which expressions or forms of social action are to be considered acts of violence. We are able to argue for different positions. Relative to our cultural heritage and our social position, the position we advocate can be related to our own interests, our own values, or both. Positions on violence in society then become linked within the contexts of culture and social structure to particular personal or political agendas. In that sense, it becomes possible for people to recognize particular acts as violent or a particular magnitude of such acts as problematic when to do so serves particular interests or conforms to particular sets of values. Or, it is also possible for people to advocate for a position that is based not on what they want or believe they need or deserve, but simply on the basis of their feelings or their sense of virtue.

The Social Reality of Violence and Violent Crime in the United States

By now, it should be clear that, like everyone else, I am a claims maker. In making claims about violence, throughout this book I have tried to ground my arguments in the findings of sound research and intelligible and meaningful statistics. When they were not available, I put my faith in reasonable assumptions and leaped over chasms of various depths from one conclusion to another. While I cannot be sure, it is probably safe to say that, when necessary, I clung to branches that were rooted in my own interests and values, and perhaps even in my own feelings and my own sense of right and wrong or good and evil. In no way, however, does this confession refute or even diminish the argument that the meaning and measure of violence in society is socially constructed. If anything, it supports and even validates that conclusion.

In some areas of social life, we have come to believe that there is *more* violence than any available evidence would lead us to believe is really there. As shown in Chapter 2, for example, some drug users do acts of violence, but they could not possibly be responsible for as much violence as Harry Anslinger or William Bennett attributed to them at various times in our history. Nonetheless, our criminal justice system has devoted vast resources to arresting, convicting, sentencing, and punishing drug users. Similarly, Chapter 4 showed that innocent people can inadvertently be the victims of violence, but not nearly as often as the news media argued they were in the last decades of the twentieth century. Nonetheless, public resources that could have been spent trying to help people who were *more* likely to be victims of violence were spent helping people who were *less* likely to be victims of violence.

In other areas of social life, we have come to believe that there is *less* violence than any available evidence would lead us to believe there really is. Chapter 5 showed that not all families are "havens in a heartless world," and, more often than we like to admit, they can be home to violence against their own members. Yet, it took generations of women and children being beaten and even killed before we came to recognize and treat domestic violence and child abuse as forms of violence worthy of the consideration of our criminal justice system.

The question, then, is why do people make claims about the nature and level of violence in our society that are *not* consistent with available and credible evidence? The reasons for doing so, as suggested in Chapter 1, are both rational and nonrational. Claims making is rational when the purpose of the claim is to achieve an objective that is reasonable and comprehensible in the context of the experience of the claims maker and his or her place in society. Similarly, claims making is nonrational when the reason for making the claim cannot be determined or understood in relation to the experience of the claims maker or his or her place in society—such as in the case of claims that are made to support a position grounded in personal feelings or morality.

Rational claims making can take place when an individual or group makes claims about something to advocate a viewpoint in support of their own interests, values, or both. For example, Chapter 2 showed how Harry Anslinger used the claim that marijuana users were violent to build his agency and enhance his own career. Chapter 9 showed how violence in the workplace traditionally has been defined in terms of what workers do as individuals rather than what managers do as representatives of business interests, thereby diverting attention from corporate decisions that place the maximization of corporate profit ahead of the minimization of public morbidity and mortality. Similarly, rational claims making can take place on behalf of a broad political agenda. Chapters 2 and 3 showed how drug users and drug dealers were used during the 1980s by the federal, state, and local governments to support a get-tough philosophy toward crime that resulted in a broad expansion of the criminal justice system and hence the diversion of public resources to crime and justice agencies. Rational claims making can also serve to simplify the task of policy makers or practitioners by defining a problem in simple, manageable terms. For example, Chapter 8 showed how, in at least one case, race was used to try to make a problem of justice that is complex and deeply rooted in American tradition appear as a simple matter of adjusting criminal case processing procedures.

Nonrational claims making takes place when an individual or group makes claims in response to personal feelings or a personal sense of right and wrong or good and evil, such as in the case of a moral panic. As shown in Chapters 2 and 3, much of drug policy in the United States during the twentieth century has been rooted in the belief that drug using and dealing are bad things to do and drug users and dealers are evil people. As shown in Chapter 7, much of the shift in juvenile justice policy and practice in the later years of the twentieth century has been grounded in claims that have generated widespread fear of increasingly violent youthful superpredators. Similarly, nonrational claims making can be supportive of social prejudices and biases. Chapter 6 showed how public attitudes about women and their role in society continue to serve as the basis for our policies concerning violence by and against women.

Implications for Public Policy

It is not my intent here to oversimplify a highly complicated and often arcane social process. By saying that claims making can be rational or nonrational, I do not mean to suggest that any individual and certainly not any group that engages in claims making for purposes of influencing social life does so for a single clear and obvious reason. Look at the number of times and ways I used the example of how and why claims have been made about drug using and dealing. Rather, the point is that, in trying to understand how and why a variety of claims makers participate in and influence the construction of social policy and practice, it helps to think about the rational and nonrational bases of their claims. Only then can we determine or even assess the extent to which particular claims are reasonable and worthy to serve as the basis for public policy and practice.

Telling stories and making claims to advocate particular positions or viewpoints is not just about getting people to believe in your ideas or to agree with your conclusions. Ultimately, the competition among claims makers is about social resources. The real competition is for society's wealth, power, and prestige. Likewise, policy making is a process of resource allocation. Given the competition among claims makers in the social arena, the allocation of social resources are as likely to be allocated on the basis of successful claims making as they are to be allocated on the basis of the best available evidence about where they are most needed and where they can do the most good.

The question, then, is what can we do about violence in our society, knowing what we know about the claims that have been made about violence and how they have been used in the construction of public policy and practice. In that there will always be competing social interests and social values, and given that people will always have their own prejudices and their own sense of morality, there is no way we can completely eliminate claims making from the processes of constructing public policy and practice. Nonetheless, there are things we can do that would make these processes more representative.

- To be able to properly assess and evaluate the variety of claims that will continue to be made about violence, we need to improve the quality of our definitions and measures of violence in society. Efforts are underway, particularly on the federal level, to improve the quality of particular measures. But we need also to distance ourselves from the definitions and measures we now use and to think about what we really mean by violence in terms of its implications for the quality of our ongoing social life. Reports that ask broad questions, such as the report prepared by The Urban Institute called *Did Getting Tough on Crime Pay?*,[11] begin to address this need, but tend to be directed at very limited audiences of policy makers and academics. These questions and issues need to be prepared in ways that are more accessible to broader elements of the public, perhaps through newspaper, magazine, and even television reports designed to appeal to people at all different levels of education, interest, and so on. Of course, for this to work, we would need to respect the intelligence and abilities of all people to participate in such a debate.

• We need public mechanisms to be put in place that assure that decisions of public policy and practice are made in the best interests of the publics being served. For example, before we decide that young people have become a breed apart from what they used to be and begin to change ways established decades ago to deal with offenders too young to understand the implications of their actions, we need to have established procedures in place for making sure that we act in the best interest of both the wider society and the youth. We need to do this before we set in motion policies and practices that will change the nature of our society's relationship with its own children for decades to come. That is, we need to assure that all claims about violence are assessed and evaluated in ways that all people can understand before we use them as a basis for policy and practice.

• We need to establish social institutions that permit and encourage open, democratic debate on violence and other social issues. The opinions of a handful of people selected as experts by media officials to speak to us through official media outlets should not be the focal point of any debate on what we mean by violence or what we consider to be our problems of violence. New forms of communication being developed, both technologically and sociologically, can be adapted to this purpose. Not long ago, communication through the Internet was limited to government officials and university professors. In just the few years before the end of the twentieth century, those lines opened to anyone who could afford access to a computer. As the technology develops, as social practices involving people using the Internet evolve, and as more people are afforded access to this form of communication, cyberspace could become a truly democratic frontier where debates about violence and other social issues can take place.

Ultimately, all this means is that we need to open the claims making process to the broadest base of people so all interests, values, and personal concerns can be addressed.

A purpose of this book has been to demonstrate how stories have been and can be used to support arguments or advocate positions. The following story supports the argument for opening the claims making process to a wider public. An article appeared in the New York *Daily News* on Friday, December 19, 1997. The article by Austin Fenner was called "They want a new bridge to the future." Taking more than two-thirds of the page, the article included two large pictures. One was of the backs of three small children leaning over a fence, overstuffed backpacks resting across their shoulders. The other was mostly of pavement littered with sharp images of crack vials in the foreground and outlined with blurred images of children in the background. The two pictures shared the same caption: "Drug vials litter bridge used by kids from Public School 75. The school children often see prostitutes and drug users." According to the text, neighborhood people have tried to reclaim the bridge for their children who must cross it daily to get to school. They formed a group called Mothers on the Move. Fifty or so people held a rally and proclaimed that the bridge would be called "The Children's Bridge." To these people, the problem is obvious. Maritza Chavez, a mother of two young boys who attend P.S. 75, told the reporter, "My children have seen junkies shooting dope into their veins, and prostitutes cleaning themselves with their bodies exposed." After ten years of complaining, the people of this neighborhood in the Bronx wonder why nothing is being done to help them. The reporter asked for a response from the city's board of education. "The principal of P.S. 75 said the problems of the bridge have not made their way into the school," he was told by a board representative. He asked the police department. A spokesperson assured him that "the 42nd Precinct will be increasing enforcement and patrols of the bridge." He asked the city's transportation department. He was told that "the bridge is state-owned." He asked a mother of one of the children who attend P.S. 75. "I think they forget about us," she told him.

Endnotes

1. Adams, A. (1983). *Examples: The Making of 40 Photographs*. Boston: Little, Brown, p. 43.

2. Adams 1983:43.

3. Weber, M. (1947). *The Theory of Social and Economic Organization*. Tr. by A. M. Henderson and T. Parsons. New York: The Free Press, p. 88.

4. Jencks, C. (1991). "Behind the Numbers—Is Violent Crime Increasing?" *The American Prospect* Winter:98–109.

5. Jencks 1991:109.

6. Jencks 1991:109.

7. Reiss, A. J., Jr, and Roth, J. A. (1993). *Understanding and Preventing Violence*. Washington, DC: National Academy Press, p. 42–43.

8. Kappeler, V. E., Blumberg, M., and Potter, G. W. (1996). *The Mythology of Crime and Criminal Justice.* Second Edition. Prospect Heights, IL: Waveland, p. 35.

9. Donohue, E., Schiraldi, V and Ziedenberg, J. (1998). *School House Hype: School Shootings and the Real Risks Kids Face in America.* Washington, DC: Justice Policy Institute, p. 2.

10. Donahue, Schiraldi and Ziedenberg 1998:6–8.

11. Lynch, J. P. and Sabol, W. J. (1997). *Did Getting Tough on Crime Pay?* Washington, DC: The Urban Institute.

References

Abrams, M. H. 1957. *A Glossary of Literary Terms*. New York: Holt, Rinehart and Winston.

Adams, Ansel. 1983. *Examples: The Making of 40 Photographs*. Boston: Little, Brown.

Adler, Freda. 1975. *Sisters in Crime: The Rise of the New Female Criminal*. New York: McGraw-Hill.

Adler, Patricia. 1985. *Wheeling and Dealing: An Ethnography of an Upper-Level Dealing and Smuggling Community*. New York: Columbia University Press.

Agnew, Robert. 1992. "Foundation for a General Strain Theory of Crime and Delinquency," *Criminology* 30:47–87

Akers, Ronald L. 1977. *Deviant Behavior: A Social Learning Approach*. Belmont, CA: Wadsworth.

Allen-Hagen, Barbara, Melissa Sickmund, and Howard Snyder. 1994. *Juveniles and Violence: Juvenile Offending and Juvenile Victimization*. Fact Sheet # 19. November. Washington, DC: Office of Juvenile Justice and Delinquency Prevention.

Altschuler, David M. and Paul J. Brounstein. 1991. "Patterns of Drug Use, Drug Trafficking, and Other Delinquency among Inner-City Adolescent Males in Washington, D.C." *Criminology* 29:589–621.

Alvarez, Rafael and Michael James. 1995. "'War' in city's streets fuels fear in residents' hearts." *The Sun* (Baltimore) August 20:C1.

American Psychological Association. 1993. *Youth and Violence: Psychology's Response*. Vol. 1: Summary Report of the American Psychological Association Commission on Violence and Youth. Washington, DC: APA Commission on Violence and Youth.

Annin, Peter. 1996. "Superpredators arrive." *Newsweek* January 22:57.

Arendt, Hannah. 1969. *On Violence*. New York: Harcourt, Brace & World.

Asher, Ramona M. 1992. *Women with Alcoholic Husbands—Ambivalence and the Trap of Codependency*. Chapel Hill: University of North Carolina Press.

Associated Press. 1992. "Guns, short tempers, drugs: kid killers." *The Sun* (Baltimore) October 27:A3.

———. 1995. "U.S. children: Armed and dangerous." *The Sun* (Baltimore) September 8:3A.

———. 1995. "Major crimes show 3–year decline." *The Boston Sunday Globe* November 19:12.

———. 1996. "Reported Serious Crime Drops for 4th Straight Year." *The Washington Post* May 6:A9.

———. 1996. "Dole urges crackdown on youth violence." *The Sun* (Baltimore) July 7:10A.

———. 1997. "Poll of U.S. Cities Finds Increase in Curfews." *The Washington Post* December 1:A4.

Attinger, Joelle. 1989. "The Decline of New York." *Time* September 17:36–41, 44.

Baccaglini, William F. et al. 1993. *Violent Offenders. Research Focus on Youth.* Rensselaer, NY: New York State Division for Youth.

Bachman, Ronet. 1994. *Violence and Theft in the Workplace.* Crime Data Brief. Washington, DC: Bureau of Justice Statistics.

Bakalar, James B. and Lester Grinspoon. 1984. *Drug Control in a Free Society.* Cambridge: Cambridge University Press.

Ball, John C., J. W. Schaeffer, and David N. Nurco. 1983. "The Day-to-Day Criminality of Heroin Addicts in Baltimore—A Study in the Continuity of Offense Rates." *Drug and Alcohol Dependence* 12:119–42.

Barron, James. 1988. "Abrams Office to Investigate Attack on Black Teen-Ager." *The New York Times* January 27:B3.

———. 1997. "Grand Jury Found Nothing to Back Claim." *The New York Times* December 4:B12.

Baskin, Deborah R. and Ira B. Sommers. 1998. *Casualties of Community Disorder—Women's Careers in Violent Crime.* Boulder, CO: Westview.

Bastian, Lisa D. and Bruce M. Taylor. 1994. *Young Black Male Victims.* National Crime Victimization Survey. Washington, DC: Bureau of Justice Statistics.

Becker, Howard S. 1963. *Outsiders—Studies in the Sociology of Deviance.* New York: The Free Press.

Beckett, Katherine. 1997. *Making Crime Pay—Law and Order in Contemporary American Politics.* New York: Oxford University Press.

Belenko, Steven. 1990. "The Impact of Drug Offenders on the Criminal Justice System." Pp. 27–78 in R. Weisheit (ed.), *Drugs, Crime and the Criminal Justice System.* Cincinnati: Anderson.

———. 1993. *Crack and the Evolution of Anti-Drug Policy.* Westport, CT: Greenwood.

Ben-Yehuda, Nachman. 1990. *The Politics and Morality of Deviance—Moral Panics, Drug Abuse, Deviant Science, and Reversed Stigmatization.* Albany, NY: State University of New York.

Bennett, William J., John J. DiIulio, Jr., and John P. Walters. 1996. *Body Count—Moral Poverty. . . and How to Win America's War against Crime and Drugs.* New York: Simon and Schuster.

Benokraitis, Nijole. 1993. *Marriages and Families.* Englewood Cliffs, NJ: Prentice-Hall.

Bensinger, Peter B. et al. 1994. *On Good Authority—Juvenile Offenders and Violent Crime.* Chicago: Illinois Criminal Justice Information Authority.

Berger, Peter L. 1963. *Invitation to Sociology: A Humanistic Perspective.* Garden City, NY: Anchor Books, Doubleday & Co.

Berger, Peter L. and Brigitte Berger. 1975. *Sociology—A Biographical Approach.* Second, Expanded Edition. New York: Basic Books.

Berger, Peter L. and Thomas Luckmann. 1966. *The Social Construction of Reality—A Treatise in the Sociology of Knowledge.* Garden City, NY: Doubleday & Co.

Best, Joel. 1989. *Images of Issues: Typifying Contemporary Social Problems.* New York: Aldine de Gruyter.

———. 1990. *Threatened Children—Rhetoric and Concern about Child-Victims.* Chicago: University of Chicago Press.

Best, Joel and Gerald T. Horiuchi. 1985. "The Razor Blade in the Apple: The Social Construction of Urban Legends." *Social Problems* 32:488–99.

Biden, Joseph R., Jr. 1990. *Fighting Drug Abuse: A National Strategy.* Washington, DC: Prepared by the Majority Staffs of the Senate Judiciary Committee and the International Narcotics Control Caucus, January.

Black, Donald J. and Albert J. Reiss, Jr. 1970. "Police Control of Juveniles." *American Sociological Review* 35:63–78.

Block, Carolyn R. and Richard Block. 1993. "Street Gang Crime in Chicago," *National Institute of Justice Journal*. August. Washington, DC: U.S. Department of Justice.

Blumenthal, Ralph. 1988. "Brawley's Texts Founds At School." *The New York Times* March 24:B1, B4.

———. 1988. "F.B.I. Pulls Back in Brawley Case." *The New York Times* April 29:B3.

———. 1988. "Abrams Urges Brawley Lawyers To Testify on What They Know." *The New York Times* June 4:31.

Blumer, Herbert. 1971. "Social Problems as Collective Behavior." *Social Problems* 18:298–306.

Blumstein, Alfred. 1982. "On the Racial Disproportionality of United States' Prison Populations." *Journal of Criminal Law and Criminology* 73:1259–81.

———. 1995. "Violence by Young People: Why the Deadly Nexus." *National Institute of Justice Journal*. August. Washington, DC: U.S. Department of Justice, pp. 2–9.

Blumstein, Alfred, Jacqueline Cohen, and Richard Rosenfeld. 1991. "Trend and Deviation in Crime Rates: A Comparison of UCR and NCS Data for Burglary and Robbery." *Criminology* 29:237–63.

———. 1992. "The UCR-NCS Relationationship Revisited: A Reply to Menard." *Criminology* 30:115–24.

Blumstein, Alfred and Graddy, E. 1983. "Prevalence and Recidivism in Index Arrests: A Feedback Model." *Law and Society Review* 16:279–80.

Bluth, Howard. 1996. "A violent generation comes of age, and we are not prepared." *The Sun* (Baltimore) January 30:7A.

Bourgois, Philippe. 1995. *In Search of Respect—Selling Crack in El Barrio*. Cambridge: Cambridge University Press.

Brookoff, Daniel. 1997. *Drugs, Alcohol, and Domestic Violence in Memphis*. NIJ Research Preview. Washington, DC: U.S. Department of Jusatice.

Brooks, Tim and Earle Marsh. 1995. *The Complete Directory to Prime Time Network and Cable TV Shows—1946–Present*. New York: Ballantine.

Brownstein, Henry H. 1991. "The Media and the Construction of Random Drug Violence." *Social Justice* 18:85–103.

———. 1992. "Making Peace in the War on Drugs." *Humanity and Society* 16:217–35.

———. 1995. "The Social Construction of Crime Problems: Insiders and the Use of Official Statistics." *Journal of Crime and Justice* 18:17–30.

———. 1996. *The Rise and Fall of a Violent Crime Wave—Crack Cocaine and the Social Construction of a Crime Problem*. Guilderland, NY: Harrow and Heston.

———. 1998. "The Drugs–Violence Connection: Constructing Policy from Research Findings." Pp. 59–69 in Jensen, E. L. and Gerber, J. (eds.), *The New War on Drugs—Symbolic Politics and Criminal Justice Policy*. Cincinnati: Anderson.

Brownstein, Henry H. et al. (1993). *1992 Crime and Justice Annual Report*. Albany, NY: New York State Division of Criminal Justice Services.

Brownstein, Henry H., Hari R. S. Baxi, Paul J. Goldstein, and Patrick J. Ryan. 1992. "The Relationship of Drugs, Drug Trafficking, and Drug Traffickers to Homicide." *Journal of Crime and Justice* 15:25–44.

Brownstein, Henry H. and Paul J. Goldstein. 1990. "Research and the Development of Public Policy: The Case of Drugs and Violent Crime." *Journal of Applied Sociology* 7:77–92.

Brownstein, Henry H., Sandra C. Langley, Susan M. Crimmins, and Barry J. Spunt. 1995. "Women Who Kill Strangers." Paper presented at the annual meeting of the American Society of Criminology, Boston, November.

Brownstein, Henry H., Barry J. Spunt, Susan M. Crimmins, and Sandra C. Langley. 1995. "Women Who Kill in Drug Market Situations." *Justice Quarterly* 12:473–98.

Budd, Robert D. 1989. "Cocaine Abuse and Violent Death." *American Journal of Drug and Alcohol Abuse* 14:375–82.

Bureau of Criminal Information and Analysis. n.d. *1995 Crime and Delinquency in California*. Sacramento: California Department of Justice.

Bureau of Justice Statistics. 1988. *Report to the Nation on Crime and Justice*. Second Edition. NCJ-105506. Washington, DC: U.S. Department of Justice.

———. 1994. *Criminal Victimization in the United States: 1973–92 Trends*. July. Washington, DC: U.S. Department of Justice.

———. 1997. *Correctional Populations in the United States, 1995*. Executive Summary. NCJ-163917. Washington, DC: U.S. Department of Justice.

Bulmer, Martin. 1982. *The Uses of Social Research*. London: George Allen & Unwin.

Butts, Jeffrey A. and Howard N. Snyder. 1997. *The Youngest Delinquents: Offenders under Age 15*. Juvenile Justice Bulletin. September. Washington, DC: Office of Juvenile Justice and Delinquency Prevention.

Campbell, Anne. 1993. *Men, Women, and Aggression—From Rage in Marriage to Violence in the Streets—How Gender Affects the Way We Act*. New York: BasicBooks.

Caplovitz, David. 1963. *The Poor Pay More—Consumer Practices of Low Income Families*. New York: The Free Press.

Centers for Disease Control. 1990. "Homicide among Young Black Males—United States, 1978–1987." *Morbidity and Mortality Weekly Report* 39:869–73.

Chaiken, Jan M. and Marcia R. Chaiken. 1990. "Drugs and Predatory Crime." Pp. 203–39 in M. Tonry and J. Q. Wilson (eds.), *Drugs and Crime*. Chicago: University of Chicago Press.

Christianson, Scott. 1981. "Our Black Prisoners." *Crime and Delinquency* 27:364–75.

Clark, Kenneth. 1965. *Dark Ghetto—Dilemmas of Social Power*. New York: Harper & Row.

Cleaver, Eldridge. 1968. *Soul on Ice*. New York: Dell.

Cloward, Richard A. and Lloyd E. Ohlin. 1960. *Delinquency and Opportunity*. New York: The Free Press.

Cockburn, Alexander. 1996. "The War on Kids." *The Nation* June 3, v. 262:7–8.

Cohen, Albert K. 1955. *Delinquent Boys*. New York: The Free Press.

Cory, Mary. 1993. "Defense mechanisms—Wary people would never think of leaving home without them." *The Sun* (Baltimore) November 19:D1.

Coordinating Council on Juvenile Justice and Delinquency Prevention. 1996. *Combating Violence and Delinquency: The National Juvenile Justice Action Plan—Report*. March. Washington, DC: Office of Juvenile Justice and Delinquency Prevention.

Crane, Verne W. 1954. *Benjamin Franklin and a Rising People*. Boston: Little, Brown.

Craven, Diane. 1996. *Female Victims of Violent Crime*. NCJ-16602. Washington, DC: Bureau of Justice Statistics.

———. 1997. *Sex Differences in Violent Victimization, 1994*. NCJ-164508. Washington, DC: Bureau of Justice Statistics.

Crowell, Nancy A. and Ann W. Burgess. (eds.). 1996. *Understanding Violence against Women*. Washington, DC: National Academy Press.

Cuomo, Mario M. 1987. *Message to the Legislature*. January 7. Albany, NY.

Curran, Daniel J. and Claire M. Renzetti. 1994. *Theories of Crime*. Boston: Allyn and Bacon.

Currie, Elliott. 1993. *Reckoning—Drugs, the Cities, and the American Future*. New York: Hill and Wang.

Curtis, Lynn A. 1974. *Criminal Violence*. Lexington, MA: Lexington Books.

———. 1989. *The National Drug Control Strategy and Inner City Policy*. Testimony before the U.S. House Select Committee on Narcotics Abuse and Control. November 15, 1989. Washington, DC: Milton Eisenhower Foundation.

Daly, Kathleen and Meda Chesney-Lind. 1988. "Feminism and Criminology." *Justice Quarterly* 5:497–538.

Dao, James. 1995. "Pataki Proposes Legislative Plan to Curb Violent Crime by Youths." *The New York Times* December 10:1, 46.

Decker, Cathleen. 1995. "Most in County Disagree With Simpson Verdicts." *Los Angeles Times* October 8:A1, A36.

Decker, Cathleen and Sheryl Stolberg. 1995. "Half of Americans Disagree With Verdict." *Los Angeles Times* October 4:A1, A11.

DeKeseredy, Walter S. and Desmond Ellis. 1997. "Sibling Violence: A Review of Canadian Sociological Research and Suggestions for Further Empirical Research." *Humanity and Society* 21:397–411.

DeKeseredy, Walter S. and Ronald Hinch. 1991. *Woman Abuse—Sociological Perspectives*. Toronto, Canada: Thompson Educational Publishing.

De La Rosa, Mario and F. I. Soriano. 1992. "Understanding Criminal Activity and Use of Alcohol and Cocaine Derivatives by Multi-Ethnic Gang Members." Pp. 24–42 in R. Cervantes (ed.), *Substance Abuse and Gang Violence*. Newbury Park, CA: Sage.

Dembo, Richard, Linda Williams, Werner Wothke, and James Schmeidler. 1994. "The Relationships among Family Problems, Friends' Troubled Behavior, and High Risk Youths' Alcohol/Other Drug Use and Delinquent Behavior: A Longitudinal Study." *The International Journal of the Addictions* 29:1419–42.

Dembo, Richard. L., Linda Williams, Werner Wothke, James Schmeidler, A. Getreu, E. Berry, E. D. Wish, and C. Christensen. 1990. "The Relationship between Cocaine Use, Drug Sales, and Other Delinquency among a Cohort of High Risk Youths Over Time." Pp. 112–35 in M. De La Rosa, E.Y. Lambert, and B. Gropper (eds.), *Drugs and Violence: Causes, Correlates, and Consequences*, NIDA Research Monograph No. 103. Rockville, MD: National Institute on Drug Abuse.

Denton, Rhonda E. and Charlene M. Kampfe. 1994. "The Relationship between Family Variables and Adolescent Substance Abuse: A Literature Review." *Adolescence* 29:475–95.

Derber, Charles. 1996. *The Wilding of America—How Greed and Violence Are Eroding Our Nation's Character*. New York: St. Martin's.

DiIulio, John J., Jr. 1994. "America's Ticking Crime Bomb and How to Defuse It." *Wisconsin Interest* Spring/Summer:1–8.

———. 1995. "Crime in America—It's Going to Get Worse." *Reader's Digest* August.55–60.

Division of Substance Abuse Services. 1986. *Study of Crack Smokers*. Albany, NY: New York State Division of Substance Abuse Services.

Dobash, R. Emerson and Russell Dobash. 1979. *Violence against Wives—A Case Against the Patriarchy.* New York: The Free Press.

Donohue, Elizabeth, Vincent Schiraldi, and Jason Ziedenberg. 1998. *School House Hype: School Shootings and the Real Risks Kids Face in America.* Washington, DC: Justice Policy Institute.

Donziger, Steven R. (ed.). 1996. *The Real War on Crime—The Report of the National Criminal Justice Commission.* New York: HarperPerennial.

Dowie, Mark. 1987. "Pinto Madness." Pp. 13–29 in S. L. Hills (ed.), *Corporate Violence—Injury and Death for Profit.* Totowa, NJ: Rowan and Littlefield.

Downs, James F. 1966. *The Two Worlds of the Washo—An Indian Tribe of California and Nevada.* New York: Holt, Rinehart and Winston.

Durkheim, Emile. 1938. *The Rules of Sociological Method.* Eighth Edition. Tr. by S. A. Solovay and J. H. Mueller and ed. by G. E. G. Catlin. New York: The Free Press.

Duster, Troy. 1970. *The Legislation of Morality—Law, Drugs, and Moral Judgment.* New York: The Free Press.

Eck, J. Ernst and Lucius J. Riccio. 1979. "Relationship between Reported Crime Rates and Victimization Survey Results: An Empirical and Analytic Study." *Journal of Criminal Justice* 7:293–308.

Elias, Robert. 1993. *Victims Still—The Political Manipulation of Crime Victims.* Newbury Park, CA: Sage.

Elliott, Delbert S. 1994. "Serious Violent Offenders: Onset, Developmental Course, and Termination—The American Society of Criminology 1993 Presidential Address." *Criminology* 32:1–21.

Ely, Richard E. et al. 1996. *1995 Crime and Justice Annual Report.* Albany, NY: New York State Division of Criminal Justice Services.

———. 1998. *1996 Crime and Justice Annual Report.* Albany, NY: New York State Division of Criminal Justice Services.

Ember, Carol R. and Melvin Ember, M. 1977. *Cultural Anthropology.* Second Edition. Englewood Cliffs, NJ: Prentice-Hall.

Fagan, Jeffrey. 1989. "The Social Organization of Drug Use and Drug Dealing among Urban Gangs." *Criminology* 27:633–69

———. 1990. "Intoxication and Aggression." Pp. 241–320 in M. Tonry and J. Q. Wilson (eds.), *Drugs and Crime.* Chicago: University of Chicago Press.

———. 1996. *The Criminalization of Domestic Violence: Promises and Limits.* National Institute of Justice Research Report. Washington, DC: U.S. Department of Justice.

Fagan, Jeffrey and Ko Lin Chin. 1990. "Violence as Regulation and Social Control in the Distribution of Crack." Pp. 8–43 in M. De La Rosa, E. Y. Lambert, and B. Gropper (eds.), *Drugs and Violence: Causes, Correlates, and Consequences.* Washington, DC: National Institute on Drug Abuse.

Fagan, Jeffrey and Sandra Wexler. 1987. "Family Origins of Violent Delinquents." *Criminology* 25:643–69.

Falco, Malthea. 1989. *Winning the Drug War: A National Strategy.* New York: Priority Press.

Federal Bureau of Investigation. 1994. *Crime in the United States, 1993.* Washington, DC: U.S. Government Printing Office.

———. 1996. *Crime in the United States, 1995.* Washington, DC: U.S. Government Printing Office.

———. 1997. *Crime in the United States, 1996*. Washington, DC: U.S. Government Printing Office.

Fendrich, Michael, Mary E. Mackesy-Amiti, Paul J. Goldstein, Barry Spunt, Henry H. Brownstein. 1995. "Substance Involvement among Juvenile Murderers: Comparisons with Older Offenders Based on Prison Inmates." *The International Journal of the Addictions* 30:1363–82.

Francke, Caitlin. 1996. "Girls' crimes worry some officials." *The Sun* (Baltimore) July 23: 1B, 10B.

———. 1997. "Schoolgirl violence on rise in region." *The Sun* (Baltimore) May16: 1A, 7A.

Fraser, Antonia. 1991. *The Wild Island*. New York: Bantam Books.

Friedan, Betty. 1963. *The Feminine Mystique*. New York: Dell.

Friedl, Ernestine. 1962. *Vasilika — A Village in Modern Greece*. New York: Holt, Rinehart and Winston.

Fyfe, James F., David A. Klinger, and Jeanne M. Flavin. 1997. "Differential Police Treatment of Male-on-Female Spousal Violence." *Criminology* 35:455–73.

Gary, Leonard E. 1986. "Drinking, Homicide, and the Black Male." *Journal of Black Studies* 17:15–31.

Garry, Eileen M. 1996. *Truancy: First Step to a Lifetime of Problems*. Juvenile Justice Bulletin. October. Washington, DC: Office of Juvenile Justice and Delinquency Prevention.

Gelles, Richard J. 1997. *Intimate Violence in Families*. Third Edition. Thousand Oaks, CA: Sage.

Gil, David. 1970. *Violence against Children: Physical Child Abuse in the United States*. Cambridge: Harvard University Press.

Gilligan, James. 1996. *Violence — Our Deadly Epidemic and Its Causes*. New York: G.P. Putnam's Sons.

Glazer, Nathan and Daniel Patrick Moynihan. 1963. *Beyond the Melting Pot — The Negroes, Puerto Ricans, Jews, Italians, and Irish of New York City*. Cambridge: The MIT Press.

———. 1975. *Ethnicity — Theory and Experience*. Cambridge: Harvard University Press.

Glueck, Sheldon and Eleanor Glueck. 1950. *Unraveling Juvenile Delinquency*. New York: Commonwealth Fund.

Goetting, Ann. 1994. "The Parenting-Crime Connection." *The Journal of Primary Prevention* 14:169–86.

Goldstein, Paul J. 1985 "The Drugs/Violence Nexus: A Tripartite Conceptual Framework." *Journal of Drug Issues* 15:493–506.

Goldstein, Paul J., Henry H. Brownstein, and Patrick J. Ryan. 1992. "Drug-Related Homicide in New York: 1984 and 1988." *Crime and Delinquency* 38:459–76.

Goldstein, Paul J., Henry H. Brownstein, Patrick J. Ryan, and Patricia A. Bellucci. 1989. "Crack and Homicide in New York City, 1988: A Conceptually-Based Event Analysis." *Contemporary Drug Problems* 16:651–87.

Goldstein, Paul J., Douglas S. Lipton, Edward Preble, Ira Sobel, Tom Miller, William Abbott, William Paige, and Franklin Soto. 1984. "The Marketing of Street Heroin in New York City." *Journal of Drug Issues* 14:553–66.

Golub, Andrew Lang and Bruce D. Johnson. 1997. *Crack's Decline: Some Surprises across U.S. Cities*. National Institute of Justice Research in Brief. Washington, DC: U.S. Department of Justice.

Gondolf, Edward W. 1989. *Man against Woman—What Every Woman Should Know about Violent Men*. Blue Ridge Summit, PA: Tab Books.

Goode, William J. 1964. *The Family*. Englewood Cliffs, NJ: Prentice-Hall.

Goodman, Richard A., James A. Mercy, Fred Loya, Mark L. Rosenberg, Jack C. Smith, Nancy H. Allen, Lewis Vargas, and Robert Kolts. 1986. "Alcohol Use and Interpersonal Violence: Alcohol Detected in Homicide Victims." *American Journal of Public Health* 76:144–49.

Gordon, Diana R. 1990. *The Justice Juggernaut—Fighting Street Crime, Controlling Citizens*. New Brunswick, NJ: Rutgers University Press.

Gordon, Milton M. 1964. *Assimilation in American Life—The Role of Race, Religion, and National Origins*. New York: Oxford University Press.

Gough, Kathleen. 1975. "The Origin of the Family." Pp. 181–91 in D. H. Spain (ed.), *The Human Experience—Readings in Sociocultural Anthropology*. Homewood, IL: Dorsey Press.

Gove, Walter R., Michael Hughes, and Michael Geerken. 1985. "Are Uniform Crime Reports a Valid Indicator of the Index Crimes? An Affirmative Answer with Minor Qualifications." *Criminology* 23:451–501.

Governor's Statewide Anti-Drug Abuse Council. 1989. *State of New York Anti-Drug Abuse Strategy Report*. Albany, NY: Governor's Statewide Anti-Drug Abuse Council.

Governor's Office of Employee Relations. 1986. "Crack—The Deadliest Cocaine of All." *GOER News*. September. Albany, NY: GOER.

Greenfeld, Lawrence A. et al. 1998. *Violence by Intimates—Analysis of Data on Crimes by Current or Former Spouses, Boyfriends, and Girlfriends*. BJS Factbook. Washington, DC: U.S. Department of Justice.

Haberman, Paul W. and Michael M. Baden. 1978. *Alcohol, Other Drugs and Violent Death*. New York: Oxford University Press.

Heffernan, Ronald, John M. Martin, and Anne T. Romano. 1982. "Homicide Related to Drug Trafficking." *Federal Probation* 46:3–7.

Hepburn, John and Harwin L. Voss. 1970. "Patterns of Criminal Homicide—A Comparison of Chicago and Philadelphia." *Criminology* 8:21–45.

Hermann, Peter. 1997. "Closer shots, larger guns mark slayings." *The Sun* (Baltimore) January 30:1B.

———. 1998. "Police plan clampdown on Baltimore youth gangs." *The Sun* (Baltimore) January 23:1A, 5A.

Heskett, Sandra L. 1996. *Workplace Violence: Before, During, and After*. Boston: Butterworth-Heinemann.

Hicks, Ralph A. and Daniel C. Gaughan. 1995. "Understanding Fatal Child Abuse." *Child Abuse and Neglect* 19:855–63.

Hills, Stuart L. (ed.). 1987. *Corporate Violence—Injury and Death for Profit*. Totowa, NJ: Rowan and Littlefield.

Hindelang, Michael J., Travis Hirschi, and Joseph G. Weis. 1979. "Correlates of Delinquency: The Illusion of Discrepancy between Self-Report and Official Measures." *American Sociological Review* 44:995–1014.

Hirschi, Travis. 1969. *Causes of Delinquency*. Berkeley: University of California Press.

Horner, Edith R. 1997. *Almanac of the 50 States—Basic Data Profiles with Comparative Tables*. Palo Alto, CA: Information Publications.

Hosler, Karen. 1997. "Tough bill on youth crime." *The Sun* (Baltimore) May 9:1A, 16A.

Howell, James C. (ed.). 1995. *Guide of Implementing the Comprehensive Strategy for Serious, Violent, and Chronic Juvenile Offenders.* June. Washington, DC: Office of Juvenile Justice and Delinquency Prevention.

Hughes, Everett C. 1945. "Dilemmas and Contradictions of Status." *American Journal of Sociology* 50:353–59.

Hughes, Patrick H. 1977. *Behind the Wall of Respect—Community Experiments in Heroin Addiction Control.* Chicago: University of Chicago Press.

Hutter, Mark. 1981. *The Changing Family—Comparative Perspectives.* New York: John Wiley.

Huxley, Aldous. 1954. *Doors of Perception.* New York: Harper and Row.

Inciardi, James A. 1989. "Beyond Cocaine: Basuco, Crack, and Other Coca Products." *Contemporary Drug Problems* 14:461–92.

———. 1992. *The War on Drugs II.* Mountain View, CA: Mayfield.

Inciardi, James A., Ruth Horowitz, and Anne E. Pottieger. 1993. *Street Kids, Street Drugs, Street Crime: An Examination of Drug Use and Serious Delinquency in Miami.* Belmont, CA: Wadsworth.

Inciardi, James A., Dorothy Lockwood, and Anne E. Pottieger. 1993. *Women and Crack-Cocaine.* New York: Macmillan.

International Association of Chiefs of Police. 1997. *Family Violence in America—Breaking the Cycle for Children Who Witness.* Alexandria, VA: International Association of Chiefs of Police.

Iverem, Esther. 1987. "Bias Cases Fuel Anger of Blacks." *The New York Times* December 14:B1, B2.

Jencks, Christopher. 1991. "Behind the Numbers—Is Violent Crime Increasing?" *The American Prospect* Winter: 98–109.

Jenkins, Philip. 1994. "The 'Ice Age'—The Social Construction of a Drug Panic." *Justice Quarterly* 11:7–31.

Jensen, Eric L. and Jurg Gerber. (1998). *The New War on Drugs: Symbolic Politics and Criminal Justice Policy.* Cincinnati: Anderson.

Jensen, Gary F. and Maryaltani Karpos. 1993. "Managing Rape: Exploratory Research on the Behavior of Rape Statistics." *Criminology* 31:363–85.

Johnson, Bruce D., Ansley Hamid, and Harry Sanabria. 1992. "Emerging Models of Crack Distribution." Pp. 56–78 in T. Mieczkowski (ed.), *Drugs, Crime, and Social Policy: Research, Issues, and Concerns.* Boston: Allyn and Bacon.

Johnson, Kevin. 1996. "Study eases fear of teen crime wave." *USA Today* December 13–15:1A.

Johnson, Kevin and Gary Fields. 1996. "Juvenile crime 'wave' may be just a ripple." *USA Today* December 13–15:4A.

Joint Committee on New York Drug Law Evaluation. 1977. *The Nation's Toughest Drug Law: Evaluation of the New York Experience.* Final Report. New York: The Association of the Bar of the City of New York.

Jurik, Nancy C. and Russ Winn. 1990. "Gender and Homicide: A Comparison of Men and Women Who Kill." *Violence and Victims* 5:227–42.

Justice Research and Statistics Association. 1997. "BJS/JRSA Conference Features Fox on 'The Young and the Ruthless.'" *The (JRSA) Forum* 15:12.

Kaplan, Abraham. 1964. *The Conduct of Inquiry—Methodology for Behavioral Science.* San Francisco: Chandler Publishing.

Kaplan, Howard B. 1995. *Drugs, Crime, and Other Deviant Adaptations—Longitudinal Studies.* New York: Plenum.

Kaplan, John. 1971. *Marijuana—The New Prohibition*. New York: Pocket Books.

Kappeler, Victor E., Mark Blumberg, and Gary W. Potter. 1996. *The Mythology of Crime and Criminal Justice*. Second Edition. Prospect Heights, IL: Waveland Press.

Kelleher, Michael D. 1996. *New Arenas for Violence—Homicide in the American Workplace*. Westport, CT: Praeger.

Kelley, Barbara Tatem, Terence P. Thornberry, and Carolyn A. Smith. 1997. *In the Wake of Childhood Maltreatment*. OJJDP Juvenile Justice Bulletin. Washington, DC: U.S. Department of Justice.

Kitsuse, John I. and Aaron V. Cicourel. 1963. "A Note on the Uses of Official Statistics." *Social Problems* 11:131–39.

Klaidman, Daniel and Evan Thomas. 1998. "Rosty's Difficult Winter." *Newsweek* January 12:36–37.

Kleck, Gary. 1985. "Life Support for Ailing Hypotheses: Modes of Summarizing the Evidence for Racial Discrimination in Sentencing." *Law and Human Behavior* 9:271–85.

Klein, Malcolm W. 1971. *Street Gangs and Street Workers*. Englewood Cliffs, NJ: Prentice-Hall.

Klein, Malcolm W., Cheryl L. Maxson, and Lea C. Cunningham. 1991. "'Crack,' Street Gangs, and Violence." *Criminology* 29:701–17.

Koch, Tom. 1990. *The News as Myth—Fact and Context in Journalism*. New York: Greenwood.

Knight-Ridder. 1991. "Bystander shooting rate mushrooms." *The Sun* (Baltimore) August 8:A23.

Kracke, Kristen and Special Emphasis Division Staff. 1996. *SafeFutures: Partnerships to Reduce Youth Violence and Delinquency*. Fact Sheet # 38. June. Washington, DC: Office of Juvenile Justice and Delinquency Prevention.

Kramer, Ronald C. 1983. "A Prolegomena to the Study of Corporate Violence." *Humanity and Society* 7:149–78.

Ladoceur, Patricia and Mark Temple. 1985. "Substance Use among Rapists: A Comparison with Other Serious Felons." *Crime and Delinquency* 31:269–94.

Landau, Elaine. 1991. *Teenage Violence*. Englewood Cliffs, NJ: Julian Messner.

Lasch, Christopher. 1977. *Haven in a Heartless World—The Family Beseiged*. New York: Basic Books.

Lattimore, Pamela K., James Trudeau, Jack K. Riley, Jordan Leiter, and Steven Edwards. 1997. *Homicide in Eight U.S. Cities: Trends, Context, and Policy Implications—An Intramural Research Project*. Washington, DC: National Institute of Justice.

LeBoeuf, Donni. 1996. *Curfew: An Answer to Juvenile Delinquency and Victimization?* Juvenile Justice Bulletin. April. Washington, DC: Office of Juvenile Justice and Delinquency Prevention.

Lee, Alfred McClung. 1973. *The Daily Newspaper in America—The Evolution of a Social Instrument*. New York: Octagon.

———. 1988. *Sociology for People—Toward a Caring Profession*. Syracuse, NY: Syracuse University Press.

Lewis, Claude. 1992. "Car jacking: Our new terrorism." *The Sun* (Baltimore). September 23:A17.

Lewis, Ray, LaLonnie Erickson, Daniel Storkamp, and Carol Weber. 1996. *1996 Crime Survey—Changing Perceptions*. St. Paul: The Criminal Justice Center at Minnesota Planning.

Libit, Howard and Jill Hudson. 1997. "Howard teacher collapses, dies after effort to break up brawl." *The Sun* (Baltimore). May 15: 1A, 15A.

Lynch, James P. and William J. Sabol. 1997. *Did Getting Tough on Crime Pay?* Washington, DC: The Urban Institute.

Maguire, Kathleen and Ann L. Pastore (eds.). 1996. *Sourcebook of Criminal Justice Statistics 1995.* U.S. Department of Justice, Bureau of Justice Statistics. Washington, DC: U.S. Government Printing Office.

———. 1997. *Sourcebook of Criminal Justice Statistics 1996.* U.S. Department of Justice, Bureau of Justice Statistics. Washington, DC: U.S. Government Printing Office.

Maher, Lisa and Rick Curtis. 1995. "In Search of the Female Urban 'Gansta': Change, Culture, and Crack Cocaine." Pp. 147–66 in B. R. Price and N. J. Sokoloff (eds.), *The Criminal Justice System and Women—Offenders, Victims, and Workers.* New York: McGraw Hill.

Maher, Lisa and Kathleen Daly. 1996. "Women in the Street-Level Drug Economy: Continuity or Change?" *Criminology* 34:465–91.

Males, Mike A. 1996. *The Scapegoat Generation—America's War on Adolescents.* Monroe, ME: Common Courage.

Maline, Karen, Nancy Michel, Laura Parisi, and Veronica Puryear. 1997. *Criminal Justice Issues in the States—1997 Directory.* Volume XIV. Washington, DC: Justice Research and Statistics Association.

Maltz, Michael D. 1975. "Crime Statistics: A Mathematical Perspective." *Journal of Criminal Justice* 3:177–94.

———. 1977. "Crime Statistics: A Historical Perspective." *Crime and Delinquency* 23:32–40.

Mann, Coramae Richey. 1993. *Unequal Justice.* Bloomington: Indiana University Press.

Martz, Larry, Mark Miller, Sue Hutchinson, Tony Emerson, and Frank Washington. 1989. "The Tide of Drug Killing." *Newsweek* January 16:44–45.

Massing, Michael. 1980. "Crack's Destructive Sprint across America." *New York Times Magazine.* October 1:38, 40–41, 58, 60, 62.

Mauer, Marc. 1990. *Young Black Men and the Criminal Justice System: A Growing National Problem.* Washington, DC: The Sentencing Project.

Mauer, Marc and Tracy Huling. 1995. *Young Black Americans and the Criminal Justice System: Five Years Later.* Washington, DC: The Sentencing Project.

Mayer, Martin. 1987. *Making News.* Garden City, NY: Doubleday.

Mayer, Robert R. and Ernest Greenwood. 1980. *The Design of Social Policy Research.* Englewood Cliffs, NJ: Prentice-Hall.

McCord, Joan. 1991. "Family Relationships, Juvenile Delinquency, and Adult Criminality." *Criminology* 29:397–417.

McCoy, H. Virginia, James A. Inciardi, Lisa R. Metsch, Anne E. Pottieger, and Christine A. Saum. 1995. "Women, Crack, and Crime: Gender Comparisons of Criminal Activity among Crack Cocaine Users." *Contemporary Drug Problems* 22:435–51.

McCuen, Gary E. 1990. *Inner-City Violence.* Hudson, WI: GEM Publications.

McDonald, Douglas C. and Kenneth E. Carlson. 1993. *Sentencing in the Federal Courts: Does Race Matter? The Transition to Sentencing Guidelines, 1986–90.* Washington, DC: Bureau of Justice Statistics.

McDowall, David and Colin Loftin. 1992. "Comparing the UCR and NCS over Time." *Criminology* 30:125–32.

McFadden, Robert D. et al. 1988. "Evidence Points to Deceit by Brawley." *The New York Times* September 27:A1, B4.

McWilliams, John C. 1990 *The Protectors: Harry J. Anslinger and the Federal Bureau of Narcotics*. Newark: University of Delaware Press.

Meisler, Stanley. 1996. "The First Drug Czar." *The Drug Policy Letter* 29:13–17.

Menard, Scott. 1991. "Encouraging News for Criminologists (in the Year 2050)? A Comment on O'Brien." *Journal of Criminal Justice* 19:563–67.

———. 1992. "Residual Gains, Reliability, and the UCR-NCS Relationship: A Comment on Blumstein, Cohen, and Rosenfeld." *Criminology* 30:105–13.

Menard, Scott and Herbert C. Covey. 1988. "UCR and NCS: Comparison over Space and Time." *Journal of Criminal Justice* 16:371–84.

Merton, Robert K. 1938. "Social Structure and Anomie." *American Sociological Review* 3:672–82.

Merton, Robert K. and Jane Z. Moss. 1985. "Basic Research and Its Potentials of Relevance." *The Mount Sinai Journal of Medicine* 52:679–84.

Mieczkowski, Tom. 1990. "Crack Distribution in Detroit." *Contemporary Drug Problems* 17:9–29.

———. 1994. "Experiences of Women Who Sell Crack: Descriptive Data from the Detroit Crack Ethnography Project." *Journal of Drug Issues* 24:227–48.

Miller, Eleanor M. 1986. *Street Women*. Philadelphia: Temple University Press.

Miller, G. and J. A. Holstein. 1993. "Constructing Social Problems: Context and Legacy." Pp. 3–18 in G. Miller and J. A. Holstein (eds.), *Constructionist Controversies—Issues in Social Problems Theory*. New York: Aldine de Gruyter.

Miller, Jody. 1998. "Up It Up: Gender and the Accomplishment of Street Robbery." *Criminology* 36:37–66.

Miller, Walter B. 1958. "Lower Class Culture as a Generating Milieu of Gang Delinquency." *The Journal of Social Issues* 14:5–19.

Millett, Kate. 1971. *Sexual Politics*. New York: Equinox.

Minor, Marianne. 1995. *Preventing Workplace Violence—Positive Management Strategies*. Menlo Park, CA: Crisp Publications.

Mohd, Sham Kasim and Haliza Mohd Shafie. 1995. "Childhood Deaths from Physical Abuse." *Child Abuse and Neglect* 19:847–54.

Montgomery, Lori. 1996. "A divide on what's fueling youth crime. Teens raised for violence or just well-armed?" *The Philadelphia Inquirer* July 28.

Moody, Wayne. 1998. *Patterson's American Education* 1998 Edition. Volume XCIV. Mount Prospect, IL: Educational Directories, p. vii.

———. 1998. *Patterson's Elementary Education*. 1998 Edition. Volume X. Mount Prospect, IL: Educational Directories, p. vii.

Moone, Joseph. 1994. *Juvenile Victimization: 1987–1992*. Fact Sheet # 17. June. Washington, DC: Office of Juvenile Justice and Delinquency Prevention.

Morganthau, Tom. 1995. "The Lull Before the Storm?" *Newsweek* December 4:40–42.

Morley, Jefferson. 1996. "White Grams' Burden." *The Drug Policy Letter* Winter:17–19.

Musto, David. 1973. *The American Disease*. New Haven: Yale University Press.

———. 1997. "Opium, Cocaine and Marijuana in American History." Pp. 21–33 in L. K. Gaines and P. B. Kraska (eds.), *Drugs, Crime, and Justice—Contemporary Perspectives*. Prospect Heights, IL: Waveland.

National Center for Health Statistics. 1996. *Health, United States 1995*. Hyattsville, MD: Public Health Service.

National Commission on the Causes and Prevention of Violence. 1969. *Final Report: To Establish Justice, to Insure Domestic Tranquility.* Washington, DC: U.S. Government Printing Office.

National Institute of Justice. 1990. *DUF—1988 Drug Use Forecasting Annual Report— Drugs and Crime in America.* Research in Action. March. Washington, DC: U.S. Department of Justice.

———. 1995. *Evaluation of Family Violence Programs.* NIJ Research Preview. Washington, DC: U.S. Department of Justice.

———. 1997. *1996 Drug Use Forecasting—Annual Report on Adult and Juvenile Arrestees.* June. Washington, DC: U.S. Department of Justice.

National Safety Council. 1997. *Accident Facts 1997 Edition.* Itasca, IL: National Safety Council.

Nelson, James F. 1991a. *The Incarceration of Minority Defendants: An Identification of Disparity in New York State, 1985–1986.* Albany, NY: New York State Division of Criminal Justice Services.

———. 1991b. *Racial and Ethnic Disparities in Processing Persons Arrested for Misdemeanor Crimes: New York State, 1985–1986.* Albany, NY: New York State Division of Criminal Justice Services.

———. 1992. "Hidden Disparities in Case Processing: New York State, 1985–86." *Journal of Criminal Justice* 20:181–200.

———. 1994. "A Dollar or a Day: Sentencing Misdemeanants in New York State." *Journal of Research in Crime and Delinquency* 31:183–201.

———. 1995. *Disparities in Processing Felony Arrests in New York State, 1990–1992.* Albany, NY: New York State Division of Criminal Justice Services.

Newman, Graeme. 1979. *Understanding Violence.* New York: J. B. Lippincott.

Newman, Philip L. 1965. *Knowing the Gururumba.* New York: Holt, Rinehart and Winston.

Newton, David E. 1995. *Teen Violence—Out of Control.* Springfield, NJ: Enslow Publishers.

Nurco, David N., Thomas F. Hanlon, Mitchell B. Balter, Timothy W. Kinlock, and Evelyn Slaght. 1991. "A Classification of Narcotics Addicts Based on Type, Amount, and Severity of Crime." *Journal of Drug Issues* 21:429–48.

Nyberg, David. 1985. "Lucking into Harvard." A review of *Choosing Elites* by R. Klitgaard. *New York Times Book Review* May 5:7.

Nye, F. Ivan. 1958. *Family Relationships and Delinquent Behavior.* New York: John Wiley.

O'Brien, Robert M. 1990. "Comparing Detrended UCR and NCS Crime Rates over Time: 1973–1986." *Journal of Criminal Justice* 16:229–38.

———. 1991. "Detrended UCR and NCS Crime Rates: Their Utility and Meaning." *Journal of Criminal Justice* 19:569–74.

———. 1996. "Police Productivity and Crime Rates:1973–1992." *Criminology* 34:183–207.

Office of the Attorney General. 1989. *Drug Trafficking: A Report to the President of the United States.* Washington, DC: U.S. Department of Justice.

Office of National Drug Control Policy. 1989. *National Drug Control Strategy.* Washington, DC: Executive Office of the President.

———. 1990. *National Drug Control Strategy.* Washington, DC: Executive Office of the President.

———. 1998. *The National Drug Control Strategy, 1998—A Ten Year Plan.* Washington, DC: Executive Office of the President.

Office of Policy Planning and Research. 1965. *The Negro Family: The Case for National Action*. Washington, DC: U.S. Department of Labor.

Orchowsky, Stan. 1998. "The Unique Nature of Domestic Violence in Rural Areas." *JRSA Forum* 16:1, 6–9.

Ostrow, Ronald J. 1995. "Sentencing Study Sees Race Disparity." *Los Angeles Times* October 5:A1, A17.

Parent, Dale, Terence Dunworth, Douglas McDonald, and William Rhodes. 1997. *Transferring Serious Juvenile Offenders to Adult Courts*. Research in Action. January. Washington, DC: National Institute of Justice.

Park, R. E., E. W. Burgess, and R. D. McKenzie. 1967. *The City*. Chicago: University of Chicago Press.

Parsons, Talcott and Robert F. Bales. 1955. *Family, Socialization and Interaction Process*. New York: The Free Press.

Pepinsky Harold and Paul Jesilow. 1985. *Myths That Cause Crime*. Second edition. Cabin John, MD: Seven Locks Press.

Peters, M., David Thomas, Christopher Zamberlan, and Caliber Associates. 1997. *Boot Camps for Juvenile Offenders*. September. Washington, DC: Office of Juvenile Justice and Delinquency Prevention.

Petersilia, Joan. 1983. *Racial Disparities in the Criminal Justice System*. Santa Monica, CA: Rand.

Pitt, David E. 1989. "Gang Attack: Unusual for its Viciousness." *The New York Times* April 25:B1.

Pooley, Eric. 1989. "Fighting Back against Crack." *New York* January 23:31–39.

Potter, Gary W. and Victor E. Kappeler. 1998. *Constructing Crime—Perspectives on Making News and Social Problems*. Prospect Heights, IL: Waveland.

President's Commission on Law Enforcement and Administration of Justice. 1968. *The Challenge of Crime in a Free Society—The Complete Official Report*. New York: Avon Books.

Prothrow-Stith, Deborah (with Michaele Weissman). 1991. *Deadly Consequences*. New York: HarperCollins.

Przybylski, Roger et al. 1997. *Trends and Issues 1997*. Chicago: Illinois Criminal Justice Information Authority.

Quinney, Richard. 1970. *The Social Reality of Crime*. Boston: Little, Brown.

Radcliffe-Brown, A. R. 1965. *Structure and Function in Primitive Society*. New York: The Free Press.

Rafter, Nicole H. 1990. "The Social Construction of Crime and Crime Control." *Journal of Research in Crime and Delinquency* 27:376–89.

———. 1992. "Claims-making and Socio-cultural Context in the First U.S. Eugenics Campaign." *Social Problems* 39:17–34.

Rainwater, Lee and William L. Yancey. 1967. *The Moynihan Report and the Politics of Controversy*. Cambridge: The M.I.T. Press.

Rand, Michael R. 1982. *Violent Crime by Strangers*. Bureau of Justice Statistics Bulletin. Washington, DC: Bureau of Justice Statistics.

———. 1997. *Violence-Related Injuries Treated in Hospital Emergency Departments*. Special Report. August. Washington, DC: Bureau of Justice Statistics.

Reiman, Jeffrey. 1998. *The Rich Get Richer and the Poor Get Prison—Ideology, Class, and Criminal Justice*. Fifth Edition. Boston: Allyn and Bacon.

Reinarman, Craig and Harry G. Levine. 1989. "Crack in Context: Politics and Media in the Making of a Drug Scare." *Contemporary Drug Problems* 16:535–77.

———. 1997a. *Crack in America—Demon Drugs and Social Justice.* Berkeley: University of California Press.

———. 1997b. "Crack in Context—America's Latest Demon Drug." Pp. 1–17 in C. Reinarman and H. G. Levine (eds.), *Crack in America—Demon Drugs and Social Justice.* Berkeley: University of California Press.

Reiss, Albert J. and Jeffrey A. Roth. 1993. *Understanding and Preventing Violence.* Washington, DC: National Academy Press.

Reuter, Peter H. and Patricia A. Ebener. 1992. *Cocaine: The First Decade.* RAND DPRC Issue Paper. April. Santa Monica, CA: RAND.

Reuter, Peter, R. MacCoun, and P. Murphy. 1990. *Money from Crime: A Study of the Economics of Drug Dealing in Washington, D.C.* Santa Monica, CA: RAND.

Riedel, Marc. 1993. *Stranger Violence: A Theoretical Inquiry.* New York: Garland.

———. 1998. "Counting Stranger Homicides—A Case Study of Statistical Prestidigitation." *Homicide Studies* 2:206–19.

Riedel, Marc, Margaret A. Zahn, and Lois Mock. 1985. *The Nature and Patterns of American Homicide.* Washington, DC: National Institute of Justice.

Riley, K. Jack. 1997. *Crack, Powder Cocaine, and Heroin: Drug Purchase and Use Patterns in Six U.S. Cities.* Washington, DC: National Institute of Justice.

Ringel, Cheryl. 1997. *Criminal Victimization 1996—Changes 1995–96 with Trends 1993–96.* November. Washington, DC: Bureau of Justice Statistics.

Rosch, Joel and Susan Ajygin. 1997. *SystemStats—Understanding Juvenile Crime Trends and What Can and Cannot Be Done about Them.* Raleigh: North Carolina Criminal Justice Analysis Center.

Rosen, Richard A. 1991. *1990 Crime and Justice Annual Report.* Albany, NY: New York State Division of Criminal Justice Services.

Rosenberg, Mark A. and James A. Mercy. 1991. "Introduction." Pp. 3–13 in Rosenberg, M. L. and Fenley, M. A. (eds)., *Violence in America—A Public Health Approach.* New York: Oxford University Press.

Rosenberg, Mark L. and Mary Ann Fenley. 1991. *Violence in America—A Public Health Approach.* New York: Oxford University Press.

Roth, Jeffrey A. 1994a. *Understanding and Preventing Violence.* National Institute of Justice Research in Brief. Washington, DC: Office of Justice Programs.

———. 1994b. *Psychoactive Substances and Violence.* Research in Brief. February. Washington, DC: National Institute of Justice.

Roth, Jeffrey A. and Mark H. Moore. 1995. *Reducing Violent Crimes and Intentional Injuries.* National Institute of Justice Research in Action. Washington, DC: Office of Justice Programs.

Sampson, Robert. 1986. "Effects of Socioeconomic Context on Official Reaction to Juvenile Delinquency." *American Sociological Review* 51:876–85.

Scalia, John. 1997. *Juvenile Delinquents in the Federal Criminal Justice System.* Special Report. January. Washington, DC: Bureau of Justice Statistics.

Schiraldi, Vincent. 1998. "The Latest Trend in Juvenile Crime: Exaggeration by the News Media." *The Washington Post* January 11:C5.

Schur, Edwin. 1962. *Narcotic Addiction in Britain and America—The Impact of Public Policy.* Bloomington: Indiana University Press.

Schusky, Ernest L. 1965. *Manual for Kinship Analysis.* New York: Holt, Rinehart and Winston.

Sellin, Thorsten. 1938. *Culture Conflict and Crime.* New York: Social Science Research Council.

Shaw, Clifford R. and Henry D. McKay. 1942. *Juvenile Delinquency and Urban Areas.* Chicago: University of Chicago Press.

Sherman, Lawrence W. 1992. *Policing Domestic Violence—Experiments and Dilemmas.* New York: The Free Press.

Sherman, Lawrence W. and Berk, Richard. 1984. "The Specific Deterrent Effects of Arrest for Domestic Assault." *American Sociological Review* 49:261–72.

Sherman, Lawrence W., Leslie Steele, Deborah Laufersweiler, Nancy Hoffer, and Sherry A. Julian. 1989. "Stray Bullets and 'Mushrooms': Random Shootings of Bystanders in Four Cities, 1977–1988." *Journal of Quantitative Criminology* 5:297–316.

Shibutani, Tamotsu and Kian M. Kwan. 1965. *Ethnic Stratification—A Comparative Approach.* London: Macmillan

Shipp, E. R. 1988. "Brawley Rejects Evidence Cited To Grand Jury." *The New York Times* September 29:B4.

Simmel, Georg. 1950. *The Sociology of Georg Simmel.* Tr., ed., and with an Introduction by K. H. Wolff. New York: The Free Press.

Simon, David and Edward Burns. 1997. *The Corner—A Year in the Life of an Inner-City Neighborhood.* New York: Broadway Books.

Simon, Rita J. 1975. *Women and Crime.* Lexington, MA: Lexington Books.

Simon, Rita J. and Jean Landis. 1991. *The Crimes Women Commit, The Punishments They Receive.* Lexington, MA: Lexington Books.

Skogan, Wesley. 1974. "The Validity of Official Crime Statistics: An Empirical Investigation." *Social Science Quarterly* 55:25–38.

Skolnick, Arlene S. and Jerome H. Skolnick. 1971. *Family in Transition; Rethinking Marriage, Sexuality, Child Rearing, and Family Organization.* Boston: Little, Brown.

Sloman, Larry. 1979. *Reefer Madness—Marijuana in America.* New York: Grove.

Smart, Carol. 1978. "The New Female Criminal: Myth and Reality." *British Journal of Criminology* 19:50–59.

Smith, M. Dwayne. 1987. "Changes in the Victimization of Women: Is There a 'New Female Victim'?" *Journal of Research in Crime and Delinquency* 24:291–301.

Smith, Merrill A. 1988. "The Drug Problem—Is There an Answer?" *Federal Probation* 52:3–6.

Smith, Michael E., Michele Sviridoff, Susan Sadd, Ric Curtis, and R. Grinc. 1992. *The Neighborhood Effects of Street-Level Drug Enforcement—Tactical Narcotics Teams in New York—AN Evaluation of TNT.* New York: The Vera Institute of Justice.

Snell, Tracy L. 1997. *Capital Punishment, 1996.* Bulletin. December. Washington, DC: Bureau of Justice Statistics.

Snyder, Howard N. 1994a. *Juvenile Violent Crime Arrest Rates 1972–1992.* Fact Sheet # 14. May. Washington, DC: Office of Juvenile Justice and Delinquency Prevention.

———. 1994b. *Are Juveniles Driving the Violent Crime Trends?* Fact Sheet #16. May. Washington, DC: Office of Juvenile Justice and Delinquency Prevention.

———. 1996. *Juvenile Arrests 1995.* Juvenile Justice Bulletin. December. Washington, DC: Office of Juvenile Justice and Delinquency Prevention.

Snyder, Howard N. and Melissa Sickmund. 1995. *Juvenile Offenders and Victims: A National Report.* August. Washington, DC: Office of Juvenile Justice and Delinquency Prevention.

Snyder, Howard N., Melissa Sickmund, and Eileen Poe-Yamagata. 1996. *Juvenile Offenders and Victims: 1996 Update on Violence—Statistics Summary.* February. Washington, DC: Office of Juvenile Justice and Delinquency Prevention.

————. 1997. *Juvenile Offenders and Victims: 1997 Update on Violence—Statistics Summary*. February. Washington, DC: Office of Juvenile Justice and Delinquency Prevention.

Sondheimer, Henry (ed.) et al. 1995. "Is Waiver to Adult Court the Best Response to Juvenile Crime?" *Juvenile Justice Update* 1:3, 13–16.

Sorel, Georges. 1950. *Reflections on Violence*. Tr. by T. E. Hulme and J. Roth. Glencoe, IL: The Free Press.

Southerland, Mittie D., Pamela A. Collins, and Kathryn E. Scarborough. 1997. *Workplace Violence—A Continuum from Threat to Death*. Cincinnati: Anderson.

Spector, Malcolm and John I. Kitsuse. 1987. *Constructing Social Problems*. New York: Aldine de Gruyter.

Spunt, Barry J., Henry H. Brownstein, Susan M. Crimmins, Sandra Langley. 1994. *Female Drug Relationships in Murder*. A Final Report submitted to the National Institute on Drug Abuse. New York: National Development and Research Institutes.

Spunt, Barry, Henry H. Brownstein, Paul J. Goldstein, Michael Fendrich, and Hilary Liberty. 1995. "Drug Use by Homicide Offenders." *Journal of Psychoactive Drugs* 27:125–34.

Steinmetz, Suzanne K. and Murray A. Straus. (eds.). 1974. *Violence in the Family*. New York: Dodd, Mead.

Stelzer, Irwin M. (1997). "Teaching the Wrong Lessons." *New York Post* December 17:29.

Stigliano, Tony. 1983. "Jean-Paul Sartre on Understanding Violence." *Crime and Social Justice* 19:52–64.

Suro, Roberto. 1996. "Violent Crime Drops among Young Teens." *The Washington Post* December 13:A1, A19.

————. 1997. "White House, Hill GOP Offer Get Tough Measures on Juvenile Crime." *The Washington Post* May 8:A4.

Sutherland, Edwin H. 1924. *Principles of Criminology*. Philadelphia: J. P. Lippincott.

Sykes, Gresham and David Matza. 1957. "Techniques of Neutralization." *American Sociological Review* 12:664–70.

Tardiff, Kenneth and Elliott M. Gross. 1986. "Homicide in New York City." *Bulletin of the New York Academy of Medicine* 62: 413–26.

Thomas, Pierre. 1995. "The New Face of Murder in America." *The Washington Post* October 23:A1, A4.

Thornberry, Terence P. 1973. "Race, Socioeconomic Status, and Sentencing in the Juvenile Justice System." *Journal of Criminal Law and Criminology* 64:90–98.

————. 1994. *Violent Families and Youth Violence*. OJJDP Fact Sheet # 21. Washington, DC: U.S. Department of Justice.

Thornberry, Terence P. and James H. Burch, II. 1997. "Gang Members and Delinquent Behavior." Juvenile Justice Bulletin. June. Washington, DC: Office of Juvenile Justice and Delinquency Prevention.

Thornberry, Terence P. and Margaret Farnworth. 1982. "Social Correlates of Crime Involvement: Further Evidence of the Relationship between Social Status and Criminal Behavior." *American Sociological Review* 47:505–18.

Thrasher, Frederic M. 1927. *The Gang*. Chicago: University of Chicago Press.

Timm, Howard W. and Callie J. Chandler. n.d. *Combating Workplace Violence—Guidelines for Employers and Law Enforcement*. Alexandria, VA: International Association of Chiefs of Police.

Timrots, Anita D. and Michael R. Rand. 1987. *Violent Crime by Strangers and Nonstrangers.* Bureau of Justice Statistics Special Report. January. Washington, DC: Bureau of Justice Statistics.

Tonry, Michael. 1995. *Malign Neglect: Race, Crime, and Punishment in America.* New York: Oxford University Press.

Trebach, Arnold S. 1982. *The Heroin Solution.* New Haven: Yale University Press.

United States Department of Health and Human Services, Children's Bureau. (1998). *Child Maltreatment 1996: Reports from the States to the National Child Abuse and Neglect Data System.* Washington, DC: U.S. Government Printing Office.

Waldorf, Dan, Craig Reinarman, and Sheigla Murphy. (1991). *Cocaine Changes—The Experience of Using and Quitting.* Philadelphia: Temple University Press.

Walker, Samuel. 1994. *Sense and Nonsense about Crime and Drugs—A Policy Guide.* Third Edition. Belmont, CA: Wadsworth.

Walker, Samuel, Cassia Spohn, and Miriam DeLone. 1996. *The Color of Justice—Race, Ethnicity, and Crime in America.* Belmont, CA: Wadsworth.

Wallace, Harvey. 1999. *Family Violence—Legal, Medical, and Social Perspectives.* Second Edition. Boston: Allyn and Bacon.

Warchol, Greg. 1998. *Workplace Violence, 1992–96.* Bureau of Justice Statistics Special Report. Washington, DC: Bureau of Justice Statistics.

Weber, Max. 1947. *The Theory of Social and Economic Organization.* Tr. by A. M. Henderson and T. Parsons and edited with an Introduction by T. Parsons. New York: The Free Press.

Weil, Andrew. 1972. *The Natural Mind—An Investigation of Drugs and Higher Consciousness.* Boston: Houghton Mifflin.

Weiner, Neil Alan, Margaret A. Zahn, and Rita J. Sagi. 1990. *Violence: Patterns, Causes, Public Policy.* San Diego: Harcourt Brace Jovanovich.

Weisheit, Ralph A. 1990. "Civil War on Drugs." Pp. 1–10 in R. A. Weisheit (ed.), *Drugs, Crime and the Criminal Justice System.* Cincinnati: Anderson.

Whyte, William F. 1943. *Street Corner Society.* Chicago: University of Chicago Press.

Widom, Cathy Spatz. 1992. *The Cycle of Violence.* National Institute of Justice Research in Brief. Washington, DC: U.S. Department of Justice.

———. 1996. *The Cycle of Violence Revisited.* National Institute of Justice Research Preview. Washington, DC: U.S. Department of Justice.

Wieczorek, William F., John W. Welte, and Ernest L. Abel. 1990. "Alcohol, Drugs, and Murder: A Study of Convicted Homicide Offenders." *Journal of Criminal Justice* 18:217–27.

Wilbanks, William. 1987. *The Myth of the Racist Criminal Justice System.* Belmont, CA: Wadsworth.

Williams, Terry. 1989. *Cocaine Kids—The Inside Story of a Teenage Drug Ring.* Reading, MA: Addison-Wesley.

———. 1992. *Crackhouse—Notes from the End of the Line.* New York: Penguin Books.

Wilt, Susan A., Susan M. Illman, and Maia BrodyField. 1997. *Female Homicide Victims in New York City 1990–1994.* New York: New York City Department of Health.

Wisotsky, Steven. 1986. *Breaking the Impasse in the War on Drugs.* New York: Greenwood.

Witkin, Gordon. 1991. "The Men Who Created Crack." *U.S. News & World Report* August 19:44–53.

Wolfgang, Marvin E. 1958. *Patterns in Criminal Homicide*. Philadelphia: University of Pennsylvania Press.

Wolfgang, Marvin E. and Franco Ferracuti. 1975. *The Subculture of Violence: Towards an Integrated Theory of Criminology*. London: Tavistock.

Wolfgang, Marvin E. and Rolf B. Strohm. 1956. "The Relationship between Alcohol and Criminal Homicide." *Quarterly Journal of Studies on Alcohol* 17:411–25.

Woolgar, Steve and Dorothy Pawluch. 1985. "Ontological Gerrymandering: The Anatomy of Social Problems Explanations." *Social Problems* 33:159–62.

Wright, Kevin N. and Karen E. Wright. 1994. *Family Life, Delinquency, and Crime: A Policymaker's Guide*. Washington, DC: Office of Juvenile Justice and Delinquency Prevention.

Yablonsky, Lewis. 1962. *The Violent Gang*. New York: Macmillan.

Yardley, Jim. 1997. "Brawley Comes to Rally and Repeats Charge of an Attack." *The New York Times* December 3:B1, B6.

Zahn, Margaret. 1980. "Homicide in the Twentieth Century United States." In J. A. Inciardi and C. E. Faupel (eds.), *History and Crime*. Beverly Hills: Sage.

Zahn, Margaret and Marc Bencivengo. 1974. "Violent Death: A Comparison between Drug Users and Nondrug Users." *Addictive Diseases* 1:283–96.

Zawitz, Marianne W. 1994. *Domestic Violence—Violence between Intimates*. Bureau of Justice Statistics Selected Findings. Washington, DC: U.S. Department of Justice.

Zimmer, Lynn and John P. Morgan. 1997. *Marijuana Myths, Marijuana Facts—A Review of the Scientific Evidence*. New York: Lindesmith Center.

Zimring, Franklin E. 1996. "Desperadoes in Diapers?" *Overcrowded Times* 7:2, 3.

Index